MARYSE CONDÉ AND THE SPACE OF LITERATURE

LEGENDA

LEGENDA, founded in 1995 by the European Humanities Research Centre of the University of Oxford, is now a joint imprint of the Modern Humanities Research Association and Maney Publishing. Titles range from medieval texts to contemporary cinema and form a widely comparative view of the modern humanities, including works on Arabic, Catalan, English, French, German, Greek, Italian, Portuguese, Russian, Spanish, and Yiddish literature. An Editorial Board of distinguished academic specialists works in collaboration with leading scholarly bodies such as the Society for French Studies and the British Comparative Literature Association.

MHRA

The Modern Humanities Research Association (MHRA) encourages and promotes advanced study and research in the field of the modern humanities, especially modern European languages and literature, including English, and also cinema. It also aims to break down the barriers between scholars working in different disciplines and to maintain the unity of humanistic scholarship in the face of increasing specialization. The Association fulfils this purpose primarily through the publication of journals, bibliographies, monographs and other aids to research.

Maney Publishing is one of the few remaining independent British academic publishers. Founded in 1900 the company has offices both in the UK, in Leeds and London, and in North America, in Boston. Since 1945 Maney Publishing has worked closely with learned societies, their editors, authors, and members, in publishing academic books and journals to the highest traditional standards of materials and production.

RESEARCH MONOGRAPHS IN FRENCH STUDIES

The *Research Monographs in French Studies* (RMFS) form a separate series within the Legenda programme and are published in association with the Society for French Studies. Individual members of the Society are entitled to purchase all RMFS titles at a discount.

The series seeks to publish the best new work in all areas of the literature, thought, theory, culture, film and language of the French-speaking world. Its distinctiveness lies in the relative brevity of its publications (50,000–60,000 words). As innovation is a priority of the series, volumes should predominantly consist of new material, although, subject to appropriate modification, previously published research may form up to one third of the whole. Proposals may include critical editions as well as critical studies. They should be sent with one or two sample chapters for consideration to Professor Ann Jefferson, New College, Oxford OX1 3BN.

PUBLISHED IN THIS SERIES

www.rmfs.mhra.org.uk

Maryse Condé and the Space of Literature

Eva Sansavior

Research Monographs in French Studies 32
Modern Humanities Research Association and Maney Publishing
2012

Published by the
Modern Humanities Research Association and Maney Publishing
1 Carlton House Terrace
London SW1Y 5AF
United Kingdom

LEGENDA *is an imprint of the*
Modern Humanities Research Association and Maney Publishing

Maney Publishing is the trading name of W. S. Maney & Son Ltd,
whose registered office is at Suite 1C, Joseph's Well, Hanover Walk, Leeds LS3 1AB

ISBN 9-781-906540-94-4

First published 2012

Printed and bound by Charlesworth Press, Wakefield, UK

Cover: 875 Design

Copy-Editor: Richard Correll

CONTENTS

FOR MY PARENTS

ACKNOWLEDGEMENTS

I am grateful to the following people for their support in the completion of this book: Celia Britton, Nicholas Harrison, Ann Jefferson, Graham Nelson, Richard Correll and John Basham. I would also like to acknowledge a debt of gratitude to Maryse Condé, whose generous and thought-provoking comments in the course of our various interviews have been an immense source of inspiration. Finally, I would like to express my thanks to Oriel College and Oxford University for providing the stimulating research and teaching environment that has served as a crucible for my thinking on this project.

E. S., Oxford, November 2011

ABBREVIATIONS OF MAIN TEXTS

Works of Maryse Condé

Desirada	*Desirada*
DesiradaE	*Desirada: A Novel*, trans. by Richard Philcox
ELB	*En attendant le bonheur*
H	*Heremakhonon: A Novel*, trans. by Richard Philcox
LCRP	*Le Cœur à rire et à pleurer: Contes vrais de mon enfance*
TFTH	*Tales from the Heart: True Stories from My Childhood*, trans. by Richard Philcox
DRM	*Les Derniers Rois mages*
LAK	*The Last of the African Kings*, trans. by Richard Philcox
MTSNS	*Moi Tituba, sorcière... Noire de Salem*
ITBWS	*I, Tituba, Black Witch of Salem*, trans. by Richard Philcox

Other works cited

CPRN	*Cahier d'un retour au pays natal*, by Aimé Césaire
NRN	*Notebook of a Return to My Native Land*, trans. by Mireille Rosello and Annie Pritchard
LTRC	*La Tragédie du Roi Christophe*, by Aimé Césaire
EMC	*Entretiens avec Maryse Condé*, by Françoise Pfaff
CMC	*Conversations with Maryse Condé*, trans. by Pfaff
CSB	*Contre Sainte-Beuve*, by Marcel Proust
PNMB	*Peau noire, masques blancs*, by Frantz Fanon
BSWM	*Black Skin White Masks*, trans. by Charles Lam Markmann
QQL	*Qu'est-ce que la littérature?*, by Jean–Paul Sartre
WIL	*What is Literature?*, trans. by Bernard Frechtman
LRCN	*La Rue Case-Nègres*, by Joseph Zobel

For full publication details see the Bibliography

INTRODUCTION

Je crois maintenant que c'est l'errance qui amène la créativité. L'enracinement est très mauvais au fond. Il faut absolument être errant, multiple au-dehors et au-dedans. Nomade. (*EMC*, 46)

[I now believe that it's this wandering that engenders creativity. In the final analysis, it's very bad to put down roots. You must be errant and multi-faceted, inside and outside. Nomadic. (*CMC*, 28)]

The nomadic impulse endorsed by the Guadeloupean female author Maryse Condé in the above quotation is emblematic of the shifting sets of relationships to different spaces configured by boundaries — geographical, institutional, generic and also experiential — that are mapped out in her work. As I shall outline in this introduction, if Condé's work suggests notions of 'space' and 'crossing' in a number of ways, these pivot around a series of literary encounters between historically and culturally specific individual and collective experiences in an increasingly globalized world.

Perhaps the most literal articulation of such encounters can be found in the author's biography. Although Condé was born in Guadeloupe and is often discussed as a 'Guadeloupean' or 'Francophone Caribbean' writer, North American academia — and in particular, the field of postcolonial studies — have served as privileged contexts for the consolidation of Condé's status as a major writer and critic and for the institutionalization of her work: it is here that Condé's texts are routinely taught (often in translation) on a range of university literature courses and — until her retirement in 2004 — that she combined her fictional writing with work as a university lecturer and literary critic.[1] At the same time, Condé's work has served as a site for various literal and metaphorical 'crossings' between her native Guadeloupe, Africa, the United States and France. Born in 1937, Condé left Guadeloupe to pursue her studies in France at the age of sixteen. In 1958, she married the Guinean actor Mamadou Condé and then spent a year teaching in Bingerville, Côte d'Ivoire. She joined her husband in Guinea in 1962, at the time of the Sekou Touré regime, but left two years later on her own for Ghana. After spending time in various African countries, Condé left Africa and returned to France where she received her PhD from the Sorbonne in 1975. In 1982 she married Richard Philcox who became the long-standing English translator for her work. A Fulbright scholarship awarded in 1985 enabled her to spend a year in Los Angeles; this was the start of a twenty-three-year period in which Condé combined her writing with academic posts at a number of North American universities.

The trajectory of Condé's career points to the paradigmatically global status of Francophone or Third World authors whose works are read predominantly outside their country of origin. However the dominant cultural frame of this status varies according to whether Condé is viewed as a 'Francophone Caribbean' or 'Third World' author. When this status is placed in the context of other major Francophone Caribbean writers, revealing paradoxes and divergences emerge. In common with many of these writers, such as Patrick Chamoiseau, Raphaël Confiant and Édouard Glissant, Condé has lived in France. But her significant stay in Africa is unique amongst her Francophone Caribbean contemporaries. In addition, with the exception of Édouard Glissant, Condé's success and long-standing residence in the United States have set her apart from other Francophone Caribbean writers. In fact, the centrality of the United States for Condé's writing places her amongst a specific group of international writers for whom that country serves as an institutional home. In their introduction to a special issue of *Paragraph* entitled 'Francophone Texts and Postcolonial Theory', Celia Britton and Michael Syrotinski characterize this group as 'the most original thinkers and internationally celebrated writers from former colonized countries who have gravitated almost irresistibly to teaching and research posts there'.[2]

In both its varied generic identity and prolific nature, Condé's writing career is also distinctive. To date, Condé has produced numerous novels aimed at both adult and young readers, two memoirs, and a growing number of essays in French and English.[3] In addition to works of prose, Condé — whose writing career began in theatre — continues to write plays which are performed in the United States and in the Francophone Caribbean.[4] While her work has attracted a significant amount of critical attention, this attention has been focused on a relatively limited number of novels and there has been a tendency to read these novels in isolation from the significant body of her critical essays and numerous interviews.[5] The complex generic profile of Condé's body of work underlines the need to adopt an integrative critical focus that accounts for the evolution of her thinking across various generic sites of writing and also of oral performances. And, as I observe in my discussion of the particular uses that she makes of the interview in Chapter 1, Condé's ongoing reflection on the varying conditions of reception of her texts allows for a reading of the field of reception as a series of culturally embedded spaces or sites. In response to the generic complexity that I highlighted above, this book aims to adopt an integrative critical approach: it combines new readings of literary texts that have already attracted significant critical attention with less widely read texts and a selection of her critical essays and interviews. It also situates these readings within a comparative study of the institutional frameworks in which the dominant critical readings of Condé's work are produced.

A cross-generic focus is a productive context for reflecting on the implications of the continuities as well as the contradictions that inform representations of space and crossing both within Condé's self-presentation as an author and in the thematic content of her work. The complexity of the generic status of that work is doubled by the shifting range of individual and collective identities that Condé claims in the predominantly North American context of postcolonial studies, one in which, as Chris Bongie observes in *Friends and Enemies: The Scribal Politics of Post/Colonial Literature*, identity politics is prioritized as the mode of intervention for critical practice.[6] Some of the identities claimed by Condé such as 'female' or 'black' are intelligible within the sectarian logic that underpins this type of politics. Other identity categories such as 'Francophone' and 'négro-bourgeois', however, draw attention to Condé's illegibility or foreignness and, specifically, to the ways in which the range of her identity positionings tests the limits of the practices of translation on which these disciplinary fields rely.[7] As I hope to demonstrate in this Introduction, such practices of translation operate necessarily (although often in oblique and incomplete ways) on the distinct literary and political cultures on which Condé draws in her highly intertextual œuvre.

Accounting for the disjuncture between the presentation of her work (and by extension, her identity) as susceptible to translations or readings and a foregrounding of their resistance to pre-existing critical and political schema is integral to an engagement with the complex sets of relationships that Condé establishes with Anglophone and Francophone institutional contexts. Condé's engagements with these two institutional contexts can be legitimately viewed as central, but they are complicated by her ambivalent positions on gender. In this respect, the masculine bias of Francophone Caribbean literary culture is one of primary targets of Condé's criticism.[8] However, this critique directed at the Francophone Caribbean context is accompanied by a rejection of the reductive North American gender politics and ambiguous representations of her status as a 'black female author', positions that suggest the strategic uses that she makes of various types of identity politics in her negotiation of Anglophone and Francophone contexts of reception (concerns that I address in Chapter 1).

Through her appeal to the freedom that she ascribes to literature, Condé also establishes thematically in her work a distance from the assumed political role of critical practice and of critics. She does so at a defining moment in the field of postcolonial studies, which Chris Bongie describes as 'a moment of doubt, renewal, and expansion'.[9] According to Bongie, this doubt centres on two related questions: first, how to account for the status of the field's representative intellectuals (or its 'scribes' as he calls them) and their complicity with the commodifying processes of the capitalist system; and, second, how to define the idea of politics, or, as he asks: 'exactly what sort of resistance has postcolonial studies been offering over the past several decades and to what extent does it really qualify as "political"?'[10] Bongie's stated position is that, in spite of appeals to an idea of politics, what actually counts as 'politics' in the field of postcolonial studies is effectively unknown. The spheres of action that he names with varying degrees of explicitness (i.e. identity politics, resistance to capitalist commodification, a diffuse idea of resistance) provide useful co-ordinates for mapping the specific political Anglo-American culture in which postcolonial studies are embedded. The thematic focus of Condé's literary work and her self-presentations in interviews raises questions that address the implicit idea of the political to which Bongie alludes, making it the subject of explicit critical and creative engagement that she maps and re-remaps across the various generic sites of her work. Condé's exploration of issues of reception along with the relationship between literature and politics also serves as a starting point for a broader reflection on the possibilities for re-framing these ideas in terms of the overlapping and

divergent histories and afterlives of the intellectual traditions in which the disciplines of French, Francophone literature and criticism and Postcolonial Studies
are located. And it is precisely Condé's status as a 'global Francophone Caribbean
writer' who moves between the roles of author, critic and educator that potentially
facilitates this process of re-framing. In this introductory chapter, I explore the
ways in which Condé's cross-generic and cross-cultural self-positionings constitute
a space in which she both addresses and participates in major contemporary debates
surrounding the relationship between literature, politics and critical reception, while
also offering a type of meta-critical engagement with the historical development of
the disciplinary fields in which her work are read.

It would be hardly be an overstatement to argue that one of the central questions
posed by Maryse Condé's work, that of the relationship between 'literature' and
'politics', is at the centre of a largely unchallenged and, arguably, global orthodoxy
within the various fields in which Condé's work is read: the idea that literature
has a necessarily political role. That this idea can be viewed as part of these fields'
orthodoxy is evidenced by the general absence of discussion that it elicits. The
political relevance of literature is thus typically presented as a given, discernible
only in asserted positions that are presented as somehow self-evident. This view
of literature as necessarily political and produced in resistance to certain kinds of
representations that are in some way 'reductive' or 'negative' is a critical commonplace
in one of the primary critical paradigms through which Maryse Condé's work is
read, namely 'black women's writing'.[11] A sample of some canonical critical texts
points to the constitutive role of such assumptions for the field. In *Out of the Kumbla*,
Carole Boyce Davies and Elaine Savory Fido identify a state of 'voicelessness' which
characterizes the experience of women and is reflected in the literature produced
by women: 'By voicelessness we mean silence: the inability to express a position in
the language of the "master" as well as the textual construction of women as silent'
(p. 1). Writing and, in particular, the first-person and/or autobiographical narrative,
is therefore presented as a politically strategic site of resistance to the historical
'voicelessness' of the black Francophone Caribbean female subject. As a response to
this experience of 'voicelessness', Julia Watson and Sidonie Smith ascribe a special
political efficacy to the practice of female autobiography in *De/Colonizing the
Subject: The Politics of Women's Autobiography*. They identify a 'subversive' practice
of feminine autobiography that produces a distinctive 'voice' by writing against
the grain of masculine autobiographical conventions. This theory of subversive
feminine autobiography relies on a conflation of 'autobiographical writing' with
social and political action, and Watson and Smith read the tendency for female
subjects to represent collective, as opposed to individual, autobiographical subjects
as a collective form of agency. While beyond the scope of this book, it is worth
noting that they locate this view of agency within the process of decolonization
itself from which it draws its revolutionary charge:

> As a process of and a product of decolonisation, autobiographical writing has
> the potential to 'transform spectators crushed with their inessentiality into
> privileged actors,' to foster 'the veritable creation of new [wo]men', to quote
> with a shift in emphasis, the revolutionary Fanon.[12]

The idea of a decolonizing agency is thus extended to the creation of a collective female autobiographical subject, who, it is assumed, works to displace the dominant position of the 'unitary' masculine subject of traditional autobiography by giving expression to, or 'witnessing', the experiences of a 'female community'.[13] In addition, this process is linked to certain formal strategies such as the use of oral history, the blurring of the boundaries between fiction and autobiography, and other forms of narrative ambiguity.[14]

If to claim a 'political' role for literature is also to make certain assumptions about what constitutes 'authentic literature', these are typically taken as unworthy of explication. Robert Young offers the following useful illumination of these assumptions in the inaugural volume of the postcolonial studies journal *Interventions*:

> Postcolonial writing, together with minority writing in the west and feminist writing generally, has achieved a revolution in aesthetics and aesthetic criteria of the literary, just at the moment when the literary was under attack as an outdated category of elitist institutions. In institutional terms, the impact of feminism and postcolonialism has radically changed the criteria that make authentic art by challenging the cultural capital from which notions of the literary are derived. Writing is now valued as much for its depiction of representative experience as for its aesthetic qualities.[15]

Young's self-confident reference to the notion of 'authentic' art acts as a key pointer to a whole range of unspoken assumptions about the representative status of literature, writers and critics within the various critical fields on behalf of which he claims a form of critical solidarity with the aims of postcolonial studies. Through the appeal to ideas of 'revolution', 'minority writing', and 'cultural capital', Young offers a vision of postcolonial studies as located within a critical genealogy that is distinctly and uncompromisingly political. But this is a vision of politics in which a universal notion of Marxist anti-colonial resistance serves to federate, culturally disparate — if ambiguously defined — political practices: North American identity politics and French Bourdieusian cultural and social critique.[16]

The emerging debate surrounding questions of the relationship between 'literature' and politics in the field (to which I alluded earlier with reference to Chris Bongie) challenges Young's vision of postcolonial studies in two ways: first, the vision of the field as culturally homogeneous and united around a common consensus that politics could be clearly distinguished from literature has come under increasing scrutiny in the context of a transatlantic dialogue between North American and British postcolonial scholars. This would suggest that the issue of the proper place or, for that matter, the nature of politics or literature, while emerging from the broader field of 'postcolonial studies', cannot be meaningfully addressed by situating this process of questioning within a general model of 'Anglophone' postcolonial studies. These topics can only be explored in relation to the interactions between specific cultures of postcolonial studies, although these cultures will of course maintain points of convergence with a broader model of postcolonial studies. Second, the very idea that postcolonial studies is inherently political reveals the fault lines in a field that maintains privileged, if conflicted, relationships, with the historically and culturally specific representations of literature and politics in

Francophone literature and French theory. As a perhaps necessary response to such complexity, the British institutional context has also shown itself to be markedly open to undertaking both extensive disciplinary self-scrutiny and historically situated theoretical investigations. In *Postcolonial Thought in the French-Speaking World*, Charles Forsdick and David Murphy offer an account of the intellectual genealogy of postcolonial studies that highlights its status as a travelling theory that is 'the result of the expatriation of two bodies of thought — the anti-colonialism of figures such as Frantz Fanon; the post-structuralism of intellectuals such as Derrida and Foucault — and their subsequent fusion in the critical practices emerging from (largely) Anglophone campuses.'[17] Forsdick and Murphy highlight the role of *passeurs* (Anglophone scholars working on French-language texts and French-speaking scholars working in Anglophone universities) in facilitating the transfer of ideas across institutional contexts.[18] Condé's role as both author and critic suggests that the work of the creative writers must also be viewed as integral to — and also complicating — the trans-national transfers of ideas and knowledge that are central to Forsdick and Murphy's definition of the *passeur*.

Condé's appeal to the literary can thus be viewed as addressing both the underlying process of translation that accompanies this flow of theoretical ideas and the power relationships between literary critics and authors that such an institutional model takes for granted. By signalling 'freedom' as central to her writing practice, Condé can be seen to be offering a negative reading of what may be characterized as orthodox postcolonial theory. This reading would endorse the position of some its most virulent critics — namely, that postcolonial theory is a cultural imposition that fails to take account of the specific historical and cultural contexts in which the Francophone literary works are produced.[19]

Such a reading would be consistent with a negative idea of space as the meaning lost in the translation — or perhaps even the incommensurability — between the Anglophone and Francophone academic cultures, what Nicholas Harrison in his introduction to a special issue of *Paragraph* entitled 'The Idea of the Literary' has called 'the divergence [...] between postcolonial criticism written mainly in English language' and 'certain strands of work in literary theory often in French'.[20] However, to argue that the transfer of theoretical ideas between these two fields may be the subject of incomplete translation is not to call for a critical disengagement from an intellectual 'lost cause'. Rather, the acknowledgement of the real challenges that bedevil this (and indeed any) transfer of intellectual ideas across cultures may serve as the starting point for a creative reflection on the possibilities (also identified by Harrison) for 'convergence', and for recovering the historically significant but occluded routes of influence between these institutional contexts. Such a process would require a more supple reading of the idea of 'travelling theory' as a spatial practice configured by varying power relationships and flows of influence between academic cultures ('the French', 'the Francophone' and 'the Anglophone') as well as between creative writers and critics. In contrast to the critical tendency to view postcolonial studies as a unidirectional imposition of Anglophone theorizations on Francophone literary texts, it would be fruitful to be attentive to what Charles Forsdick and David Murphy (citing James Clifford) characterize as 'feedback loops, the ambivalent appropriations and resistances that characterize the travel of theories, and theorists'.[21] An awareness of the multi-directional flows of influence between Anglophone and Francophone contexts would also allow for an extended conception of the role of *passeur*. An extended view of this role would take account not just of the work of critics but also the theoretical and literary interventions of writers such as Condé.

By adopting an approach that places the interventions of critics in dialogue with those of authors, this process can thus be approached in a number of ways. One such way would be to bring attention to the critical assumptions and the institutional practices of the disciplinary fields of reception for international Francophone or Third World authors such as Condé.[22] The field of Francophone Postcolonial Studies has sought to account for the specifically Francophone contribution to postcolonial studies, situating this process of investigation within a broad historical framework. Emerging from a British institutional context, the term 'Francophone Postcolonial Studies' was first used by Charles Forsdick and David Murphy in 2003. In their introduction to *Postcolonial Thought in the French-Speaking World* they define two primary research objectives for this new field: first, to consolidate the research activities of the emergent disciplinary field and second, to 'explore how a Francophone postcolonial debate might challenge and interrogate what was then the primarily English-language field of postcolonial studies.'[23] In line with this focus, their volume has provided a more extensive Francophone genealogy for postcolonial studies, moving beyond the field's privileged focus on the theorizations of Frantz Fanon to explore the contributions of the anti-colonial thought of the Martinican Aimé Césaire and the Tunisian Albert Memmi. By presenting essays with a broad thematic range, their study has also placed these Francophone theorizations in dialogue with readings of the anti-colonial legacy of the metropolitan French theorist, Jacques Derrida as well as with the complex critical and political positionings of contemporary Francophone authors such as Maryse Condé and Assia Djebar.

Another possible critical response to Condé's expressed concern with the possibilities for achieving literary freedom would be to focus on defining the idea of the literary itself and, with it, the role of the author. This focus has produced interventions from scholars from different cultures of Anglophone postcolonial studies such as Nicholas Harrison, Gayatri Chakravorty Spivak, and Graham Huggan, with critical enquiry centred around questions of 'authenticity', 'representativity' and 'reception'.[24] While these questions will serve essentially as a key theoretical context for my analysis of Condé's work, I also bring these into dialogue with Condé's preoccupation with the relationship between literature and freedom, as well as with the specific Francophone Caribbean writers Aimé Césaire and Fanon, and the broader notion of *Créolité*. What I hope to demonstrate is that Condé's work draws much of its critical energy from a longer debate in the broader field of 'French Studies' about the relationship between literature and the politics *after* Sartrean *engagement*. While the focus of my discussion will be on theoretical responses to Sartrean *engagement*, I would argue that the questioning of the relationship between literature and politics articulated in Sartre's œuvre can be viewed as a theoretical bridge between modernist and post-structuralist articulations of these concerns in the French context. As David Hopkins argues in *Dada and Surrealism: A Short Introduction*, Sartre's definition of a politicized role for literature was based on a rejection of the bourgeois conception of autonomous art that would make him (along with Bourdieu) an heir to the Surrealists who situated *praxis* in daily life (p. 2).[25]

Sartrean *engagement* is thus significant as a theoretical contribution, in its own right, as well as for its complex implication in antecedent and succeeding theoretical positions. As such, it is shaped by a simultaneous rejection of the bourgeois conception of autonomous art and an extension of the Surrealists' fusing of artistic practice with social and political activism. It also serves to generate a diverse range of broadly (post)-structuralist responses — which although varied are united around a common questioning of the indissoluble link that Sartre forges between 'literature' and 'politics' — from individual theorists such as Roland Barthes, Jacques Derrida and Maurice Blanchot as well as avant-garde theoretical and literary schools such as the *nouveaux romanciers*. A key concern of this book will be to track, through the reading of a diverse range of French theoretical positions in parallel with works by major Francophone Caribbean theorists such as Aimé Césaire, Frantz Fanon and Édouard Glissant, how Condé's work participates in this broader debate in the field of 'French Studies' by serving as the site of interchange between 'metropolitan French' and Francophone Caribbean theorizations of politics and literature. My broader aim is to highlight the complex sets of relationships that Condé's œuvre establishes with both French and international modernist aesthetic and political projects.

In schematic terms, it is possible to situate the emerging debate in Francophone Postcolonial Studies in relation to two main critical responses to the Sartrean view of literature as necessarily political: on the one hand, a Bourdieusian analysis has questioned the assumed political efficacy of literary and critical work and has instead focused on the mechanisms by which these very practices create the social and economic hierarchies that enshrine their superior status through appeals to notions of taste and value as well as 'the aesthetic'.[26] On the other hand, an alternative critical debate has emerged around a defence of the literary within a broad grouping of theories. French thinkers such as Roland Barthes, Jacques Derrida and Maurice Blanchot have argued for a renewed attention to the specificity of literature as text and 'space' and to an ethics of reading.[27] What is distinctive about this group of theorists is that their appeal to the specificity of literature as a theoretical position tended to coexist with concrete political action. Indeed, as Celia Britton observes in *The Nouveau Roman: Fiction, Theory and Politics*, what defines the broad grouping of avant-garde positions that draws together Barthes, Derrida, the *nouveaux romanciers* and (to a lesser extent) also Blanchot is precisely their intense and emotional political engagement in a range of political struggles that include de-Stalinization in the Soviet Union, the Algerian war and the events of May 1968.[28] The rest of this introduction will therefore explore how these debates articulated initially in the broader field of French Studies, come to be refracted in what I shall argue is the mutually illuminating traffic between Condé's œuvre and the emerging discussion in the fields of Francophone/Postcolonial Studies and in 'Francophone Caribbean' literature, concerning not only the nature and place of politics and literature but also possibilities for forging individual and collective identities.

Graham Huggan's study of the international reception of Third World authors in *The Postcolonial Exotic: Marketing the Margins* develops a Bourdieusian scepticism about the political claims made for literature and the writer-critic along with a concern to cast light on with the ways in which literature and criticism work together to produce and shore up various forms of cultural prestige or 'cultural capital'. Following Bourdieu, Huggan emphasizes the mediating role played by metropolitan critics in assigning value and legitimacy to the work of Third World authors.[29] He locates the literary field within a contested site of cultural production 'in which what is at stake is the power to impose the dominant definition of the writer and therefore to delimit the population of those entitled to take part in the struggle to define the writer.'[30] Questions of authenticity are central to this process of legitimization and, as Young's comments illustrate, to use the term 'authentic art' takes for granted that the critic is equipped to make a judgement as to which works constitute 'authentic art'. However, as Huggan points out, this judgement typically draws its legitimacy from assumptions about the author's 'representativity' that are necessarily bound up in the market-driven imperatives for 'exotic cultural products' (pp. 151–62).[31] He also draws attention to the implicit censure that is directed at any critical preoccupation with exploring the literary aspects of the texts, as he highlights the occasional tendency to 'view postcolonial literary criticism as little more than an anachronism — a symptom of the nostalgic desire to return to earlier, over-aestheticized formations'.[32] Huggan therefore emphasizes that in this context, literary criticism is viewed as both politically and critically suspect. It is politically suspect because if critics and their critical work are assumed to be politically accountable, then (as Young also suggests) a concern with literary textual analysis seems somehow trivial and therefore politically irresponsible. Or, perhaps even more damningly in line with Young's criticism, 'elitist'.

In spite of what Huggan argues is an ingrained institutional suspicion of any concern with the 'aesthetic dimension' in postcolonial studies and a related tendency to view literature exclusively in terms of its political viability, he nevertheless attempts (in a marked divergence from the Bourdieusian suspicion of the aesthetic realm) an uneasy accommodation of both sides of the theoretical divide. Huggan appeals to some idea of the aesthetic realm — or the literary — when he argues that international female Aboriginal female writers are able to disrupt representative readings through an ironic awareness that puts the conflicting expectations of their various readerships into play in the paratextual sphere (pp. 165–76).[33] An arguably attenuated version of the Sartrean idea of committed writing also finds space here too as he notes that these writers are 'singularly adept in "playing the market" to their own ideological ends' (p. 176). Huggan concludes with a paradoxical recuperation of the political viability of the field noting that while 'postcolonial studies is — to some degree — constrained by the exoticist machinery of representations in which it is made to operate, it still has the potential to turn that machinery against itself, adapting it for future use' (p. 262). The notion of political action that emerges here is therefore centred on a seemingly ceaseless pointing up and disruption of the field's entrapment within an 'exoticizing' capitalist system. Within the ongoing process of resistance that Huggan envisages, literature thus maintains its position — historically and widely sanctioned — as a form of instrumentalist writing, whose role it is simply to be 'useful' to the political cause.

While Condé displays a marked and strategic awareness of the field of reception, her defence of literature as a space of freedom suggests not the conflation of the aesthetic and the political against which Deepika Bahri argues in *Native Intelligence*, but rather what as I will show are a series of performative 'prisings open' of the 'political' and 'aesthetic' that lead to a 'questioning of the assumption that the rightful content of political action is already known and understood'.[34] Such a questioning suggests that a reflection on the literary itself may be a necessary precondition for determining what Bahri calls 'the rightful content of political action'.[35] Nicholas Harrison shares both Huggan's and Bahri's scepticism about assigning a taken-for-granted political value to literature, and like Huggan, he is particularly attentive to the assumptions of 'representativity' that inform the reading of works by 'Third World' authors. The questioning of the specific claims of representativity brought to these authors is the basis for a reflection on the nature of literature itself and an exploration of a renewed, non-instrumentalist practice of reading. In *Postcolonial Criticism: History Theory and the Work of Fiction*, Harrison draws on Derrida's notions of *suspense* and *dependence* to define literature as follows: 'There is no literature without a *suspended* relation to meaning and reference. *Suspended* means *suspense*, but also *dependence*, condition, conditionality.'[36] By alluding to the complex and multi-layered relationship between the literary text and elements of reference, Harrison's reading of the 'literary' as characterized by 'suspense' effectively nuances Huggan's criticism of the imposition of implicitly quite inappropriate politicized readings on the texts. In his article 'The Idea of the Literary' Harrison characterizes the experience of the literary text as 'an experience of the non-literary [...] mixed and multi-faceted, engaging on one level with issues of reference (history, one might say, or experience), and on another level with those aspects of the text that defer or frustrate reference.'[37] He argues that the inextricability of 'reference' and 'suspension' in the literary text means that 'even if it appears to offer "information" of one sort or another, the literary text cannot itself ever indicate reliably which "information" within it is truthful or "representative" or, [...] is drawn from the author's own experience.'[38] Crucially, Harrison underscores the role of the field of reception in bringing to light the strategic possibilities of this suspension of referentiality as he notes that the text's claims to suspension of referentiality take place within a dialectic between text and reader.[39]

This dialectic is central to Bahri's conception of literature in *Native Intelligence*. Like Harrison, Bahri privileges qualities of literary evasiveness or a type of literature that makes 'comprehension a moving target'.[40] Bahri views this inconclusiveness as an invitation to adopt '[a] mode of reading that accepts the necessary pause and allows the reader to inhabit the experience of being confounded', and that 'presents us with a way of understanding the challenge of communication across differences and the ethical positions necessary to it.'[41] Such a challenge to the 'general reader' has far-reaching implications for the practice of professional reading that underpins criticism as well as for the political aims that are attached to this practice. Bahri points to a critical obligation to reconsider the traditional relationship between literature and theory, with literature traditionally figured as the object of theory.[42] One possibility presented by Bahri's argument in support of maintaining the 'tension between subject and object' — that I explore in the course of this book — is that the generic crossings between literature and criticism that are a distinctive feature of Condé's œuvre may constitute what Bahri refers to as 'the very key to emancipatory theory and practice'.[43] Bahri makes it clear, however, that such emancipatory potential should in no way be assimilated with traditional political action. Nevertheless, her striking use of political language to describe the resistance of literature and criticism to political instrumentalization gestures towards the terms of the radical rethinking of political activity that is central to the modernist project. One implication of Bahri's arguments is that any attempt to define the nature of political action in the field of postcolonial studies would not as, Bongie avers, rule out the possibilities of 'a re-energized modernist politics and aesthetics of resistance' but, rather, would reconsider the uses of the modernist-defined tensions between 'literature' and 'politics'.[44]

* * * * *

Centred around questions of literary freedom and generically positioned between the manifesto, literature, criticism and autobiography, Condé's 1993 essay 'Order, Disorder, Freedom and the West Indian Writer' makes a key intervention in the critical debate that I have sketched out above, an intervention that also offers possibilities for a creative re-framing of the terms of this debate. In this essay, Condé uses manifesto-like strategies and what may be called 'style' as both the symbolic articulation of the complex relationships between 'literature' and 'politics' and as a space for re-thinking these relationships. To read Condé's text as a manifesto is to consider its *essential* relationship to modernist aesthetic and political practices, since, as Janet Lyon notes in her study *Manifestoes: Provocations of the Modern*, the proliferation of manifesto texts since the 1960s situates this genre at the centre of the historical evolution of Western modernity.[45] At the same time, Lyon notes that the manifesto's history can be traced back as far as the twelfth century implying that its 'constitutive discourses'[46] are shaped by the preoccupations of a range of different historical epochs that pre-date what may be configured as the 'modern' period. Among the constitutive discourses that Lyon identifies are 'discourses of religious prophecy and chiliasm (or millennialism); the martial language of war and siege, the forensic mode of persuasive rhetoric'.[47] The manifesto's complex genealogy is matched by its protean generic form. Borrowing from, synthesizing, as well as moving between forms that include the political tract, the editorial letter, advertising and the philosophical essay, the manifesto can be viewed as a paradigmatically liminal genre. This generic liminality offers a productive entry into both its aims and style. For if the manifesto is typically concerned with defending the interests of a group defined as marginal in relation to a more powerful, dominant group (making it particularly well suited to the requirements of identity politics), it is a type of writing that draws its contestatory and creative force from extreme emotional states. Lyon describes these as 'passional' states that include frustration, disappointment and aggressive resolve, arising out of unfulfilled expectations or a breach of contractual relations.[48] In addition, she identifies a commitment to plain-speaking or truth–telling as pivotal to the manifesto's aims.[49] The formal and rhetorical strategies employed by the manifesto are the context for the conjoining of these 'passional' states with political objectives expressed in three main conventions outlined by Lyon. First, the manifesto constructs a 'foreshortened, impassioned, and highly selective history which chronicles the oppression leading to the present moment of crisis.'[50] Second, it entails the 'forceful enumeration of grievances' of a group, defining these in terms of a starkly polarized struggle between 'the empowered and the disempowered'.[51] Third, it employs numbered lists to mark 'its refusal of mediated prose and synthesized transitions [...] allowing it to move relentlessly from one diverse demand to another.'[52] This is accompanied by its use of 'epigrammatic, declarative rhetoric which directly challenges a named oppressor', one that may be only evoked vaguely, 'while uniting its audience in an exhortation to action'.[53] All these strategies can be seen at work in Condé's essay.

'Order, Disorder' starts with a reference to a moment of crisis that is signalled by quoted comments about literature made by Édouard Glissant during an interview: 'I don't believe that West Indian literature exists yet since literature supposes a reaction between a public and an audience'.[54] These comments lead to a discussion of the Creolists' paean to Creole literature, 'Éloge de la Créolité', another text that may also be viewed as a literary manifesto. *ELC* posits a radical break with an earlier, imitative literary model, what it dismissively calls, 'une littérature empruntée, ancrée dans les valeurs françaises' [a borrowed writing, steeped in French values] (*ELC*, 14; *IPC*, 76). At the same time, *ELC* is what Lyon describes as 'generically functional',[55] in the sense that with its powerful assertion of a Creole identity at the start of the work, it effectively serves as a birth narrative for this people: 'Ni Européeens, ni Africains, ni Asiatiques, nous nous proclamons Créoles' [Neither Europeans, nor Africans, nor Asians, we proclaim ourselves Creoles] (*ELC*, 13; *IPC*, 75). The birth of a Creole people is intimately linked to a future literature that gestures beyond the unsatisfying current state of affairs characterized by Chamoiseau et al. as 'un état de prélittérature' [a state of preliterature] (*ELC*, 14, *IPC*, 76). The future conditions that would enable the realization of this literature are explicitly stated in *ELC* and paraphrased in English in Condé's essay as 'the interaction between writers/readers which is necessary for any literature to exist' (p. 121).[56] So, for the Creolists, reading emerges as the basis of a type of engagement that allows for the interpellation of a unique community even as it brings about the transformation of collective consciousness through this new literature's transcendence of the range of inauthentic literary models that it cites from Césaire, to the Surrealists and the broader classical French literary tradition.

Condé's essay establishes a dialogue with the Creolists' political claims in ways that foreground the strategic role of reading as a form of criticism and creative practice that harnesses the rhetorical energy of the manifesto for the definition of a marginal female Francophone Caribbean literary tradition. Her initial response to the Creolists' claims at the start of 'Order, Disorder' suggests an intention to nuance what she implies is an overstated position. Condé also occupies the position of interpellated reader who responds to the Creolists' 'call to arms' as she observes: 'Although it seems difficult to state seriously that West Indian literature doesn't exist, we easily agree that there is a crisis, a malaise.'[57] Her apparent acceptance of a form of politicized resistance to this particular crisis is the basis for a series of critical readings of the Creolists' manifesto that proceed by establishing what in the course of the essay is shown to be two unstable polarized positions: on the one hand, an order associated with the Creolists and, on the other hand, a creative disorder that is linked to a marginalized female identity.

The establishment of both positions necessitates multi-directional readings that overlap with and also diverge from the rhetorical strategies employed within *ELC*. Condé's response to what Lyon characterizes as the manifesto's tendency to construct a 'mythic present' is to provide a historical context for the Creolists' claims, which she situates within her own broadly linear historical narrative that extends from the immediate pre-World War II period to 1993 (the date the essay was written).[58] This narrative is made up of a complex range of French, Francophone Caribbean, Haitian and Latin American texts (that may themselves be read as literary manifestos), all produced in the service of various forms of anti-colonial resistance. Crucially, however — with the exception of Césaire's *Cahier d'un retour au pays natal* — the narrative provided in Condé's essay privileges the role of texts absent from *ELC*. She starts with the 1927 assertion by a group of young Haitian intellectuals in the journal *La Trouée*, published during the American occupation of Haiti, that 'Literature is the cry of a people who want to say what boils in them' (p. 122). This is succeeded by a discussion of a diverse range of texts that include the work of the Haitian writer Jacques Roumain, the "Légitime Défense" manifesto, Suzanne Césaire's 'Misère d'une Poésie' published in *Tropiques* in 1939, Aimé Césaire's *Cahier d'un retour au pays natal*, references to social realism and Sartre's 1948 preface to the anthology to black poetry 'Orphée Noir', Frantz Fanon's *Les Damnés de la terre* and Édouard Glissant's *Le Discours antillais*. Condé's aim here is also to suggest a type of horizontal reading of these texts with a view to situating them — at least provisionally — in a literary tradition of Condé's own making. Thus the Creolists' theorizations of the relationship between politics and literature are shown to be indebted to a tradition of Sartrean *engagement* that bears the mark of the very French values from which the Creolists had sought to distance themselves. And it is certainly significant that Condé chooses to reference explicitly not *Qu'est-ce que la littérature?* (the major work in the which Sartre develops his theory of engagement) but rather his preface to *Orphée Noir*, a text that arguably serves not only to articulate political solidarity with the Négritude writers but also as a linear, unidirectional model of influence that effectively identifies Sartrean engagement as a catalyst or progenitor for the Négritude writers' aesthetic and political ambitions. Condé identifies Sartre's 1948 introduction to what she refers to as 'the first anthology of French-speaking black poetry' as central to the generation of key tenets of the order to which she links the Creolists. These tenets are presented in the form of a list:

(1). Individualism was chastised. Only the collectivity had the right to express itself.

(2). The masses were the sole producers of Beauty, and the poet had to take inspiration from them.

(3). The main, if not the sole, purpose of writing was to denounce one's political and social conditions, and in so doing, bring about one's liberation.

(4). Poetic and political ambition were one and the same.[59]

Through the use of this list Condé's reading highlights the programmatic nature of the tenets provided by Sartre's preface. Later in the essay, she lists prescriptions from texts such as Roumain's *Les Gouverneurs de la rosée* and Glissant's *DA*, thereby employing the list as a formal linking device that serves as a material marker of the Sartrean tradition of engagement within which she situates these texts.

Condé also points to areas of divergence from Sartre's tenets. In particular, she argues that the privileging of heroic male characters in the Francophone Caribbean texts that she cites is accompanied by a tendency either to exclude representations of female characters or to confine these characters to stereotypically passive roles.[60] On this basis, she ascribes a marginal status to female writers to which she implicitly links herself. With a rhetorical gesture typical of the manifesto, her dismissal of a previous inauthentic representational order is the context for the articulation of a collective identity: that of women and female writers. If these two amorphous collective identities are linked by a common propensity to a creative disorder, their definition is based on the use of distinct rhetorical gestures. Condé's definition of womanhood recruits the Bambara myth of origin, thereby making explicitly central to the rhetorical structure of her argument the underlying but typically implicit recourse to mythification that characterizes the representational project of the manifesto: 'In a Bambara myth of origin, after the creation of the earth, and the organization of everything on its surface, disorder was introduced by a woman'.[61]

The political claims that Condé seeks to make on behalf of female writers also rely on drawing attention to their absence from a materially situated literary tradition: 'Apart from one or two names, the female writers of the West Indies are little known, their works are forgotten, out of print, misunderstood.'[62] The experience of being ignored or misunderstood is therefore shown to be constitutive of the marginal identity that Condé ascribes to these writers and the marginal female literary tradition that she simultaneously constructs through her references to the works of female authors such as Mayotte Capécia, Michèle Lacrosil, Miriam Warner-Vieyra, as well as to one of her own semi-autobiographical texts *La Vie scélérate*. This marginality is itself figured as an enabling creativity that has distinct implications for the representational role that is implicitly ascribed to these authors' practice of literature. On the one hand, these female writers are empowered to bear witness to the experiences of their specific constituency and, to this end, Condé draws attention to their depiction of themes that are particularly relevant to the experiences of Francophone Caribbean women. On the other hand, this focus allows her to recuperate Mayotte Capécia's *Je suis martiniquaise*, the subject of excoriating criticism in Fanon's *Peau noire, masques blancs*, as a foundational instance of the marginalization of writing by women. The emotive tone in the following quotation underscores an oblique identification with Capécia's fate:

> The best example of incomprehension remains the criticism of Mayotte Capécia's *Je suis martiniquaise* by Frantz Fanon. In *Black Skin, White Masks*, he singled her out to illustrate what he calls the 'le complexe de lactification,' the desire to be white and thereby to go down in history. [...] Frantz Fanon takes a very dangerous stand. He deliberately confuses *the author* and the *object of her fiction.*[63]

In defence of Capécia's text, Condé stresses its specific representational value or authenticity as a 'precious written testimony [...] of the mentality of a West Indian girl' in 1948. But the representational ambit of these texts is also presented as extending beyond the concerns of a narrowly defined female constituency. Indeed, female writers are charged with a type of uncompromising truth-telling in the face of a whole range of societal realities that include the persistence of the colour hierarchy that privileges lighter skin, the exclusion of female sexuality from West Indian literature, and the absenteeism and irresponsibility of fathers within the family. The descanting role of writing by female writers is also expressed in its challenge to mythical representations of Francophone Caribbean men as 'messianic heroes'.[64]

Interestingly, the sentence that follows on directly from this one suggests that this female disorder also targets the very idea that women are marginal. This would imply that the idea of female marginality is (like the representation of men) a 'myth': 'In *Pluie et vent sur Télumée Miracle*, Simone Schwarz-Bart was the first to dare to shatter this myth and place West Indian women where they belong — at the forefront of the daily battle for survival.'[65] Crucially, this questioning of the very state presented as intrinsic to the collective identity previously claimed by Condé exemplifies the provisional and strategic constructions of identity on which the manifesto's claims are based. In effect, collective identities are pulled into the service of a cause — political or creative — for as long as they are useful and are then discarded. Such an instrumentalist approach to the construction of collective identities means that the gendered 'we' that emerges in Condé's essay can only be viewed, in line with Lyon's observations, as 'highly unstable, inflectable, expansive and mobile'.[66]

If for Condé, as I noted earlier, the marginal status of female writers has a strategic potential that is figured in terms of creativity, the same can be said of this paradoxical state of central-marginality to which she alludes at this stage of her argument. The ways in which female writing and, by extension, Condé's essays 'feeds off' this paradoxical state is suggested in the section entitled 'Order'. Condé draws attention in this section to the role of a female author, Suzanne Césaire, in the development of the masculine 'order' against which she would later define the female disorder: 'On the eve of World War II, Suzanne Césaire [...] uttered her famous command: "Martinican poetry shall be cannibalistic or shall not be".'[67] In this way, Condé highlights the role of women at the centre of the development of this literature and their paradoxical relationship to the masculine 'order' that underpins it. Suzanne Césaire's reference to a type of literary cannibalism thus provides a productive means for reflecting on how a marginal female identity may be viewed as sustained by the very masculine tradition or order against which Condé defines it, as well as by a range of traditions that extend beyond this 'order'. The form and content of Suzanne Césaire's injunction make it clear that her political and aesthetic ambitions are influenced not just by texts belonging to a strictly Francophone Caribbean literary tradition but also by those from metropolitan French and Latin American modernist traditions that include the *Le Manifeste du surréalisme*, and the 1928 'Manifesto Antropófago' [Cannibal Manifesto] published by the Brazilian modernist writer Oswald de Andrade. If, as I have observed, 'female writing' is fed by the exclusions and also the myths of a normative masculine order, then an idea of literary cannibalism is an apposite description of the creative strategies employed in works by women. Viewing the practice of literary cannibalism as focused on the incorporation of other texts also illuminates Condé's own creative and rhetorical strategies in the essay.[68] The use of reading as a form of creative incorporation is represented formally through the various manifesto-style lists that Condé reproduces in the essay. A practice of creative incorporation is also arguably implicit in the complex intertextual patterning of the essay which refers to texts by authors from a variety of cultural contexts. Through her readings of these works, Condé appears to be seeking to identify provisionally with their discursive positions. These identifications serve as the basis on which to construct a shifting range of literary and communitarian associations and an evolving set of demands that Condé characterizes in the final section of her essay as a type of literary freedom.

The possibility of attaining this type of freedom is reliant on relinquishing the identification with the marginalized female identity that Condé had appeared to defend in the section on disorder. Her decision to abandon at this stage of the essay the arguably satirical gender-based polarization of positions is thus strategic: she does so in order to claim another set of polarized positions broadly congruent with 'defenders' and 'enemies' of literary freedom. This idea of 'literary freedom' is in turn shared out between three discursive positions that also pivot around an idea of 'false revolutionary literature'. Condé begins by quoting the comments by the Argentinean modernist writer Julio Cortázar made during a lecture given at University of California, Berkeley, in 1977: 'It is the destiny of literature to provide for beauty. It is its duty to provide for truth in this beauty.'[69]

This is followed by a quotation from an English translation of Maurice Blanchot's *Le Livre à venir*: 'The essence of literature is to escape any fundamental determination, any assertion which could stabilize it or even fix it. It is never already there, it is always to be found and invented again.'[70] Thus, the essay appears to align both Cortázar's and Blanchot's views on literature with a defence of literary freedom that could be contrasted with what is implicitly the false revolutionary claims of a West Indian literature (associated with *ELC*) that inhibits freedom by 'respecting a stereotypical portrayal of themselves (reader and writer) and their society'.[71]

At the end of the essay, Condé projects a future in which the implicit question concerning the possibility of 'a new era of freedom in West Indian writing', raised at the start of the essay, is restated explicitly in the final paragraph. Both questions are, nevertheless, only partially 'answered':

> Can we expect the liberation of the West Indian Writer in the years to come? *Éloge de la Créolité* gives a negative answer. However other forces are at work [...]. Among the writers themselves, a few dissenting voices, not just female voices [...] make themselves heard and give cause for hope.[72]

This unresolved questioning is the context of as yet unrealized solidarities between 'dissenting voices' that are 'not just female voices'. In fact, the conception of literary freedom outlined in the essay's ending appears to juxtapose two positions that have been presented throughout as antithetical: a notion of irreducible or absolute literary freedom and a diffuse idea of political action that employs the language of conventional political discourse with references to 'revolution', 'forces' and 'dissenting voices'. However, the fact that this politically charged literary freedom is projected into an indefinite future that is 'a cause for hope' lends it a distinctly utopian inflection. In this way, Condé's manifesto-essay 'feeds' on the symbolic economy and impassioned rhetorical style of political discourse, shifting its claims away from an established idea of political engagement (associated with ideas of revolution or — in the case of North American academic culture — identity politics) towards a defence of the specificity of the literary sphere, in a process that perhaps gestures towards the possibility for a re-configuration of the political sphere itself. Such a re-configuration is ultimately the source of a dialogue with the various literary and critical traditions with which Condé forges connections.

Viewed in the context of the debate I have sketched out above, Condé's use of manifesto strategies poses the following key questions: in light of the manifesto's close association with an international or global modernist project, what uses may be envisaged for specific avant-garde creative and formal practices and the accompanying political positions?[73] Another is the question of the relationship that exists between an idea of 'the literary absolute' posited by Blanchot, and the attempts by both Cortázar and Condé to define types of socially responsible and socially situated literary freedom. As Leslie Hill observes in *Blanchot: Extreme Contemporary*, Blanchot's view of literature aims to 'put in place an absolute absence of world' and 'could not be made subject to worldly, moral criteria such as authenticity or intersubjective freedom'.[73] Such an uncompromising view of literature's independence would thus render it incompatible with any attempt at instrumentalization, even in the service of a notion of 'literary freedom' (defined in the case of Cortázar in terms of truth-telling and by Condé as providing a context for various forms of communitarian relations). It is perhaps fitting then that Condé's essay does not resolve the tensions between literature and politics that accompany these positions but rather puts them in play in the space of the manifesto-essay. Through close attention to the relationships between different forms of politics — identity politics, anti-colonial resistance, cultural and literary politics — this book aims to track these tensions as they are mobilized across a range of textual and generic sites in Condé's œuvre. The notion of space will be read with a view to highlighting various metaphorical possibilities for addressing key but as yet under-theorized concerns in Condé's œuvre: ideas of genre, performance, representation and the imaginary. A wider aim of this book is also to situate the notions of politics, literature and space within fresh readings of the themes in Condé's work that have attracted greater critical attention: questions of history, memory, individual and collective identity.

Chapter 1, 'Performing "the Personal" in the Interview', considers the implications of Condé's marked use of interviews and also the related use of these as the context in which interviewers seek to establish a connection between her life and work. Drawing together theorizations of the interview, exoticism and representativity with a close reading of a selection of her interviews, the chapter reads the interviews as spaces of literary and identitarian performances.

Chapter 2, 'Re-writing the Journey to Africa or "finding the wrong ancestors" in *En attendant le bonheur*', builds on the discussion of Condé's engagement with the field of reception and considers the reading assumptions that are brought to her work in the United States. Reading against the grain of the critical orthodoxy that situates the text in relation to the ethnic and gender-based constituency allegiances that are taken for granted within North American identity politics, I account for the complex sets of relationships that *En attendant le bonheur* establishes between the Francophone Caribbean and African-American texts that it references.

Against the critical backdrop of testimonial literature, Chapter 3, 'Voice, Irony and History in *Moi Tituba, sorcière...Noire de Salem*', extends the discussion of the ways in which Condé's work resists critical expectations of representativity, highlighting the use of different of forms of irony in *Moi Tituba, sorcière...Noire de Salem*. The chapter argues that through this use of irony the text undertakes an ambiguous series of engagements with and re-formulations of questions of 'voice', 'history', 'agency' and 'community'.

Chapter 4, 'Autobiography and Reading in *Le Cœur à rire et à pleurer: Contes vrais de mon enfance*', reads the specific generic and stylistic choices employed in Condé's memoir as expressions of literary agency. Through a reading of the work as a type of 'literary autobiography', the chapter explores the strategic potential presented by the interaction between the marked intertextual patterning of the text and the complex blurring between its fictional and autobiographical elements.

Chapter 5, 'Literature, Art and Identity Politics in *Les Derniers Rois mages*', defines the notion of 'literature' or 'the literary' in relation to the themes of 'quest' and 'origins'. The chapter situates this process in the context of an enlarged cultural and geographical matrix exploring the experiences of a male Guadeloupean artist married to an African-American woman and living in the United States. Reading the protagonist's failed quest for identity in terms of the questioning of notions of 'authenticity' and 'origins', the chapter discusses the distinctive relationship between literature, art, representation and African-American identity politics that is constructed in the novel.

Chapter 6, 'On the Creative Uses of Gaps: (Re)-imagining Identity in *Desirada*', examines the role of immigration and the related trend towards globalization on re-shaping existing conceptions of Francophone Caribbean or 'black' identity. Against the backdrop of a discussion of the transformation of the notion of politics in the context of globalization, the chapter highlights the ways in which the novel points to possibilities for a creative re-visioning of traditional building blocks of identity such as 'family', 'home', 'race' and 'collective memory' and, ultimately, the very notions of 'identity' and 'the imaginary'.

Notes to the Introduction

1. For a discussion of the complex role of English translations of Condé's novels in framing both the critical reception of Condé's work and the dialogue that she establishes with this process in her work, see Dawn Fulton, *Signs of Dissent: Maryse Condé and Postcolonial Criticism* (Charlottesville and London: University of Virginia Press, 2008), pp. 143–50. In this respect, Fulton notes that the fact that many critical readings of Condé's work rely on translations adds an important dimension to the critical dialogue that Condé undertakes in her fiction (p. 143).

2. Celia Britton and Michael Syrotinski, 'Introduction', in *Francophone Texts and Postcolonial Theory*, ed. by Britton and Syrotinski (= *Paragraph: Journal of Modern Critical Theory*, 24, 3 (2001)), 1–11 (p. 2).

3. For a regularly updated list of Maryse Condé's publications see the City University website dedicated to the work of Francophone writers: <www.lehman.cuny.edu/ile.en.ile/paroles/conde.html>.

4. For a discussion of Condé's plays as part of a dynamic tradition of Francophone Caribbean theatre see Stephanie Bérard, *Théâtres des Antilles, Traditions et Scènes Contemporaines* (préface d'Ina Césaire) (Paris: L'Harmattan, 2009).

5. Exceptions to this approach include Dawn Fulton, *Signs of Dissent*.

6. Chris Bongie, *Friends and Enemies: The Scribal Politics of Post/Colonial Literature* (Liverpool: Liverpool University Press, 2009). Bongie describes this as the 'the ready-made homology between culture and politics' (p. 5).

7. This is not say that Condé has no positively articulated political position. In fact, in 1992 Condé was an unsuccessful candidate in regional elections in Guadeloupe on the electoral platform of the pro-independence party. As Condé reveals in Françoise Pfaff's *Entretiens avec Maryse Condé*, 'Ce sont deux domaines totalement différents. Mais l'énergie qu'il faudrait déployer pour avoir un poste politique, pour aller à des meetings, pour aller haranguer la foule, cette énergie-là, je n'ai pas envie de la consacrer qu'à l'écriture' [These are two entirely different matters. The energy you have to exert to seek political office, to go to meetings, to address crowds, I prefer to dedicate to writing] (*EMC*, 133; *CMC*, 90).

8. See for example Maryse Condé, 'Order, Disorder, Freedom and the West Indian Writer', *Yale French Studies*, 83 (1993), 121–35; 'The Stealers of Fire: The French-Speaking Writers of the Caribbean and Their Strategies of Liberation', *Journal of Black Studies*, 35 (2004), 154–64.

9. Bongie, *Friends and Enemies*, pp. 2–3.

10. Bongie, *Friends and Enemies*, p. 3.

11. See for example Joanne M. Braxton, *Black Women Writing Autobiography: A Tradition within a Tradition* (Philadelphia, PA: Temple University Press, 1989); Carole Boyce Davies, *Black Women, Writing and Identity: Migrations of the Subject* (London and New York: Routledge, 1994); Anne McClintock, *Imperial Leather: Race, Gender and Sexuality in the Colonial Contest* (New York and London: Routledge, 1995); *Women, Autobiography, Theory: A Reader*, ed. by Sidonie Smith and Julia Watson (Madison, Wisconsin and London: University of Wisconsin Press, 1998); Johnnie M. Stover, *Rhetoric and Resistance in Black Women's Autobiography* (Gainesville: University Press of Florida, 2003).

12. Julia Watson and Sidonie Smith, 'De/Colonization and the Politics of Discourse in Women's Autobiographical Practices', in *De/Colonizing the Subject: The Politics of Women's Autobiography*, ed. by Sidonie Smith and Julia Watson (Minneapolis: University of Minnesota Press, 1992), pp. xiii–xxxi (p. xxi).

13. See Doris Sommer, '"Not Just a Personal Story": Women's *Testimonios* and the Plural Self', in *Life/Lines: Theorizing Women's Autobiography*, ed. by Bella Brodzki and Celeste Schenck (Ithaca, NY, and London: Cornell University Press, 1988), pp. 107–30.

14. See Braxton, *Black Women Writing Autobiography*; Boyce Davies, *Black Women, Writing and Identity*; McClintock, *Imperial Leather*; Smith and Watson, eds, *Women, Autobiography, Theory*; Stover, *Rhetoric and Resistance*.

15. Robert Young, 'Ideologies of the Postcolonial', Editorial in *Interventions*, 1 (1998/99), 4–8 (p. 7) (quoted in Nicholas Harrison, 'Who Needs an Idea of the Literary?', in *The Idea of the Literary*, ed. by Nicholas Harrison (= *Paragraph*, 28, 2 (2005)), 1–17 (p. 1)).

16. See Pierre Bourdieu, *La Distinction: Critique sociale du jugement* (Paris: Minuit, 1979); *Les Règles de l'art: Génèse et structure du champ littéraire* (Paris: Seuil, 1992).

17. Charles Forsdick and David Murphy, 'Introduction: Situating Postcolonial Thought', in *Postcolonial Thought in the French-Speaking World*, ed. by Charles Forsdick and David Murphy (Liverpool: Liverpool University Press, 2009), pp. 1–27 (p. 11).

18. Forsdick and Murphy, p. 8.

19. See for example Ahmad Aijaz, *In Theory: Class, Nations, Literatures* (London: Verso, 1992); Richard Serrano, *'Francophone' Writers at the Ends of the French Empire* (Lanham, MD: Lexington Books, 2005).

20. Nicholas Harrison, 'Preface', in *The Idea of the Literary*, ed. by Nicholas Harrison (= *Paragraph*, 28, 2 (2005)), iii–iv (p. iii).

21. Forsdick and Murphy, 'Introduction: Situating Postcolonial Thought', in *Postcolonial Thought in the French-Speaking World*, p. 11.

22. The last decade has seen a proliferation of monographs, edited volumes and special issues of journals dedicated to these questions. Examples include: Celia Britton, *Edouard Glissant and Postcolonial Theory: Strategies of Language and Resistance* (Charlottesville and London: University Press of Virginia, 1999); Peter Hallward, *Absolutely Postcolonial: Writing between the Singular and the Specific* (Manchester: Manchester University Press, 2001); Graham Huggan, *The Postcolonial Exotic: Marketing the Margins* (London and New York: Routledge, 2001); Britton and Syrotinski, eds, *Paragraph: Journal of Modern Critical Theory*, 24 (2001); *Francophone Postcolonial Studies: A Critical Introduction*, ed. by Charles Forsdick and David Murphy (London and New York: Arnold, 2003); Nicholas Harrison, *Postcolonial Criticism: History, Theory and the Work of Fiction* (Cambridge: Polity, 2003); Richard Serrano, *'Francophone' Writers at the Ends of the French Empire* (Lanham, MD: Lexington Books, 2005); *Francophone Postcolonial Cultures*, ed. by Kamal Salhi (Oxford and Lanham, MD: Lexington, 2003); *Francophone Postcolonial Studies*, 1 (2003); Forsdick and Murphy, eds, *Postcolonial Thought in the French-Speaking World* (Liverpool: Liverpool University Press, 2009).

23. Forsdick and Murphy, 'Introduction: Situating Postcolonial Thought', in *Postcolonial Thought in the French-Speaking World*, p. 4.

24. See for example Harrison, *Postcolonial Criticism*; Huggan, *The Postcolonial Exotic*; Deepika Bahri, *Native Intelligence: Aesthetics, Politics and Postcolonial Literature* (Minneapolis and London: University of Minnesota Press, 2003).

25. David Hopkins, *Surrealism: A Very Short Introduction* (Oxford: Oxford University Press, 2004), p. 2. I would argue however that their focus on the unconscious processes shaping creative activity would make their view of literature inconsistent with the political instrumentalization that Sartre effects.

26. See Pierre Bourdieu, *La Distinction*; *Les Règles de l'art*.

27. See for example Maurice Blanchot, *L'Espace littéraire* (Paris: Gallimard, 1968); Jacques Derrida, *Writing and Difference*, trans. by Alan Bass (Chicago, IL: University of Chicago Press, 1978); Roland Barthes, *Le Bruissement de la langue: Essais Critiques IV* (Paris: Editions du Seuil, 1993).

28. Celia Britton, *The Nouveau Roman: Fiction, Theory and Politics* (New York: St. Martin's Press Inc., 1992), p. 5.

29. Huggan, *The Postcolonial Exotic*, p. 5.

30. Huggan, *The Postcolonial Exotic*, p. 4–5.

31. Huggan, *The Postcolonial Exotic*, p. 5.

32. Huggan, *The Postcolonial Exotic*, p. 239.

33. Huggan, *The Postcolonial Exotic*, pp. 165–76.

34. Bahri, *Native Intelligence*, p. 9.

35. Bahri, *Native Intelligence*, p. 9.

36. Harrison, *Postcolonial Criticism*, p. 139.

37. Nicholas Harrison, 'Who Needs an Idea of the Literary?', pp. 12–13.

38. Harrison, 'Who Needs an Idea of the Literary?', p. 13.

39. Harrison, 'Who Needs an Idea of the Literary?', p. 13.

40. Bahri, *Native Intelligence*, p. 21.

41. Bahri, *Native Intelligence*, p. 21.

42. Bahri, *Native Intelligence*, p. 6.
43. Bahri, *Native Intelligence*, p. 6.
44. Bongie, *Friends and Enemies*, p. 3.
45. Janet Lyon, *Manifestoes: Provocations of the Modern* (Ithaca, NY: Cornell University Press, 1999), p. 1
46. Lyon, *Manifestoes*, p. 13.
47. Lyon, *Manifestoes*, p. 13.
48. Lyon, *Manifestoes*, p. 61.
49. Lyon, *Manifestoes*, p. 14.
50. Lyon, *Manifestoes*, p. 14.
51. Lyon, *Manifestoes*, p. 15.
52. Lyons, *Manifestoes*, p. 15.
53. Lyon, *Manifestoes*, p. 15.
54. Condé, 'Order, Disorder', p. 121.
55. Lyon, *Manifestoes*, p. 42.
56. Jean Bernabé, Patrick Chamoiseau and Raphaël Confiant, *Éloge de la Créolité* (Paris: Gallimard, 1993); *In Praise of Creoleness*, trans. by Mohamed B. Taleb-Khyar (Baltimore, MD: Johns Hopkins University Press, 1990). This argument and its translation are presented as follows: 'l'interaction auteurs/lecteurs où s'élabore une littérature' [the authors/readers interaction which is the primary condition of the development of a literature] (p. 14; p. 76).
57. Condé, 'Order, Disorder', p. 121.
58. Lyon, *Manifestoes*, p. 59.
59. Condé, 'Order, Disorder', p. 123.
60. Condé, 'Order, Disorder', p. 126. For example, Condé parodies the representation of women as willingly subservient to men in this 'order'. 'I cannot resist the pleasure of quoting the passage in *Masters of the Dew* [...] "Yes", she says, "I shall be the mistress of your house. [...] I shall stay standing while you eat [...]. At night, I shall lie by your side [...] I shall be the servant of your desire"' (p. 126).
61. Condé, 'Order, Disorder', p. 130.
62. Condé, 'Order, Disorder', p. 130.
63. Condé, 'Order, Disorder', pp. 130–31.
64. Condé, 'Order, Disorder', p. 125.
65. Condé, 'Order, Disorder', p. 133.
66. Lyon, *Manifestoes*, p. 36.
67. Condé, 'Order, Disorder', p. 122.
68. My reading of Condé's use of literary cannibalism here diverges from that offered by Nicole Simek, *Eating Well, Reading Well: Maryse Condé and the Ethics of Interpretation* (Amsterdam and New York: Rodopi, 2008). Simek defines this practice as 'the hungry consumption of another's writing spurred by a desire to fuse with the text or the characters' (p. 169).
69. Condé, 'Order, Disorder', p. 134. Cortázar is associated by with an Argentinean modernist tradition and is famous for the 1963 short story *Hopscotch* (*Rayuela*) written in Paris and first published in Spanish that adopts a distinctive narrative strategy based on inviting the reader to choose his own path through 155 expendable chapters thereby realizing through the process of reading multiple endings.
70. Condé, 'Order, Disorder', p. 134.
71. Conde, 'Order, Disorder', p. 134.
72. Condé, 'Order, Disorder', pp. 134–35.
73. The essay quotes in English from Alain Robbe-Grillet, *Pour un nouveau roman* (Paris: Gallimard, 1946), p. 131: 'There are no masterpieces for eternity; merely works marked by their time' (p. 126).
74. Leslie Hill, *Blanchot: Extreme Contemporary* (London and New York: Routledge, 1997), p. 107.

CHAPTER 1

Performing 'the Personal'
in the Interview

As an international Guadeloupean female author Maryse Condé negotiates the categories of writer, critic and academic with an acute awareness of the conditions of reception of her work. Although nominally a 'Guadeloupean writer', Condé's reputation as 'an important writer' has largely been consolidated in the United States and in France where she has been awarded a number of literary prizes.[1] One of the distinguishing — and also critically overlooked — features of Condé's work has been the significant number of interviews that she has given during this period in a variety of media in both the United States and France.[2] In these interviews, Condé's numerous interviewers have all revealed a more or less pronounced concern with engaging her in a process of reflection on the influence of her own life experiences on her fiction. If Condé has typically submitted willingly and, apparently, with some relish, to this line of questioning, she has also used her interventions in these interviews (as well as her literary and critical writings) to unsettle the assumption that her fiction is a transparent reflection of her life. Condé's questioning has in turn been anchored in a marked and ongoing discussion of the conditions of reception faced by her work and an appeal to the freedom of 'literature' and 'the author'. Through a comparative analysis of two sets of published interviews conducted with Condé between 1991 and 2004, this chapter examines the uses to which Condé puts her varied and often ambiguous representations of 'the personal', 'the field of reception', 'literature' and 'the author'.

The study of the particular uses to which the interview is put by writers has attracted relatively little critical attention. In the introduction to a special issue of *Nottingham French Studies* entitled 'Thinking in Dialogue: The Role of the Interview in Post-war French thought', Christopher Johnson notes that the interview is a recent genre whose emergence in the middle of the nineteenth century coincided with the growth of mass media in Europe and the United States, and points to a related tendency to view the interview as a 'marginal' or 'parasitic' part of the author's work that is implicitly undeserving of critical attention.[3] Gérard Genette accords a spatial dimension to the interview's assumed marginal status, classifying it as 'epitext', part of the paratext that he defines as follows: '[it is] neither on the interior nor the exterior, it is both; it is on the threshold.'[4] But this 'threshold' space does possess a strategic viability. Drawing on Genette's analysis, Katherine Larson emphasizes the dual use of the interview to encourage the reader to approach the text in the way prescribed by the author and also to defend the text against misreadings.[5] Larson's privileging of the relationship between reader and author in the interview is suggestive of the individual nature of the relationship that is constructed between reader and author (a relationship that I explore in the final part of this chapter).

Johnson's analysis of the interview as situated within a nexus of relations structured both by societal expectations and authorial intention points to a broadening of the implicitly particular or individual relationship between author and reader in terms of author and 'reading public' or 'society'. In line with this, Johnson emphasizes the influence of the field of reception of the author's work on the demand for access to the author via the interview, noting that 'the interview could be said to respond to the fundamental requirement of modern civilization, that is, the desire for presence, the immediacy of the word, the authority and *authenticity* of a certain kind of testimony' (my emphasis).[6] However, crucially, he also recognizes that the interview is not simply something to which the intellectual is subjected. In fact, by providing opportunities for 'performance' and 'improvisation', the interview may potentially serve as a strategic site of intervention.[7] This emphasis on features that point to interview as a site of performance or improvisation serves to highlight the inherent instability of its effects and also of its relationship to what Johnson characterizes as 'society's demand for verification of the relationship between the author's life and work'.[8]

As I highlighted in my introduction, a socially sanctioned concern with linking an author's work and life has particular implications for the ways in which works by 'Third World' and 'female' authors such as Condé are read, since this typically translates into reading the author and their work as 'representative'.[9] In his study of the international reception of 'Third World' authors, Graham Huggan highlights the particular, and often conflicting, claims of authenticity that inform the reception of works by 'Third World' authors.[10] Graham Huggan argues that within the context of reception of non-Western authors whose work has an international and largely metropolitan readership, the idea of 'authenticity' is necessarily a contested category of evaluation which serves as 'a bargaining chip' in the ongoing negotiation of rival interests between these authors' different readerships'.[11] However, in common with Johnson, Huggan suggests that the paratextual sphere may offer such authors some room for manoeuvre. According to Huggan, it is in the paratextual frame — 'cover design, front and back cover, blurbs, glossary, notes, epigraphs, italicized quotations and so on' — that the author undertakes a process of negotiation between different expectations of authenticity by simultaneously demonstrating an awareness of these expectations and putting these into play.[12] While Huggan does not explore the specific role of the interview in this process, my argument in this chapter is that his analysis is relevant to Condé's use of the interview to address these varying reading expectations. The idea of play or improvisation that Johnson and Huggan attribute to the use of the interview suggests that it shares key characteristics with the notion of literature that Condé defines in her fiction and critical writings and it is worthwhile returning to the Blanchotian definition of literature (cited in my Introduction) that Condé provides: 'The essence of literature is to escape any fundamental determination, any assertion which could stabilize it or even fix it. It is never already there, it is always to be found or invented again.'[13] The indeterminacy that Condé associates with the practice of literature is arguably relevant to the mixed generic status of the interview, a spoken encounter between interviewer and author that is transcribed in writing and read as a 'text'.

An idea of indeterminacy or play can also be ascribed to the markedly complex and shifting representations that Condé makes of her field of reception. In Condé's collection of interviews with Françoise Pfaff entitled *Entretiens avec Maryse Condé* she identifies her two main contexts of reception as France and the United States, designating her native Guadeloupe as an absent field of reception where people did not read.[14] However in my interview with Condé, while she continues to represent France and the United States as important contexts for the reception of her work, she emphasizes the role of book clubs in the development of a larger readership for her work in Guadeloupe.[15] If Condé presents her relationship to these readerships as necessarily conflicted, she assimilates her experience to that of 'l'écrivain noir' [the Black writer], faced with competing expectations from on the one hand, 'son peuple, les siens, ceux qui le lisent localement et attendent une certaine chose' [their own people who read them locally and expect certain things] and, on the other, 'la presse qui fait le succès littéraire, qui chosifie, exotifie et demande autre chose' [the press which creates literary success, objectifies, stresses exoticism and expects something else] (*EMC*, 150; *CMC*, 103).

Condé's response to these conflicting expectations is the oblique injunction that '[i]l faut donc se retrouver entre ces deux exigencies' [[i]n between these two types of demands, writers have to find themselves] (*EMC*, 150; *CMC*, 103). This comment is richly suggestive of Condé's ongoing negotiation with the constraints that are implicitly encoded within different readings of her work in the 'local' and 'foreign' contexts of reception. In the rest of this chapter, I shall examine in detail the mobile sets of representations that Condé makes of the Guadeloupean, French and North American fields of reception, drawing out the relationships between literature and criticism, her readers and the various authorial identities that Condé constructs in her interviews.

★　★　★　★　★

The significance of Guadeloupe as a field of reception for Condé's work is rendered evident by her repeated and often contradictory comments concerning her relationship to her country of 'origin'. In her interviews with Pfaff, Condé argues that Guadeloupe could not be considered as a viable field of reception for her work since '[i]l semblerait donc que Guadeloupe offre un climat moins favorable au développement de la littérature' [It would seem that Guadeloupe offers a climate less favourable to the development of literature] (*EMC*, 43; *CMC*, 26). Condé is highly critical of the lack of reading culture in Guadeloupe, a state of affairs which, in her view, contrasts markedly with Martinique, where writers such as Aimé Césaire, Frantz Fanon and Édouard Glissant have been instrumental in forging a literary culture.[16] Condé attributes this lack of interest in reading to a cultural preoccupation with attaining tangible forms of social prestige such as money and power.[17]

However, in my interview with Condé, she points to an evolution in the conditions of reception that her work faces in Guadeloupe reflected in the development of a local readership in the context of book clubs.[18] Yet, these are readers who 'lisent sans comprendre' [who read without understanding] and in relation to whom she takes on the task of discussing and explaining her books, noting in my interview with her that 'il y a un important travail à faire [...] au niveau de la lecture' [there is a significant amount of work to be done [...] at the level of reading] (Sansavior, pp. 28–29). Condé's emphasis on explaining her texts to her local readership thus implies a challenge to the Blanchotian view of literature as predicated on play. This process of explaining her texts to local readers is in turn linked to a broader (and also oblique) function of 'Diaspora literacy' that Condé attributes to her work as a writer, that of educating 'the people of the Black Diaspora' about culturally significant artists and writers: 'Je pense que pour nous, les gens de la diaspora noire, il y a certains noms qui devraient être connus et reconnus' [I believe that we, the people of the Black Diaspora, should know and recognize certain names] (*EMC*, 144; *CMC*, 98–99).

Condé's use of her interviews with Pfaff to engage with the views expressed by Guadeloupean critics about her fiction serves to designate the interview as a key site of intervention for the author, and conforms to Johnson's Bourdieusian-inspired conception of the interview as an 'antagonistic' public space in which the intellectual 'situates himself in relation to other inhabitants of the intellectual sphere'.[19] For Condé, this process of positioning involves complex sets of interchanges between the critical and literary fields. Crucially, these interchanges foreground the role of her creative 'misreadings' in constructing these very fields and in occupying various positions in relation to her own constructions. In effect, what characterizes Condé's engagement with the Francophone Caribbean literary culture is its marked dramatic sensibility as she makes multiple runs at 'representing' this cultural space while also articulating strategic positions of marginality from it. Drawing on her own readings of the critical positions of Glissant and the Créolité school, Condé illustrates that a shared idea of authenticity informs the expectations that are brought to the role of authors and the nature of their creative output. Indeed, as Condé observes, this idea of an 'authentic West Indian writer' translates into a prescriptive vision of the role of the novelist that also has implications for the content and style of these writers' creative output. According to this vision, Condé argues that the writer is required to fulfil the role of a political representative for his people and produce works of literature that engage with political and social problems.[20] Condé also draws attention to the imperative that the novel should be written exclusively or predominantly in Creole.[21]

Yet, Condé occupies a consciously marginal position in relation to these prescriptions and thus deploys individual experiences and philosophical positions strategically. All instances of marginality — be they 'imposed' or 'claimed' — are shown to be open to recuperation within her ambiguous self-representations. By way of pointing to her marginalization from the dominant Francophone Caribbean critical tradition, Condé quotes in some detail from a particularly misogynistic review of her first novel in the journal, *Le Naïf* in which she is described as a 'voyeur'

[voyeur] and 'prostituée' [prostitute], adding that the review 'me comparant à Mayotte Capécia' [[was] comparing me to Mayotte Capécia] (*EMC*, 72; *CMC*, 46)

Condé's marginality is also a state to which she is 'born' as she draws attention to her experience of growing up in a very prosperous middle-class family in which no Creole was spoken in order to problematize the assumption that she should or indeed *could* act as representative for her people. In this way, Condé challenges the validity of the prescription that it was only through the use of Creole that the novelist was able to express an authentically Francophone Caribbean cultural experience. Condé underscores the risks of exclusion that are implicit in equating West Indian identity with Creole as she asks whether the 'second-generation' French West Indians living in France who do not speak Creole should be excluded from the category of 'West Indian people'.[22]

In addition, Condé presents Francophone Caribbean writers as potentially subject to this risk of exclusion and she thus warns that an over-eager promotion of Creole as the authentic language of Francophone Caribbean literary production carries with it the threat of becoming 'un terrorisme culturel' [a cultural terrorism] (*EMC*, 165; *CMC*, 114).[23] Faced with this perceived constraint to creative freedom, Condé asserts the following right for each writer: 'A chacun sa créolité, [...] à chacun son rapport avec la tradition, à chacun sa façon de l'exprimer dans la littérature écrite' [To each his or her own créolité [...] to each his or her own relationship with oral materials and the oral tradition and to each his or her own way of expressing it in written literature] (*EMC*, 165; *CMC*, 114). As a non-native speaker of Creole, the tension between this prescriptive use of Creole and the freedom that Condé claims for writers is creatively productive, and she characterizes her work on the language as 'à la fois un travail de recréation et d'invention' [a work of both re-creation and invention] (thereby undermining the very idea that there exists an authentic Creole language that can be faithfully reproduced in writing as opposed to, as Condé suggests, constantly re-imagined) (*EMC*, 160; *CMC*, 110).[24]

Condé also situates her refusal to fulfil the role of a 'politically engaged' novelist in terms in a firm philsosphical commitment to 'the freedom of expression' of the 'writer', noting the fundamental incompatibility that, in her view, exists between the roles of politician and novelist.[25] Condé points to a similar incompatibility between the work of the writer and commercial success, and her refusal to conform to the prescriptions concerning the role of the writer is the context for a reflection on the marketability of attempts to define an authentic Francophone Caribbean literature. Commenting on the award of the Prix Goncourt to Patrick Chamoiseau for *Texaco*, Condé observes that Chamoiseau's treatment of language may be 'seduisant' [attractive] for a French readership and the interest shown by the French media can be explained by 'des raisons exotiques' [[its] exotic appeal] (*EMC*, 164–65; *CMC*, 113–14). Interestingly, when asked whether she thinks that Créolité may lead to exoticism, Condé responds with characteristic obliqueness: 'C'est un danger. On risque de tomber dans le piège qui consiste à plaire à l'autre' [It's a danger. You risk falling into the trap of appealing to the Other] (*EMC*, 165; *CMC*, 114). Condé's use of the pronoun 'on' (which can be variously translated as 'one' 'we', or 'you' or 'I') implies both a diffuse identification with and a distance from

Chamoiseau's position of susceptibility to 'the trap of appealing to the Other'. Her response certainly begs the question: how might an 'international Guadeloupean author' such as Condé negotiate her susceptibility to this risk? Asked whether she can be said to benefit from her status as a marginal author, Condé observes in my interview with her: 'Tout le monde joue un peu parce que finalement si vous êtes exclu, vous vous complaisez dans l'exclusion. Vous jouez le rôle de l'écrivain exclu. Donc, je pense que jouer un rôle pour un écrivain est inévitable' [Everyone plays a role to some degree and finally if you are excluded, you become comfortable with exclusion. You play the role of the excluded writer. So I think that for a writer playing a role is inevitable].[26] Condé's appeal to the writer as a type of inevitable role-player underscores the strategic uses that she makes of ideas of 'marginality' and 'exoticism' in the play of the interview, a process that I discuss in the rest of this chapter.

★   ★   ★   ★   ★

Commenting on the reception of her work in France, Condé characterizes the general tenor of reviews of her work in the French media (press and radio) as 'exoticizing'.[27] This idea of exoticism is germane to a reflection on how certain assumptions about the authenticity of the author's work shape its reception in this field. In the *Postcolonial Exotic* Huggan, citing Stephen Foster, defines exoticism as a political and aesthetic practice that involves 'the systematic assimilation of cultural difference, ascribing familiar meanings and associations to unfamiliar things, it also denotes an expanded, if inevitably distorted, comprehension of diversity which effectively limits diversity "since the exotic [...] is kept at arm's length rather than taken as one's own"'.[28] This view of exoticism as both negating and *entrenching* difference means that authenticity operates as a dual category of evaluation. On the one hand, the marketing of Condé's work in mainstream media can be interpreted as assigning the status of 'authentic' (in the sense of true) French writer to Condé that implicitly negates her cultural specificity. On the other hand, the French reviewers' use of adjectives such as 'exotique', 'savoureux', 'drôlatre' ['exotic', 'appetizing' and 'humorous'] to describe Condé's work serves to signal the operation of authenticity as what Huggan refers to as 'compensatory' or 'redemptive strategy' whose effects are exclusively negative (*EMC*, 154; *CMC*, 105, translation adapted).[29] In line with this, Condé argues that the tendency among French reviewers to read her work as 'representative' of a 'Caribbean oral tradition' and produced 'de façon instinctive' [instinctively] effectively confines Francophone Caribbean literature to 'un ghetto exotique' [exotic ghetto] (*EMC*, 147; *CMC*, 100).

As in the case of Condé's response to 'representative' readings of her work in Guadeloupe, she undermines the readings of her work in France through the strategic use of references to biographical details of her life (as someone who grew up in a prosperous, middle-class, non-Creolophone family) and the appeal to the literary work involved in '[une] recherche de technique et de narrativité' [[a] search for technique and narrativity] (*EMC*, 146; *CMC*, 100).

The interventions that Condé makes concerning the reception of her work in France do not only resist directly specific assumptions as they relate to her reception in France. They also enact comparative readings of the conditions of reception in her 'foreign' and 'local' contexts of reception. By way of comparing the reception of her work in the foreign contexts, Condé establishes a contrast between the 'exotic fashion' in which Caribbean literature is 'perhaps perceived' in France and the more 'nuanced' American critical gaze:

> En France, je pense que je suis toujours un peu perçue d'une manière exotique. Il faut regarder dans les journaux. [...]. En France, j'ai un peu de mal à vaincre ce regard exotique qui est peut-être porté sur l'ensemble de la littérature antillaise. En Amérique, le regard est plus nuancé mais les critiques connaissent mal la société dont je parle et cela apporte des déformations dans leur appréciation de l'œuvre. Néanmoins, dans l'ensemble, le regard du critique américain est moins exotique que celui du français. (*EMC*, 153–54)

> [In France, I always feel perceived in a somewhat exotic fashion. You should read the reviews of my books in the French newspapers. [...]. In France, I have rather a hard time countering the exotic fashion in which West Indian literature as a whole is perceived. In the United States my works are seen in a more nuanced manner but here critics aren't really familiar with the society I depict, which causes distortions in their appreciation of the works. However, in general, the gaze of American critics is less exotic than that of their French counterparts. (*CMC*, 106)]

By appealing to differences in the degree of exoticizing reading practices in the French and American contexts, Condé suggests a moderation of the exclusively negative effects ascribed to exoticism by Huggan. Condé's comments therefore construct (what turns out be an unstable) contrast between a 'good' exoticism in the United States and a 'bad' exoticism in France.

The very fact of imputing positive effects to the practice of exoticism is not entirely unproblematic since, as Charles Forsdick observes, the term is traditionally assigned a wholly negative value within postcolonial discourse and used to connote 'a stimulating or exciting difference, something with which the domestic could be (safely) spiced'.[30] Forsdick notes that this critical focus has failed to take account of the semantic shifts that the term has undergone and argues for a need to move beyond contemporary postcolonial readings of the term as possessing 'almost universally pejorative overtones', with a view to harnessing its potential reflexivity.[31] According to Forsdick, the term, which was coined in the nineteenth century, has shifted between two semantic poles, one signifying an idea of 'radical otherness', and the other describing 'the process whereby such radical otherness is experienced by a traveller or translated, transported and represented for consumption at home'.[32] The attitude of a culture or group to radical 'otherness' or 'difference' is thus central to apprehending how exoticism informs reading practices. This is because, as Alec Hargreaves points out, 'all aesthetic categories involve some quality or other of subjective experience, which they mediate within a given culture.'[33] Hargreaves argues that it is the particular difficulty inherent in assigning a clear, stable meaning to the objects and experiences that are perceived as radically different that characterizes the exotic encounter between reader and writer. This is because '[t]he exotic lies by definition beyond our culture, and strikes us as essentially strange.'[34] Two potential responses to the disorientation that accompanies this perception of difference are designated: on the one hand, there is an attempt to attenuate the disorientation that results from this contact with alterity by attempting to assimilate or translate the culture or object into known frameworks of meaning, while, on the other hand, there is an accommodation of this difference.[35]

These two contrasting attitudes to difference are evident in the distinction that Condé makes between North American and French students: 'Les Américains ne savent rien de ces choses. [...] ils découvrent et ils écoutent tout ce qu'on leur dit. [...] Les Français, eux, sont plus ou moins allés en vacances dans les départements d'outre-mer et en Afrique, et ils pensent qu'ils connaissent tout' [Americans don't know about the subject. [...] they discover things and listen to everything that they're told. [...] French students have been on vacation to an Overseas French department or Africa and think they know it all] (*EMC*, 155; *CMC*, 107). The all-knowing attitude that Condé attributes to French students is suggestive of the form of exoticism that seeks to assimilate and domesticate difference. It is this same attitude that is subjected to a knowingly humorous imitative reading in my interview with Condé. By extending the performative idiom established in her use of the interview to that of impersonation, she satirizes French readers' pleasurable attachment to the reassuring clichés that she argues are provided by some of the texts that belong to the Créolité school: 'Les gens s'imaginent que c'est un créole authentique. Les gens s'imaginent que c'est l'aventure des djobeurs. Ils adorent ça. Ils s'imaginent: "Ah ! Oui, c'est ça, on fait comme ça"' [People imagine that it's an authentic Creole. People imagine that it's the adventure of the djobeurs. They love that. They imagine: 'Ah, yes, that's right, that's how things work there'].[36] Condé's satirical reading of the exoticist expectations of French readers therefore undertakes a strategic reversal of the effects of the 'bad exoticism' that she associates with the French context. Such a reversal presents a challenge to the fixity of the subject and object positions upon which the practice of this form of exoticism relies by highlighting the possibility for undercutting exoticist readings through direct critique. In addition, Condé's performance points to her ability to harness the dramatic potential of these very readings with a view to directing them towards the very context in which they emerge.

A similar potential for reversal of the effects of 'good exoticism', is also evident in Condé's representation of the role of difference in her reception in the United States. While Condé presents the lack of knowledge or understanding of Guadeloupe in the United States as having a largely positive impact that translates into a positive openness to her difference, in my interview with Condé, she implies with humour that it is nevertheless her status as '[u]ne étrangère' [a foreigner] with 'un accent francophone' [a Francophone accent] that is an intrinsic part of her appeal to her North American readers (Sansavior, p. 24).[37] She therefore appears to concede that her American readers are (like the French readers) also, at least partly, titillated by her 'difference'. Condé's characterization of a potential overlap in the motivations of readers in both contexts as of a love of difference for the sake of difference, as it were, serves to undercut the implicit distinction that she appears to make between 'good' exoticism in the United States and 'bad' exoticism in France. Rather than articulating a clear-cut contrast between two forms of exoticism, Condé's discourse in her interviews and critical writings enacts a fluid ongoing movement between what Charles Forsdick describes as the two semantic poles of 'radical otherness' and 'translation or assimilation'.[38] However, the effect of this movement is to challenge the fixity of these very poles.

Condé's comparison of the promotion of her texts in the United States and France thus leads to seemingly paradoxical conclusions: the 'bad exoticism' attributed to the French context is presented as having potentially positive implications for the reception of her work, while the 'good exoticism' in the United States is shown to have negative implications. When asked by Pfaff whether being a black female writer has affected her career adversely in France (a complaint frequently made by African-American female writers concerning their reception in the United States) she asserts that it is precisely her status as a black female writer that creates publishing opportunities for her work in France, as publishers are 'curieux de voir ce qu'une femme noire avait à dire, ce qu'elle avait dans la tête' [curious to see what a Black woman had to say and what she was thinking] (EMC, 41; CMC, 24).

This apparent openness of French publishers towards her work is linked to a more inclusive marketing strategy for her fiction, as Condé notes that her books are marketed both in national French and 'ethnic minority' media (EMC, 146; CMC, 100). In contrast, Condé suggests that the freedom and positive predisposition to her difference that she associates with the United States are potentially undermined by this society's preoccupation with racial politics, a preoccupation that means that her books are marketed exclusively in the 'ethnic minority' media (EMC, 146; CMC, 100). Questions concerning the publishing and marketing of her texts in interviews with Condé serve as the context in which she asserts her marginality from racial politics. This marginality is expressed in comments that are at turns sharply critical and dismissive of the predominance of discourses of racial politics in the United States. For example, she observes in relation to the marketing of her books in her interviews with Pfaff that 'l'Africain-Américain vit dans une société qui l'enferme dans la race' [African-Americans live in a society that locks them inside their race] (EMC, 146; CMC, 100). She is also dismissive of 'les Américaines' [American women] noting that '[elles] ont toujours des idées excessives sur tout' [[they] have exaggerated ideas on everything] (EMC, 41; CMC, 24).

While with these comments Condé apparently claims an oblique position beyond identity politics (race as well as gender), the claiming of an identity as 'black' and 'female' is nevertheless central to the symbolic resistance that she expresses in my interview with her to the representations of black women in France, 'une société fondamentalement raciste' [a fundamentally racist society] which, she argues, 'lui enlève toute possibilité de création autonome' [takes away from her all possibility of creative autonomy].[39]

Condé's shifting engagements with the reception of her work in Guadeloupe, France and the United States foreground a shared investment in an idea of authenticity in both political and exoticist readings. In particular, Condé's speculation on the various motivations that underpin this investment (for example, the quest for the new or the pleasure of the familiar in the foreign context of reception or the gaining of international literary plaudits in the local context) are revelatory of the overlapping representational strategies of discourses of representativity and exoticism, that Celia Britton and Michael Syrotinski characterize as a common tendency to 'fetichise difference'.[40] Thus, Condé's critique of the different assumptions of authenticity that are brought to the reading of her work in the different contexts of reception can be viewed as a type of 'literary play' that draws attention to and contests critical readings that present difference as 'fixed' or 'eternal'. More broadly, through this use of the interview to effectively offer readings of the critical process to which her work is subjected, Condé undertakes a reversal of the traditional relationship between literature and criticism (with literature as the object of criticism) that, as I highlighted in the introduction, Deepika Bahri attributes to the practice of literature.[41] By using her interviews as the context in which to challenge this established power relationship between 'literature' and 'criticism', Condé therefore gestures towards a broader questioning of the generic boundaries of literature itself.

A literary practice predicated on the play of difference and marginality is also exploited creatively by Condé in her interviews, sites of irreducible strangeness, in which she constructs a range of ambiguous authorial figures. In her interviews with Pfaff, Condé identifies the state of being a stranger as beneficial to the practice of writing:

> Je crois à présent qu'il est bon qu'un écrivain soit un étranger au monde, à tous les mondes dans lesquels il se trouve. C'est le regard de l'étranger qui est le regard de la découverte, de l'étonnement, de l'approfondissement. Si on est trop familier avec un lieu [...] on ne peut pas écrire avec vérité sur ce lieu. (*EMC*, 46)

> [I now believe that it is good for writers to be strangers to the world and to the various environments in which they find themselves. A stranger's gaze allows for discovery, astonishment and in-depth analysis. If you are overly familiar with a place [...] you cannot write truthfully about it. (*CMC*, 28)]

Moreover, this sense of strangeness is doubled by the shifting relationship that emerges in Condé's interviews between this 'real author' and her fictional characters. In my interview with Condé she observes:

> Quand je parle des choses que j'ai ressenties profondément, si j'essaie d'écrire un livre à la troisième personne, le livre est raté. Donc l'autobiographie, c'est un moyen pour moi de donner à mon texte une force, peut-être une sincérité, qu'autrement, il n'aurait pas eues. [...] c'est une stratégie d'authenticité.[42]

> [When I talk about deeply experienced emotions, if I try to write a book in the third person, the book is a failure. So autobiography is a way for me to give a force and perhaps a sincerity to my text that it would not otherwise have had. [...] it is a strategy for creating authenticity.]

Condé therefore appears to distinguish between 'intimacy' associated with the representation of her 'feelings' in fictional works and 'autobiography', the distillation of biographical facts of her life, a distinction that is richly suggestive of the complex relationship between the two unstable sites of 'the fictional' and 'the real' in her work.

This distinction between Condé's feelings and the biographical facts of her life points to an idea of 'authenticity' or 'sincerity' that is subsequently undercut later by her appeal to autobiography as part of 'une stratégie d'authenticité'. In this way, Condé appeals to an idea of literary authenticity as an 'effect' that is produced by the fictional process. More broadly, this observation casts light on the ways in which her critique of the various reading practices that I have discussed above is involved in unveiling the constructed or 'fictional' nature of such expectations. Condé's acknowledgement of the essentially constructed nature of authenticity is itself a creative prompt that allows for the realization of a type of 'spatialized' literary freedom that Condé defines as follows:

> Un roman, c'est pour faire un lieu d'abandon. On écrit un roman parce qu'on a des choses à dire et d'une certaine manière, on se trouve dans un périmètre absolument libre, fécond dans lequel on dit ce qu'on a envie de dire.[43]

> [You write a novel to create a space of spontaneity. You write a novel because you have things to say, and in a certain way. You find yourself in an arena of complete freedom and limitless creativity in which you say what you want to say.]

In effect, for Condé, literary authenticity is indistinguishable from a practice of 'making space' that is not subject to expectations of political and cultural authenticity.

This literary space is also one of constitution and dissolution of the authorial identity of Condé herself. Condé's shifting positions within her interviews serve to enact a model of open-ended individual subjectivity that is constructed at the intersection of fiction and the real world. In her interview with Marie-Agnès Sourieau, Condé characterizes her view of identity as follows: 'On se définit soi-même au fur et à mesure de son expérience personnelle et individuelle' [You define yourself in line with your personal and individual experience].[44] Interestingly, continuing in the same interview, Condé points to the distanced, subjective implication in social reality that underpins this identity as she observes: 'je m'efforce de faire une littérature qui échappe à toutes les rigidités, tous les canons, tous les interdits, tous les mots d'ordre et qui corresponde à ce que moi, Maryse Condé, je suis face aux problèmes du monde qui nous entoure' [I try to create a literature that is beyond all types of prescriptions, canons, restrictions and all literary formulae, a literature that corresponds to what, I, Maryse Condé, am when confronted with the problems of the world around us].[45] But, crucially, this is an identity that is subject to an ongoing effort and is not necessarily fully realized or, for that matter, even attainable.

The fact that Condé's views and the subject to which they point are open to a process of ongoing revision in turn has implications for the type of relationship that the Condé constructs with readers. In her study of the reception of Condé's work, Nicole Simek argues that the interviews serve two key interrelated functions: first, they provide facts which enable her to communicate to the reader her intentions and guide the interpretation of her works. Second, they serve to construct a relationship with the interviewer/reader that acts to disrupt the critics' or readers' expectations.[46] These functions do not so much impose certain interpretations of the text but rather evoke a form of freedom that Simek defines in terms of 'continually sending readers back to the texts, to reconsider their possibilities'.[47] Indeed, in my interview with Condé, she notes that while 'les entretiens servent dans l'imagination de l'écrivain à mettre au point certaines choses, [...] finalement le lecteur en fait ce qu'il veut' [in writers' imagination the interview serves to clarify certain points [...] ultimately the reader does what s/he wants with it].[48] Condé also characterizes a potential value of the freedom to read literature 'as one wishes' in terms of the capacity to '[f]aire sortir le lecteur de lui-même, l'obliger à s'auto-critiquer' [to take the reader out of himself, require him to undertake self-criticism].[49]

However, Condé stresses that this role does not translate into serving as a 'model' for her readers, noting in her interviews with Pfaff: 'Moi, je n'écris pas de livres exemplaires, il n'y a pas d'exemplarité et de personnages parfaits' [I do not write exemplary books, there are no exemplary situations or perfect characters] (*EMC*, 152; *CMC*, 105). The possibility that Condé may serve as a model for her readers, and also, by extension, that her work will be read in terms of expectations of authenticity that I discussed above, is continuously disrupted by a dual impulse towards self-disclosure and self-veiling that according to Madeleine Cottenet-Hage means that 'elle est bien de la race de ces écrivains pour qui le recours à l'écriture est un masque qui permet de dire sans se trahir' [she is among those writers who use writing as a mask, a mask that allows her to speak without revealing herself].[50]

Cottenet-Hage's characterization of 'literature' in terms of 'a mask that enables Condé to speak without revealing herself' points to the ambivalent nature of Condé's repeated recourse to the personal in her interviews. In this respect, a comparative reading of two comments in Condé's interviews with Sourieau is revelatory. Early in this interview, Condé appears to claim a wholly subjective, individual identity that she characterizes as follows: 'On se définit soi-même au fur et à mesure de son expérience personnelle et individuelle' [one defines oneself gradually, bit by bit, in line with one's personal and individual experience].[51] However, later on in the interview, she appears to express a desire to produce 'une écriture transparente' [transparent writing] and observes: 'je tâche d'aller droit à ce que je veux dire avec une grande économie, j'essaie d'éviter un trop-plein de paroles qui forment un écran entre le lecteur et l'auteur' [I try to avoid excessively dense prose that forms a screen between the reader and the writer].[52]

By implicitly ascribing this desire for transparent communication to 'the author', Condé suggests an oblique and perhaps also unbridgeable gap or 'screen' between the figure of the author and the 'personal' identity that she claims in the first comment. In addition, the potential for Condé's comments to be situated both within the context of other comments in this same interview and in an ever increasing number of other interviews (and critical writings) also generates the possibility for multiple reconfigurations of this oblique relationship between the authorial figure and the subjective identity to which she alludes at this point in the interview. In this way, the authorial identity that is presented in the interview emerges as not a single performance, as is suggested by Cottenet-Hage (with the idea of 'mask'), but one that is the subject of multiple, yet temporally bound performances.[53]

In the final analysis, Condé's interviews can be viewed as sites of performance onto which she projects a series of highly ambiguous and strategic performances of the personal. This idea of performance is pertinent to a consideration of the seemingly contradictory positions that Condé adopts in relation to her reading expectations. Indeed, Condé responds to these conflicting expectations with great astuteness. On the surface, she appears to conform to the demand for information about her life that enables her to be identified as a writer that 'represents' a specific community. To this end, in her numerous interviews, she provides repeated accounts of her experiences in Guadeloupe, France, the United States and Africa. In addition, at times, she claims a range of collective identities such as 'black', 'Francophone', 'Caribbean' and 'woman'. However, these representations are articulated alongside her ongoing appeal to the idea of a universal author 'who needs no native country' and her wide-ranging critique of all identitarian affiliations as well as her defence of individual freedom.[54] Condé's shifting positions within her interviews allow her to claim a strategic marginality that is perhaps instrumental in keeping the field of reading of both her fiction and her life infinitely open and in that sense 'unreadable'. What remains perhaps necessarily unreadable too is the extent to which Condé may herself function as a highly marketable 'licensed rebel' within the international marketplace for literary authenticity.[55]

Notes to Chapter 1

1. Condé's literary awards in France include Le Grand Prix Littéraire de la Femme, Le Prix Marguerite Yourcenar, Le Prix Alain Boucheron, for *Moi Tituba, sorcière... Noire de Salem* and Le Prix de l'Académie Française for *La Vie scélérate*. In 2001 she was awarded the Commandeur de l'Ordre des Arts et des Lettres. In the United States, she was the first woman to receive the Puterbaugh Award for her whole body of work, in 1993.
2. Interviews with Condé have been carried out in a range of newspapers and academic journals, on radio stations and on the Internet, in France and the United States. The author's interventions include articles written in journals and the press, contributions to critical anthologies, and a number of speeches.
3. Christopher Johnson, 'Introduction', in *Thinking in Dialogue: The Role of the Interview in Post-war French Thought*, ed. by Johnson (= *Nottingham French Studies*, 42 (2003)), 1–4. Johnson cites the following comment on the interview by Lévi-Strauss made ironically in the context of an interview: 'On the whole, and all things considered, the interview is a detestable genre, to which the intellectual poverty of the age obliges one to submit more often than one would like' (p. 1).
4. Gérard Genette, *Paratexts: Thresholds of Interpretation* (Cambridge: Cambridge University Press, 1997), p. xvii.
5. Katherine Larson, 'Resistance from the Margins in George Elliott Clarke's *Beatrice Chancy*', *Canadian Literature*, 189 (2006), 103–18 (p. 104).
6. Johnson, 'Introduction', p. 2.
7. Johnson, 'Introduction', p. 2.
8. Johnson, 'Introduction', p. 2.
9. See for example, Nicholas Harrison, *Postcolonial Criticism*; Graham Huggan, *The Postcolonial Exotic*; Gayatri Chakravorty Spivak, *A Critique of Postcolonial Reason: Toward a History of the Vanishing Present* (Cambridge, MA, and London: Harvard University Press, 1999).
10. Huggan, *The Postcolonial Exotic*.
11. Huggan, *The Postcolonial Exotic*, p. 176.
12. Huggan, pp. 164–65.
13. Condé, 'Order, Disorder', p. 134.
14. Françoise Pfaff, *Entretiens avec Maryse Condé* (Paris: Karthala, 1993), pp. 43–44.

15. Eva Sansavior, 'Entretien avec Maryse Conde', *Francophone Postcolonial Studies*, 2 (2004), pp. 7–33. In my interview with Condé she notes: 'Quand je repars en Guadeloupe, les gens commencent à m'écouter' [When I go back to Guadeloupe, the people are beginning to listen to me] (p. 28).

16. Pfaff, *Entretiens*, p. 43.

17. Pfaff, *Entretiens*, p. 43.

18. Sansavior, 'Entretien avec Maryse Condé', pp. 28–29.

19. Johnson, 'Introduction', pp. 3–4.

20. Françoise Pfaff, *Conversations with Maryse Condé* (London and Nebraska: University of Nebraska Press, 1996), p. 124.

21. Pfaff, *Entretiens*, p. 112.

22. Pfaff, *Entretiens*, p. 112.

23. Condé's use of the term 'terrorisme culturel' to describe what are, in her view, the Creolists' attempts to impose politicized prescriptions on Francophone Caribbean literature bears a striking similarity to Alain Robbe-Grillet's defence of the freedom of literature. Alain Robbe-Grillet, *Pour un nouveau roman* (Paris: Les Editions de Minuit, 1961):

> Il nous faut donc maintenant, une fois pour toutes, cesser de prendre au sérieux les accusations de gratuité, cesser de craindre 'l'art pour l'art' comme le pire des maux, récuser tout cet *appareil terroriste* que l'on brandit devant nous sitôt que nous parlons d'autre chose que de la lutte des classes ou de la guerre anticolonialiste. (p. 36, my emphasis)

> [We must now, once and for all, stop taking seriously accusations of irresponsibility, desist from fearing the idea of 'art for art's sake' as the worst of possible ills, and challenge this *terrorist apparatus* which is brandished before us as soon as we talk about anything other than class struggle or the fight against colonialism.]

24. For an insightful reading of the invention of the Creole language and culture by the Créolité school see, Maeve McCusker, '"This Creole culture, miraculously forged": The Contradictions of Créolité', in *Francophone Postcolonial Studies: A Critical Introduction*, ed. by Charles Forsdick and David Murphy (London and New York: Arnold, 2003), pp. 112–21.

25. Pfaff, *Entretiens*, p. 133.

26. Sansavior, 'Entretien avec Maryse Condé', p. 25.

27. Pfaff, *Entretiens*, p. 153.

28. Huggan, p. 14.

29. Huggan (in *The Postcolonial Exotic*) speculates that it is the fear of a loss of authenticity that leads metropolitan readers to invest 'Third World' literature with qualities (such as spirituality) that are perceived to have been irretrievably lost in a 'Western culture rendered inauthentic by its attachment to material excess' (p. 158).

30. Charles Forsdick, 'Travelling Concepts: Postcolonial Approaches to Exoticism', in *Francophone Texts and Postcolonial Theory*, ed. by Celia Britton and Michael Syrotinski (= *Paragraph*, 24, 3 (2001)), 12–29 (p. 14).

31. Forsdick, 'Travelling Concepts', p. 14.

32. Forsdick, 'Travelling Concepts', p. 14.

33. Alec Hargreaves, 'Exoticism in Literature and History', *Text and Context*, 1 (1986), 7–18 (p. 7).

34. Hargreaves, 'Exoticism in Literature and History', p. 7.

35. In 'Exoticism in Literature and History', Hargreaves describes this as 'a perceived inability, and perhaps at times a positive disinclination, to articulate the structures of cultural worlds beyond one's own' (p. 9).

36. Sansavior, 'Entretien avec Maryse Condé', p. 27.

37. As in the case of the French readers, Condé mines the dramatic potential for impersonating her readers' imagined responses as she observes sardonically: 'Oui, aux États-Unis, quand j'ai des choses à dire, tout le monde s'accourt. Une étrangère, elle parle avec un accent francophone, on ne comprend pas tellement ce qu'elle dit ("d'où vient-elle? Oui, de la Guadeloupe")' [Yes, in the United States, when I have things to say, everyone rushes to listen. A foreigner, who speaks with a Francophone accent, we don't really understand what she's saying ('Where's she from? Ah yes, from Guadeloupe')] (p. 24).

38. Forsdick, 'Travelling Concepts', p. 14.
39. Sansavior, 'Entretien avec Maryse Condé', p. 30.
40. Britton and Syrotinski, 'Introduction', pp. 6–7.
41. Bahri, *Native Intelligence*, p. 6.
42. Sansavior, 'Entretien avec Maryse Condé', pp. 18–19.
43. Sansavior, 'Entretien avec Maryse Condé', pp. 31–32.
44. Marie-Agnès Sourieau, 'Entretien avec Maryse Condé: De l'identité culturelle', *The French Review*, 72 (1999), 1091–98 (pp. 1091–92).
45. Sourieau, 'Entretien avec Maryse Condé', p. 1995.
46. Nicole Simek, *Eating Well, Reading Well*, p. 116.
47. Simek, p. 116.
48. Sansavior, 'Entretien avec Maryse Condé', p. 12.
49. Sourieau, 'Entretien avec Maryse Condé', p. 1097.
50. Madeleine Cottenet-Hage, '*Traversée de la Mangrove*: Réflexion sur les interviews', in *L'Œuvre de Maryse Condé: Questions et réponses à propos d'une écrivaine politiquement incorrecte*, ed. by Nara Araujo (Paris: L'Harmattan, 1996), pp. 157–71 (p. 158).
51. Sourieau, 'Entretien avec Maryse Condé', pp. 1091–92.
52. Sourieau,'Entretien avec Maryse Condé', p. 1093.
53. Condé's frequent use of temporal qualifiers such as 'maintenant' and 'à présent' also underlines the provisional or 'time-limited' nature of the positions she adopts in interviews.
54. Condé, 'Notes sur un retour au pays natal', p. 23. Condé muses: 'Est-ce qu'un écrivain doit avoir un pays natal? Est-ce qu'un écrivain doit avoir une identité définie? Est-ce qu'un écrivain ne pourrait pas être constamment errant, constamment à la recherche des autres hommes?' [Must a writer have a native land? Must a writer have a defined identity? Can't a writer be constantly wandering, constantly seeking out other men?] (p. 23).
55. Graham Huggan's analysis of the academic 'star system' points to the marked benefits to be derived from such self-conscious play. Huggan's observations that Margaret Atwood's construction of a 'reputation as at once ironic expert and artful popularizer has helped produce her canonical status, both as a versatile revisionist specialist and as a wittily amateurish bricoleur' are potentially applicable to Condé (p. 223). For a related discussion of Condé as part of the 'postcolonial middlebrow' see also Chris Bongie, *Friends and Enemies*, pp. 280–321.

CHAPTER 2

Re-writing the Journey to Africa or 'finding the wrong ancestors' in *En attendant le bonheur*

In the previous chapter, I highlighted Condé's ongoing and explicit engagement with the conditions of reception of her work in France and Guadeloupe and argued that this throws into sharp focus the ways in which ideas of 'representativity' and 'authenticity' inform the reception of her work not just in these two contexts but also in the United States. In particular, Condé points to the risk of misunderstanding that accompanies the benign form of exoticism that implicitly exists in this context, the result of critics' limited understanding of the cultural context in which the works are produced. The critical reception of Condé's first novel *En attendant le bonheur* in the United States is a paradigmatic instance of the omissions that stem from a misunderstanding of the complex social and cultural and political contexts in which Condé's novel was produced. *ELB* was published initially in 1976 under the title 'Heremakhonon'.[1] Following the novel's lack of commercial success, it was then re-issued in 1988 under the title *En attendant le bonheur*. The title's reference to 'deferred happiness' implicitly associates 'le bonheur' with an as yet unrealized state of authenticity. In this way, the title acts as a highly evocative touchstone to the motivations that drive and also render untenable the identitarian quest of the novel's protagonist, Véronica. Véronica is a young Guadeloupean intellectual from a prosperous middle-class background who leaves France to work as a teacher in an unnamed African country that is reminiscent of Guinea in the 1960s. From the outset, the protagonist characterizes the motivations for her journey in terms of a search for her lost African origins. By the end of the novel, however, the protagonist has abandoned her quest and is on her way back to France, having recognized that that she has simply got 'the wrong ancestors'.

The elements of the text's narrative highlighted above and Véronica's characterization of her journey as a straightforward case of 'mistaken ancestors' have lead to comparisons with Aimé Césaire's *Cahier d'un retour au pays natal*. The readings of *ELB* produced within American academia can be broadly distinguished in terms of the extent to which Césaire's text provides a viable model for the identity quest of Condé's protagonist. In her article 'Caribbean Insularization of Identities in Maryse Condé's Work from *En attendant le bonheur* to *Les Derniers Rois mages*', Mireille Rosello observes:

> A certain relatively dominant critical discourse (to which my voice implicitly belongs) is now ready to consider the trip to Africa as a step in the wrong historical and cultural direction, as a denial of some true, more authentic Caribbean identity.[2]

Rosello's comments endorse a critical orthodoxy surrounding the reading of the text that may be summarized as follows: the protagonist's failed quest is the result of her attempt to adopt an inauthentic Africa-centred identity and her concomitant failure to acknowledge the potential — if as yet unrealized — 'authentic Caribbean identity'.[3] As Christopher Miller highlights, this common reading of the outcome of Véronica's quest has been accompanied by a critical tendency to see Condé's novel as 'the antidote to Négritude and its vision of Africa as One'.[4] An alternative — and, arguably, more positive reading of Véronica's failed quest — has viewed the novel as a rewriting of the masculinist Césairian narrative that allows for the articulation of a distinctive feminine Caribbean identity.[5] In both cases, however, there is an assumption that *ELB* establishes a privileged relationship with *CRPN*. It is on the basis of this privileged relationship that an implicit judgement is made on the sense of identity that emerges from Véronica's identitarian quest: that is, the authenticity of this identity is linked to the extent to which *ELB* 'revises' or 'transcends' the Césairian narrative. Authenticity is also evoked on another and, arguably, less explicit level: an institutional one. In effect, if North American critics are able to correctly diagnose the outcome of Véronica's quest this is also because the institutional context in which they are embedded is assumed to occupy a similarly transcendent position in relation to the Négritude discourse represented by Césaire's narrative. The suggestion is therefore that their critical and political positions can be considered to be more 'relevant' or authentic for having moved beyond or perhaps even developed independently of the now outdated Césairian or Négritude vision of identity.

Reading against the grain of this critical orthodoxy, my argument is that this dominant critical approach fails to account for the complex sets of relationships that *ELB* establishes between the Francophone Caribbean and African-American texts that it references. In particular, the novel's numerous intertextual references to Césaire's *CRPN* and other major Francophone Caribbean texts point to the need to situate it explicitly in the context of these texts as well as their complex critical and historical trajectories. Against the backdrop of a reading of the relationship between intertextuality, identity and authenticity sketched out in *ELB*, I shall examine the implications of the text's numerous — and often oblique — intertextual references to major Francophone Caribbean and African-American texts.

★   ★   ★   ★   ★

It is certainly significant that the novel's starting point is in 1960s Paris, a context in which as Véronica observes wryly '[l]'Afrique se fait beaucoup' [Africa is very much the thing to do lately] (*ELB*, 19; *H*, 3). From the outset, the novel therefore invites a reflection on the generative role of earlier waves of interest in African culture for the various Francophone Caribbean and African-American texts that are referenced in the narrative. A brief consideration of the historical and cultural context in which Césaire's *CRPN* is produced is particularly revealing. There are marked similarities between the context of the production of Césaire's text and the intellectual and cultural milieu that Véronica describes at the start of *ELB*. Written in 1939, *CRPN* is widely considered to be the founding text of the Négritude movement, a movement dedicated to the definition of a distinctive black identity. Both the text and the movement can be situated within a resurgence of interest in African culture in a specific historical moment — 1930s Paris. A number of recent studies (including an essay by Condé herself entitled 'O Brave New World') on the transatlantic routes of black modernist culture have identified Négritude's role as part of a much more extensive history of black consciousness movements that brought together African-American, African, Francophone and Anglophone Caribbean intellectuals in Paris from the early to the mid-twentieth century.[6] One study, in particular, by Michel Fabre, highlights the role of Paris in serving as a meeting ground for 'different groups of the black diaspora'.[7] Fabre's analysis of the histories of these various groups stresses that the evolution of these movements is best understood not in terms of a linear process with the ideas of one group feeding directly into another but rather as a more oblique, multi-directional process. Fabre illustrates that this multi-directionality is a defining feature of the historical development of all these movements, one that is articulated throughout the whole period of their development. Viewed from the vantage point of the twenty-first century, the complex genesis and afterlives of their seminal texts, amongst which *CRPN* can certainly be included, become apparent. Fabre identifies the awarding of the Prix Goncourt to René Maran for the anti-colonialist novel *Batouala* in 1921 as playing a formative role in the development of the New Negro aesthetic in African-American literature in the early 1920s. However, at the same time he highlights that the African-American writer Claude McKay's novel *Banjo* (published in 1930) in turn influenced the founders of the Négritude movement from which *CRPN* emerges, noting that Aimé Césaire, Léon-Gontron Damas, and Léopold-Sédar Senghor had all read *Banjo* in translation.[8] According to Fabre, the Négritude writers found in the novel's celebration of primitivism a conceptual foundation for 'the cultural unity of the oppressed diaspora' represented in their work, a foundation on which Césaire drew directly in his celebration of the 'proud nigger' in *CRPN*.[9] More generally, Fabre argues that The New Negro and Harlem Renaissance Movements along with Négritude were part of a broader and mutually enriching dialogue taking place in Paris in the 1930s and 40s. According to Fabre, by the 1950s, Négritude ideology was being exported to the United States by black writers such as Samuel Allen and Langston Hughes and integrated into themes of 'blackness' and 'soul' (p. 6). At a broader level therefore, these studies of transatlantic black identity demonstrate that Francophone and African-American black consciousness movements emerge out of the crossing of influences between various black writers living in France throughout the first half of the twentieth century.

★   ★   ★   ★   ★

In spite of the transatlantic history of black consciousness movements that I have sketched above, there are a number of ways in which the novel suggests that

CRPN is the dominant precursor to Véronica's project to recover her authentic black identity. At the start of *ELB*, the protagonist's quest is clearly inspired by the Césairian promise of 'restored plenitude' realized through contact with a maternal Africa. The optimism that she displays during her first meeting with her African supervisor echoes the belief expressed by the Césairian hero that the lost plenitude of her African past had been recovered in this instant: 'Trois siècles et demi d'effacés!'[Three and a half centuries wiped out!] (*ELB*, 23; *H*, 5).[10]

This sense of optimism is however undercut immediately by the protagonist's sarcastic internal reconstruction of the first encounter between European slavers and the Africans:

> — Les Blancs débarquent! Les Blancs débarquent!
> Il paraît qu'on les prenait pour les revenants. Des ancêtres réincarnés et qu'on répandait du lait caillé devant eux pour les apaiser. Du lait caillé contre des boulets de canon. Pas étonnant qu'on en soit là où on est! (*ELB*, 23)

> [The whites are coming! The whites are coming! It seems that they took them for ghosts. Ancestors reincarnated. Curdled milk was splashed in front of them as an act of propitiation. Curdled milk against cannon balls. Not at all surprising that they had not gone very far. (*H*, 5)]

In figuring slavery as the result of this initial case of 'mistaken ancestry', the protagonist expresses through her sarcasm a distance from the desire for reconnection that she initially expresses (and this foreshadows her own later acknowledgment that she has found 'the wrong ancestors').

The sarcastic tenor of Véronica's comments acts as a pointer to the ambiguous intertextual relationship that the text establishes with Césaire's *CRPN*. Certain features of this relationship suggest perhaps a feminist-centred practice of inter-textuality centred on revisioning or 're-imagining'. The revisions that Condé's text makes to the normative masculine identity presented in *CRPN* are an integral part of this process.[11] For example, the fact that *ELB*'s female protagonist chooses to undertake her own identitarian quest presented as a narrative can be interpreted as expressing a form of agency that contests the traditionally passive characterization of female protagonists in male-authored Caribbean texts that include Césaire's narrative.[12] Shaped by Véronica's fragmented interior monologue, the novel's narrative is threaded through with flashbacks, imaginary, dream-like scenes, and filtered dialogue. In addition, seemingly random memorized lines from a range of texts that include *CRPN* serve as prompts for the protagonist's often sharply ironic internal philosophical disquisitions. If through *ELB*'s intertextual patterning, Véronica constructs a self-conscious dialogue with *CRPN*, this dialogue is presented as a necessarily open-ended process, one that designates neither a stable point of origin nor a clear transition towards an alternative, more 'authentic', identitarian position.

A close analysis of the text's opening (to which I made brief reference earlier) reveals the protagonist's marked ambivalence towards the assumptions that underpin the sense of identity portrayed in *CRPN* highlighting her complex evaluative implication in this discourse of identity as a modern, cosmopolitan subject. The novel starts with the protagonist ruminating sardonically on the motivations for her trip to Africa, insisting on the uniquely individual nature of her quest for identity:

Franchement on pourrait croire que j'obéis à la mode. L'Afrique se fait beaucoup en ce moment. On écrit des masses à son sujet, des Européens et d'autres. On voit s'ouvrir des centres d'Artisanat Rive gauche. Des blondes se teignent les lèvres au henné et on achète des piments [...] rue Moufettard. Or c'est faux. (*ELB*, 19)

[Honestly! You'd think I'm going because it is the in thing to do. Africa is very much the thing to do lately. Europeans and a good many others are writing volumes on it. Arts and craft centres are opening up all over the Left Bank. Blondes are dying their lips with henna and running to the open market for their peppers [...]. Well, I'm not! (*H*, 3)]

This starting point foregrounds Véronica's intellectual sophistication as evidenced by her capacity to deploy a type of philosophical scepticism in the face of the multiplicity of representations of Africa with which she is confronted in 1960s Paris. The sceptical stance that she adopts in relation to these representations is mirrored by her parents' imagined dismissive attitude towards her trip to Africa, conveyed in their facial gestures: 'Je les imagine. Ma mère soupirant. Mon père tordant ses lèvres minces' [I can see them now. My mother, sighing as usual and my father pinching his thin lips] (*ELB*, 19; *H*, 3). By situating Véronica's trip at the intersection of a dramatically conscious rejection of fashionable representations of, and familial indifference to Africa, the novel highlights the protagonist's conception of authenticity as a state to which one aspires intellectually and also one that is achieved through the disavowal of inauthenticity. The protagonist's journey at this stage is motivated by a desire to move beyond the well-worn and implicitly inauthentic performances of a type of commodified African identity available within the metropolitan popular and intellectual cultural market place. Yet, it is the protagonist's obsessively re-imagined familial context that both generates this desire for authenticity and circumscribes the possibilities for realizing this state.

If Véronica's family is the site of an absence of representations of Africa, it is also one of multiple performances of mimicry. What activates Véronica's quest is her father's failure to provide her with any information that would allow her to situate his triumphant representations of her family's social ascension in a broader African history. The girl who questions her father about her African past is concerned to know about the time '[a]vant la saga familiale. L'arrière-grand-père ou l'arrière-arrière-grand-père esclave qui à force de patience et d'efforts avait acheté sa liberté...' ['Before the family saga. The great-grandfather or the great-great grandfather who had bought his freedom with a lot of patience and hard work...'] (*ELB*, 31; *H*, 11). The familial universe is structured by two competing narratives of identity on which the protagonist draws here: Césaire's *CRPN* and the aspirational African-American autobiographical narrative by Booker T. Washington, *Up from Slavery*:

— Eia pour le Kailcédrat royal!
Sa liberté est un lopin de terre. Qui s'était mis en case avec la négresse Florimonde brave et travailleuse et dont la descendance avait gravi un à un les barreaux de l'échelle humaine. *Up from slavery*. Booker T. Washington. (*ELB*, 31)

[Eia for the royal cailcedra...
His freedom is a plot of land. Set up house with Florimonde, an honest and

hardworking negress Florimande whose children had, one by one, climbed the
rungs of the ladder of humanity. Good old Booker T. (*H*, 11, translation adapted)]

Yet, the ideal of freedom that these discourses are taken to enshrine is diverted
towards her father's mimicry of upper-class French behaviours which shore up his
prejudicial attitudes towards other black people. Véronica recalls and undercuts his
contemptuous assertions about the relationship between 'freedom' and 'dancing'
with irony:

> Il faudrait leur interdire de danser, disait le marabout mandingue. Ah s'ils ne
> dansaient pas, ils seraient déjà libres! [...] Car lui bien sûr, il était libre. Libre de
> ne pas marcher sur la chair de ses pieds. Libre de s'enserrer le cou dans un nœud
> papillon. Et d'accueillir les invités du dimanche:
> — Elaïse, vous êtes divine! (*ELB*, 25)

> [The Mandingo marabout used to say such dances should be forbidden. 'If they
> did not dance, they would already be free [...]'. *He*, of course was free. Free to
> no longer to walk on the soles of his feet. Free to stick his neck in a bowtie and
> to welcome Sundays' guests with a pompous 'Eloise, you look divine!' (*H*, 7)]

Through these memories, the protagonist adjudicates internally between the
representations of Africa provided by the popular and academic cultural spheres
and those produced by the familial context from which she emerges. Crucially,
however, it is implied that the identities produced in these different contexts are all
types of inauthentic performances.

The way in which this process of adjudication is enacted as a set of 'roles' into
which the protagonist projects herself during her identity quest is suggested by her
response to a routine question by a policeman at the airport concerning the reason
for her trip: 'Raison du voyage? Ni commerçante. Ni missionnaire. Ni touriste.
Touriste peut-être. Mais d'une espèce particulière à la découverte de soi-même'
[Purpose of visit? No, I am not a tradesman. Not a missionary. Not even a tourist.
Well, perhaps a tourist but one of a new breed, searching out herself, not landscapes]
(*ELB*, 20; *H*, 3). Her explanation of her journey in terms of a desire for 'self-
discovery' appears to be informed by the belief evoked in *CRPN* that Africa could
legitimately be viewed as the ancestral home for all Caribbean subjects and therefore
serve as the matrix for the definition of an authentic identity. However, in describing
herself as a 'tourist' who is also 'looking for herself' she privileges the motivations of
'choice' 'consumerism' and 'self-fulfilment'. In so doing, the protagonist expresses
a dual sense of emotional investment and estrangement from the very idea of an
authentic identity. This also serves to highlight her distinct relationship to the
notions of 'exile' and 'identity' as well as to the potential 'solutions' to these issues
that discourses of identity may offer. In 'Questions of Travel: Postmodern Narratives
of Displacement', Caren Kaplan highlights the traditional tendency to situate
'exile' and 'tourism' on two opposing poles of modern experience. According to
Kaplan, while exile is typically represented as a state into which an individual or
group is 'forced' or 'coerced', tourism is presented as celebrating an idea of choice
that forms part of a larger culture of superficial 'consumerism'.[13] This bringing
together of two seemingly opposing *states* (of 'coercion' and 'choice') in Véronica's
representation of the motivations for her journey to Africa is thus emblematic of the

wide-ranging and mobile intertextual practice that the text articulates. It is mobile in the sense of not suggesting a resolution of the protagonist's quest that is based on the transcendence of one position in favour of another. Instead, this practice is predicated on an ongoing movement within and between the various narratives to which the novel makes reference.

An idea of movement between narratives is suggested by the text's references to African-American and Francophone Caribbean (autobiographical) works (such as those provided by Booker T. Washington and Fanon). Césaire's text is thus placed in dialogue with alternative or competing narratives of 'black' identity. Arguably, the African-American and Francophone Caribbean texts referenced in *ELB* serve as discourses of identity and are used in contrasting ways. In general terms, African-American discourses of identity provided by the magazine *Ebony* and by Booker T. Washington are cited only to be dismissed as providing an aspirational but a materially de-politicized script for her family. This script is shown to be at odds with her parents' avid imitation of upper-class French behaviours and their concomitant disengagement from the lived experiences of the majority of their less privileged countrymen. For example, the protagonist imagines how she would be greeted on her return home by her family and thus points to the fact that her welcome would be governed by her parents' calculated assessment of the political viability of appearances:

> Si je rentrais, ils seraient tous à l'aéroport du Raizet. Le marabout mandingue comme les autres. Car le linge sale se lave en famille. J'accueille ma famille. Et puis, en un sens, je fais honneur par-delà la famille à la Race, puisque je suis universitaire. Booker T. Washington n'aurait pas hésité à m'embrasser sur les deux joues. Et je pourrais avoir ma place dans 'Ebony'. (*ELB*, 36)

> [If I went back, they would all be at the airport. The Mandingo marabout like the others. Dirty linen is kept in the family. And, in a way, I'm paying homage through the family to the whole race as I am studying at university in France. Booker T. Washington would not have hesitated to kiss me on both cheeks. And I would have my place in *Ebony*. (*H*, 14)]

The protagonist's references to African-American discourses of identity (such as 'la Race') suggest that her sense of blackness is an international or transatlantic one, inviting a reflection on the common roots of African-American and Francophone Caribbean black consciousness movements of which Césaire's text is a part. But her use of these works imply that they are merely names, that, serve at best as free-floating, empty concepts within the familial culture of which she is a part. Véronica's appeal to these discourses may thus be viewed as a further instance of the inauthentic identity performances of which she appears to be so acutely aware.

In contrast, her engagement with the works of Fanon and Césaire point to her marked intellectual and emotional implication in these discourses of identity. Nevertheless, this implication is also critically conscious. In particular, her references to Fanon's *PNMB* and *Les Damnés de la terre* confront Césaire's narrative with a body of critique that undermines its implicit position as the sole and dominant articulation of 'black identity' in the Francophone Caribbean context.[14] This relativizing of the role of *CRPN* in Véronica's quest is also suggested by her specific engagement with other texts by Césaire such as *La Tragédie du Roi Christophe*. In the following quotation, the protagonist's irreverent humour expresses a playful questioning of the opinions expressed by the eponymous protagonist in *LTRC*:

> Je ne suis pas d'accord avec Césaire quand il proclame par la grâce de Christophe:
> — J'en demande trop aux hommes. Mais pas assez aux Nègres, madame. (Parce que ne vous y trompez pas, j'ai lu Césaire comme tout le monde. Je veux dire comme tous ceux de notre monde, le tiers monde).
> A mon avis les Nègres, il serait grand temps qu'on leur foute la paix, qu'on les laisse danser, se saouler et faire l'amour, ils l'ont bien mérité. (*ELB*, 123)

> [I don't agree with Césaire when he proclaims by the grace of Christophe: 'I ask too much of men. But not enough of black men, Madame.' I have read Césaire too like everybody else. I mean like everybody from of our world, the Third World. In my opinion, it's high time they left the niggers in peace, let them dance, get drunk and make love. They've deserved it. (*H*, 71)]

The protagonist's ironic commentary on this specific text serves to emphasize that her critical engagement with Césaire's work extends beyond *CRPN* and points to her generalized questioning stance towards his œuvre and to the works that may be read (by the type of politicized critical practice outlined in the first part of this chapter) as part of a unitary black Francophone Caribbean literary tradition. In line with this, the protagonist's personal and highly irreverent reading of *LTRC* satirizes the critical tendency to read Césaire's work and, more broadly, literary works by 'black authors', for the uplifting and socially viable political messages transmitted by fictional characters *on behalf of* their authors. Another level of satire is generated by using Véronica as a mouthpiece for this approach. In effect, it is by precisely by dramatizing her wrong-headed readings that that the novel debunks the imagined pronouncements of Césaire's politicized author-protagonist.

The oblique questioning of Césaire's political ideas that emerges in this imagined dialogue between the two fictional characters Véronica and Christophe and the 'real' playwright Césaire does not however translate into an unambiguous endorsement of any of the other works cited by Véronica as a viable alternative in which to ground her identitarian quest.[15] As I illustrated above, the protagonist's ironic readings of other works by Césaire potentially raises questions about the viability of Césaire's œuvre as a whole for the construction of her identity. Similarly, her ironic attitude to the texts by the other authors that she references problematizes a reading of her quest in terms of a transcendence of Césaire's implicitly 'inauthentic' discourse in favour of a more 'authentic' one. Fanon's discourse, for example, is repeatedly satirized. One of the key elements of Fanon's work that attracts the protagonist's ambivalent irony is his excoriating dismissal of Mayotte Capécia as being preoccupied with 'lactification' or self-whitening.[16] There are elements in the narrative that bear out some of Fanon's ideas. For example, in the following quotation, the protagonist reflects on her infatuation with a mulatto boy, Jean-Marie Roseval: 'Ce jeune mulâtre au teint de prince hindou (à quinze ans on a des comparaisons idiotes), les yeux verts [...] Depuis, je ne me suis jamais guérie de ma fascination pour les yeux clairs, ou peut-être l'avais-je déjà. Oui sûrement' [This light-skinned mulatto with green eyes and the complexion of a young Oriental prince (a fifteen year old's comparisons are always silly). Since then I have never gotten over my fascination for light-colored eyes. Perhaps I already had it. Very likely (*ELB*, 24; *H*, 6)].

In highlighting her 'fascination' for light eyes and characterizing it implicitly in terms of an illness or an affliction from which she is 'never cured', the protagonist appears to display the preoccupation with 'self-whitening' that Fanon critiques. But the self-criticism implicit in this remembrance is undercut by an ironic puzzling as to the 'origins' of this fascination (was this an affliction that was inspired by Jean-Marie Roseval or was it a trait with which she was perhaps 'born'?) and by the ambiguous closure of this process of questioning ('Oui sûrement'). This ironic puzzling also gestures towards, and obliquely satirizes, Fanon's characterization of 'lactification' as inherent to all Martinican women. A similarly ambivalent relationship between the novel's depiction of Véronica's sexuality and Fanon's characterization of black female sexuality in *PNMB* is suggested in the following quotation, in which the protagonist attempts to rationalize her preference for white suitors:

> Répétons-le, j'ai aimé ces deux hommes parce que je les aimais. Et que tous ces jeunes mâles noirs que me présentait ma famille me faisaient horreur? *Pas parce qu'ils étaient noirs.* Absurde! Je ne suis pas une Mayotte Capécia. Ah non! Pas mon souci, éclaircir la Race! Je le jure... (*ELB*, 55)

> [Once again, I loved those two men because I was in love. All those young black males my family introduced to me made me shudder. Why? Not because they were black. Ridiculous! I'm no Mayotte Capécia. No! I'm not interested in whitening the race! I swear... (*H*, 28)]

The fact that she again draws on Fanon's condemnation of Capécia as the framework in which to articulate a defence of her choices is significant. This is because although the arch tone of this reference to Mayotte Capécia ('Je le jure...') implies an ironic questioning of his ideas, this tone nevertheless underscores the enduringly powerful influence that Fanon's work exerts on the types of representations that are available for the protagonist to draw on in her attempt to make sense of her own identity (and also to translate this sense of identity to others). On the one hand, the comment appears to endorse Fanon's criticism of Mayotte Capécia while on the other, the ellipses at the end of this reference gesture towards the unresolved quality of the protagonist's ambiguous implication in Fanon's text and also the ways in which this state of implication exceeds representation.[17]

Indeed, Véronica's ambivalence to both Césaire's and Fanon's works is emblematic of a more generalized questioning of the whole range of texts to which she refers in the course of the novel. This process of questioning is suggested partly by the distinctive typographical structuring of the narrative. The text's use of italics has a seemingly random or idiosyncratic quality that merits attention. Some of the examples of the use of italics do appear to conform to literary conventions as they signal titles of works of literature or music as in the following quotation: 'Mes sœurs en robe d'organza, leurs mi-bas blancs bien tirés sur leurs mollets chocolats jouaient *La Pavane pour une infante défunte*' [My sisters dressed in their white muslin dresses their white socks pulled up tight over their chocolate calves playing Ravel's *Pavane pour une infante défunte*] (*ELB*, 24; *H*, 6). In some cases the italicized comments are attributed. But italics are also used to convey an idea of reported discourse that is not necessarily clearly attributed: 'Le marabout mandingue aimait à dire que l'instruction était *la porte ouverte*' [The Mandingo marabout was fond of saying that education is the key] (*ELB*, 30; *H*, 12). However, the vast majority of these italicized fragments tantalizingly suggest the traces of unnamed speakers whose identity is neither confirmed nor revealed. This ambiguity concerning the origins of a discourse that is presented via the use of italics as implicitly *reported* is evident in the following quotation in which the protagonist speaks sardonically about her white ancestors:

> Je suis sûre qu'ils ignoraient qu'une goutte de sperme de leur aïeul était responsable de notre famille maternelle. Nous, cette goutte, nous l'avons enchâssée, embaumée. Elle était à l'origine du teint clair de ma mère et du nez droit d'Aïda. Cette goutte tenace et bienfaisante nous empêchait d'être des négresses *noires comme du charbon* et faisait de nous des *négresses rouges*.
> (Bien sûr, cela n'avait pas d'importance.) (*ELB*, 33)
>
> [I am sure they didn't know that a drop of their grandfather's sperm had started our family line. We, on the other hand, had mounted and embalmed it. It was responsible for my mother's relatively light skin and Aida's straight nose. Its long-lasting quality kept us from being as black as coal. We were *négresses-rouges*.
> (Of course, all that is of no importance.)[18] (*H*, 12)]

This proliferation of unattributed italicized fragments problematizes the very idea of origins by inhibiting access to the sources that would enable their identification. Thus, in a narrative in which the protagonist's engagement with texts is an integral part of her identity quest, it is the possibility of establishing an original identity for the protagonist that is also constantly disrupted. The intertextual practice articulated by *ELB* is therefore not easily congruent with an idea of Caribbean female writing predicated precisely on the recovery and expression of an under-represented, *original* identity.[19] In addition, the introduction of these fragments into the protagonist's discourse potentially serves to signal her distance from these highlighted ideas. The ambivalent self-consciousness of the protagonist's qualification of this account of her family origins '(Bien sûr, cela n'avait pas d'importance)' nevertheless underscores her persistent, yet disavowed, emotional attachment (that is also at least partly unconscious and perhaps also 'pleasurable') to an *idea* of authentic origins.

The implications of this shifting yet enduring attachment to an idea of identity become apparent in the light of the ambivalence that the protagonist expresses towards the acceptance of any redemptive and politically viable conceptions of collective identity. In contrast with the Césairian male hero who sees in the definition of a collective identity the possibility of transcending his state of exile, the ambivalence that Véronica displays towards this vision reveals her distinctive relationship to exile and to the very possibility of an authentic, heroic community. Despite asserting her desire for reconnection with an African 'race', the protagonist is torn between two views of the people that she encounters. On the one hand, she displays a tendency to view them through the frame of exoticist or colonialist stereotypes endorsing, for example, the brutality of the slave trade. On the other hand, such stereotypes are undermined by exposure to 'real' Africans. For example, the dignified air of one of Sory's male servants impresses Véronica who muses: 'Alors le nègre exubérant, spontané comme un enfant, encore une invention de l'Europe?' [Is the exuberant nigger, spontaneous like a child, another of Europe's inventions?] (*ELB*, 174; *H*, 116). This vacillation between the belief in an idealized African identity and a contemptuous dismissal of this idea is accompanied by consistent, almost obsessive ruminations on the inauthenticity and sickness that defines her and the various relationships that she both forges and rejects. In this sense, Véronica gestures towards the possibility of inauthenticity as the basis for the formation of various types of community. Her only female friend is the former prostitute, Adama, and this relationship serves as the context for her claiming of a provisional identity as a prostitute (p. 108).[20] In addition, while she expresses a contemptuous rejection of her bourgeois family, it is to this family that she contemplates returning when she ruminates on the possibility of returning 'chez moi' [home] (*ELB*, 110). She also repeatedly uses images of sickness to refer to herself: she is 'une malade [...] à la recherche d'une thérapie' ['an invalid [...] in search of therapy'] (*ELB*, 53; *H*, 26). Interestingly, her individual sickness is shown to be the basis of a type of transatlantic community that links her own identitarian struggles to that of African-Americans who, in their common quest for healing in Africa, are part of 'les névrosés de la diaspora' [neurotics from the diaspora] (*ELB*, 86; *H*, 49). What emerges then from the protagonist's ambivalent relationships to notions of group identity is a revalorization of the uses of individual and collective inauthenticity. Inauthenticity is expressed through the more or less conscious sense of estrangement from an ideal cultural or political identity that defines the various characters in *ELB* as well as the sceptical process of reflecting upon such states.

The protagonist's ongoing reflections on, and critique of, the shortcomings of these various discourses of identity seem to suggest that there is a political rationale for her ambivalence towards the expression of a redemptive sense of collective identity. Indeed, she reflects on the betrayal of the dream of postcolonial liberation in the African country in which she is working and pits this reality against what she represents as the romantic, even naïve, optimism of Négritude-inspired discourses that celebrate an idealized Africa: 'Ceux qui écrivent "Couleurs d'Afrique-Pour-nos-yeux-atteints-du-gris-de-nos-villes-elles-brouillent-nos-sens-éclatent-en-cris-en parfums." Comment font-ils? Que voient-ils que, moi, je ne vois pas?' [Those who write 'Colors of Africa — For our eyes attacked by the grey of our towns — they blur our senses — burst into shouts — into perfume.' How do they do it? What do they see that I don't?] (*ELB*, 124; *H*, 78–79). The protagonist contrasts this romanticized vision with the reality of the people's dissatisfaction with a corrupt regime. During a visit by president Mwalimwana to the school where she teaches she draws on the revolutionary consciousness evoked by Fanon in *LDT* to imagine her students' criticism of the regime for the abuse of its economic power:

> Ils comptent vos Mercedes et s'indignent des parures de vos femmes. Ils disent qu'une oligarchie avide a pris la relève de l'Europe. Au lieu du Coran, ils psalmodient Fanon. Hier ils ont voulu m'entraîner dans une discussion des *Damnés* que je n'ai pas lus. *Mea culpa! Mea maxima culpa!* (*ELB*, 58)

[They count your Mercedes and vent their anger against your wives' jewels.
They say an oligarchy of greed has taken over from Europe. Instead of the
Koran, they recite Fanon. Yesterday, they wanted to drag me into a discussion
of *The Wretched of the Earth* that I have not read. Mea culpa! Mea maxima culpa!
(*H*, 30)]

These comments underscore her scepticism towards the political possibilities presented by the discourses that she references that, in her opinion, serve not the
interests of the people but those of their corrupt leaders. However, the ironic tone
of her admission that she has not read Fanon's *LDT* simultaneously draws attention
to and undercuts the tendency to conflate reading with political action. There is a
somewhat self-conscious quality to Véronica's irreverent attitude here that points
to her ambiguous endorsement of the very assumption that appears to challenge
her implicit use of this attitude to cast judgement on her own lack of political
credibility. In addition, by recalling the disapproving looks that she attracts from
members of the Black Panthers when she takes her white boyfriend to a Caribbean
festival, she gestures towards the potentially repressive implications of discourses
by Fanon and other political writers for individuals: 'Jean-Michel m'accompagnait
avec un petit goût d'exotisme [...]. Et il y avait ces jeunes Antillais coiffés du
béret noir des Black Panthers. Tout le mépris de leur regard. C'était, comme des
années auparavant, leurs regards sur moi' [Jean-Michel was accompanying me,
with a little touch of exoticism [...]. And there were these young West Indians
with the Black Panther berets. All contempt. As in years before, all eyes on me]
(*ELB*, 41; *H*, 18).

It is certainly significant then that the protagonist appears to offer a purely
theoretical or intellectual response to the assumed political failings of these discourses. For example, she observes dismissively: 'Des discours, on en fait partout'
[Everybody makes speeches] (*ELB*, 59; *H*, 30). This dismissal is, however, ambiguous
as it does not provide an alternative to 'discourse', in the sense of both philosophical
idea and political speech, nor does it posit a clear response to the political challenges
that Véronica suggests are thrown up by their mendacious use. Indeed, she appears
to take for granted that it is possible to remain outside such concerns.

In spite of this questioning of the utility of ethno-geographical discourses for the
definition of a viable sense of identity, the solution that she envisages for the transcendence of her individual state of exile points to the inconsistencies that bedevil her
position. The limitations of the protagonist's position become apparent in the light
of her relationship with the corrupt government minister Sory (her only significant
relationship). Certainly, she appears to invest him with the role of privileged
facilitator of her quest and therefore appears to express a fleeting belief, at least, in the
idea of an authentic identity: 'J'ai la conviction qu'il peut me sauver. Me réconcilier
avec moi-même, c'est-à-dire avec ma race' [I am convinced that he can save me.
Reconcile me with myself, in other words my race] (*ELB*, 104; *H*, 63). However, in
the following quotation, this is shown to be an essentially discursive process (based on
the construction of 'idées') that also produces emotional effects for the protagonist:

J'aime cet homme ou une certaine idée dont j'ai besoin à travers de lui, de me
faire de l'Afrique? A bien réfléchir aimer c'est toujours se faire une idée. Dans

mon cas, c'est plus grave, parce que l'idée que je me fais de lui et par conséquent de l'Afrique est vitale, et en même temps si vague, si imprécise. Quelle est cette idée?... (*ELB*, 119)

[Do I love this man or a certain idea that I have of Africa? When you think about it, it's the same thing. Loving a man is the myth you create around him. Or with him in mind. In my case, perhaps it's a bit more serious because the idea I have is vital and yet so vague, so blurred. What is this idea? (*H*, 73)]

The repetition throughout this quotation of the subject pronoun 'je' highlights how Véronica takes it for granted that this discursive process is 'une aventure purement individuelle' [a purely individual adventure] (p. 188). This resolutely individual focus therefore means that her decision to have a relationship with this corrupt government minister is symbolic of her flight from the sense of connection that, in other respects, she seems to be seeking, as their entire relationship is conducted in a private cadre that reinforces her isolation from the experiences of the community.

In light of Véronica's overriding preoccupation with the individual and affective implications of her quest, it is ironic that her desire to gain access to her original, authentic lost African identity is frustrated precisely by her lover's dismissal of the emotional plight that accompanies her specific experience of exile as 'les petits problèmes personnels, la sentimentalité, les caprices' [little personal problems, sentimentality, whims] (*ELB*, 119; *H*, 73). If her decision to return to France is prompted partly by the invalidation of her quest expressed through Sory's dismissive attitude towards her, it is ultimately her realization that her lover is implicated in the disappearance of one of her politically active students that renders her position untenable: 'Si je comprends bien, dans ce pays, faire l'amour revient à faire un choix politique?' [If I understand correctly, making love in this country comes down to making a political choice] (*ELB*, 106; *H*, 64). Indeed, the political fall-out from this relationship with Sory suggests that the pursuit of purely individual authenticity may be viewed as a theoretical ideal that implies a position outside of politics. What Véronica's experiences make clear however, is that such a position is likely to have implications — ethical and perhaps also 'political' — that extend beyond the individual.

The literary or even theatrical terms in which she characterizes the end of her quest suggests that the novel also resists the temptation to invest literature with any particular political efficacy. This is accompanied by a radical revalorization of the various forms of inauthentic cultural performances (that include the fashionable 'displays' at the start of the novel and those enacted within Véronica's family). The text ends with Véronica reflecting whimsically on an imagined missed opportunity to join the people in a political protest:

Je me persuade que si, cette nuit-là, la ville n'avait pas dormi, si les hommes, les femmes, les adolescents étaient sortis des cases, alors oui, j'aurais marché avec eux; j'aurais trouvé le courage dans leur détermination. (*ELB*, 244)

[I imagine that if, that night, the city had not slept, if the men, women and youngsters had come out of their huts, then I would certainly have marched with them. Their determination would have given me strength. (*H*, 166, translation adapted)]

Nevertheless, the choice of the verbal structure 'Je me persuade' suggests that she is not fully convinced by her own assertion of political will. Indeed, there is a performative inflection to the way in which she presents this scene; it is as though she is projecting herself into the role of a politically committed, heroic 'woman of the people' for her own enjoyment and perhaps also that of the reader. While she appears to convey an almost palpable sense of enthusiasm for this heroic self, ultimately, this has a staged quality that undermines her expressed commitment to collective political action. This sense of doubt is intensified by the use of the conditional tense, which effectively projects the performance itself and the real political engagement that it represents onto an imaginary plane. Crucially, it is also the possibility for Véronica's assumption of a 'politically engaged' collective identity that is projected into this imaginary plane. What is expressed then by Véronica's ambiguous assertion at the end of the text that she has simply 'chosen the wrong ancestors' is in fact this indefinite deferral of the obligation to choose *any* identity: 'Je me suis trompée d'aïeux, voilà tout. J'ai cherché mon salut là où il ne fallait pas. Parmi les assassins. Allons, pas de grands mots! Toujours ce goût de drame' [My ancestors led me on. What can I say? I looked for myself in the wrong place. In the arms of an assassin. Come now, don't use big words. Always dramatizing] (*ELB*, 244; *H*, 167). Indeed, if the implication of claiming that she has chosen the wrong ancestors is that it would be possible (under different or more favourable conditions) for her to choose the right ancestors, it is noteworthy that she does not actually name these alternative precursors. Nor for that matter does she speculate on the conditions that would facilitate the successful realization of this alternative quest. The successful realization of her quest might thus be figured as the exploration of a series of open-ended possibilities.

In conclusion, the oblique terms of Véronica's final characterization of her quest reflects her ambivalence towards collective identitarian discourses as a means of resolving various forms of individual inauthenticity. By describing her quest as 'une erreur tragique', the protagonist evokes an idea of 'pre-destined' inauthenticity, a state that is at least partly inscribed in the very discourses that she uses as the basis for the expression of her ambiguous sense of identity. Indeed, her reflections on the political failings of discourses and her own failure to endorse a clear political position point to a questioning of the viability of collective discourses of identity for the definition of individual identity. It is important to note however that the protagonist's position at the end of the text does not translate into a clear-cut rejection of the very possibility that collective and individual identities may coincide. In fact, by pointing to the possibility of (eventually) finding the 'right' ancestors, Véronica appears to endorse an idea of identity that potentially links her to an as yet unknown collective grouping of 'ancestors'. Nevertheless the linking of this oblique potential to 'her taste for drama', is also an acknowledgement that this possibility is perhaps, ultimately, a reflection of the fugitive effects of her individual imagination or even a projection of sorts. Perhaps unsurprisingly, at the novel's close, the protagonist appears to remain ambivalent about the political viability of all identities. Yet this ambivalence eloquently conveys her enduring affective attachment to a diffuse idea of identity — configured as both authentic and inauthentic — and the imaginary constructions that make its performance possible.

Notes to Chapter 2

1. The word 'Heremakhonon' is from Malinké, a Guinean language and translates in French as 'attend le bonheur'.

2. Mireille Rosello, 'Caribbean Insularization of Identities in Maryse Condé's Work from *En attendant le bonheur* to *Les Derniers Rois mages*', *Callaloo* (Maryse Condé: A Special Edition), 18 (1995), 565–78 (p. 567).

3. For similar arguments see for example, Françoise Lionnet, *Autobiographical Voices: Race, Gender and Self-Portraiture* (Ithaca, NY, and London: Cornell University Press, 1989); Arlette M. Smith, 'The Semiotics of Exile in Maryse Condé's Fictional Works', *Callaloo*, 14 (1991), 381–88 (p. 382); Christopher L. Miller, 'After Negation: Africa in Two Novels by Maryse Condé', in *Postcolonial Subjects: Francophone Women Writers*, ed. by Mary Jean Green et al. (Minneapolis and London: University of Minnesota Press, 1996), pp. 173–85 (p. 174).

4. Miller, p. 174. See also, Wangari wa Nyatetu-Waigwa, 'From Liminality to a Home of her Own? The Quest Motif in Maryse Condé's Fiction from *En attendant le bonheur* to *Les Derniers Rois mages*', *Callaloo* (Maryse Condé: A Special Edition), 18 (1995), 551–64.

5. For readings of *En attendant le bonheur* as articulating a distinctive Francophone Caribbean female identity expressed partly in terms of a rewriting of Négritude discourse see Elizabeth Wilson, '"Le Voyage et l'Espace clos" — Island and Journey Metaphor: Aspects of Women's Experience in the Works of Francophone Caribbean Women Novelists', in *Out of the Kumbla: Caribbean Women and Literature*, ed. by Carole Boyce Davies and Elaine Savory Fido (Trenton, NJ: Africa World Press, 1990), pp. 45–58; Wangari wa Nyatetu-Waigwa, 'From Liminality to a Home of her Own?; Samantha Haigh, *Mapping a Tradition: Francophone Women's Writing from Guadeloupe* (Leeds: Maney Publishing, 2001).

6. See for example, Michel Fabre, *From Harlem to Paris: Black American Writers in France 1840–1980* (Urbana and Chicago: University of Illinois Press, 1991); Paul Gilroy, *The Black Atlantic: Identity and Double Consciousness* (London: Verso, 1993); Maryse Condé, 'O Brave New World', *Research in African Literatures*, 29 (1998) 1–7; Brent Hayes Edwards, *The Practice of Diaspora: Literature, Translation and the Rise of Black Nationalism* (Cambridge, MA, and London: Harvard University Press, 2003); *Black Modern: Journey Through the Black Atlantic*, ed. by Tanya Barson and Peter Gorschulter (Liverpool: Tate Publishing, 2010).

7. Fabre, p. 8.

8. Fabre, p. 4.

9. Fabre, p. 4.

10. In Aimé Césaire, *Cahier d'un retour au pays natal*, the restorative effects of this imagined contact with Africa are represented as follows: 'Il me suffirait d'une gorgée de ton lait jiculi pour qu'en toi, je découvre toujours à même distance de mirage — [...] la terre où tout est libre, et fraternel, ma terre' [I would only need one mouthful of your jiculi milk to discover in you always as distant as a mirage — [...] a land where everything is free and fraternal, my land] (*CRPN*, 86; *NRNL*, 89).

11. For a discussion of the representation of women in *CRPN*, see A. J. Arnold, *Modernism and Negritude: The Poetics and Poetry of Aimé Césaire* (Cambridge, MA: Harvard University Press, 1998), pp. 140–42.

12. For further discussion of the symbolic role of the rewriting of male-authored texts by female writers in the Caribbean context see *Caribbean Women Writers: Essays from the First International Conference*, ed. by Selwyn R. Cudjoe (Wellesley, MA: Calaloux Publications, 1990); Evelyn O'Callaghan, *Woman Version: Theoretical Approaches to West Indian Fiction by Women*, Warwick University Caribbean Studies (London and Basingstoke: Macmillan Caribbean, 1993); Emilia Ippolito, *Caribbean Women Writers: Identity and Gender* (Rochester, NY: Camden House, 2000); Caroline Rody, *The Daughter's Return: African-American and Caribbean Women's Fictions of History* (New York and London: Oxford University Press, 2001).

13. Caren Kaplan, *Questions of Travel: Postmodern Discourses of Displacement* (Durham, NC, and London: Duke University Press, 1996), p. 27.

14. Fanon's description of Négritude in *PNMB* as 'ce romantisme malheureux' [this unfortunate romanticism], can be interpreted as offering a reading of Négritude as a fictional 'narrative of identification', whose political viability is also implicitly called into question (p. 100).

15. Arguably, in the context of the dialogue constructed here, Césaire may also be viewed as at least partly 'fictional'.

16. See Fanon, *PNMB*, 31–50.

17. This sense of unresolved attachment can also be discerned in her ongoing, oblique engagement with Césaire's work throughout the text.

18. This is my own translation as this line is omitted in the English translation of the text.

19. For a reading of the text as articulating a form of female-centred 'Creole' identity, see H. Adlai Murdoch, *Creole Identity and the French Caribbean Novel* (Gainesville: University Press of Florida, 2001).

20. Veronica describes Adama as 'ma sœur en putainerie' [my sister in whoredom] (*ELB*, 108; *H*, 66).

CHAPTER 3

Voice, Irony and History in
Moi Tituba, sorcière... Noire de Salem

In the introduction to this book, I highlighted the idea of 'coming to voice' as a dominant trope in paradigms of 'female-centred autobiographical writing'. Through its depiction of collective female subjects, this form of writing is assumed to undercut the authority of the individual masculine subject of traditional autobiography and therefore to give expression to a collective feminine agency. In this chapter, through a close reading of *Moi Tituba, sorcière... Noire de Salem*, I explore the implications of reading resistance by female subjects as a process of 'coming to voice'. *MTSNS* is a 'testimonial text' of sorts which recounts the experiences of a Barbadian slave, Tituba, who was imprisoned on charges of witchcraft during the Salem witch trials. To begin with, it is necessary to situate testimonial literature briefly in the context of autobiographical women's writing.

In an article entitled 'Resisting Autobiography: Out-Law Genres and Trans-national Feminist Subjects', Caren Kaplan defines testimonial literature as work that 'takes the form of first-person narrative elicited, transcribed and edited by another person [...]'.[1] In the context of autobiographical women's writing, testimonial literature occupies a contradictory position. It is commonplace for critical antho-logies dedicated to autobiographical writing to include a section on testimonial literature and this would appear to point to its position as constitutive of a larger category of 'resistance writing'. Indeed, Caren Kaplan's article appears in a collection of essays entitled *De/Colonizing the Subject: The Politics of Women's Autobiography*. At the same time, the tendency to highlight the marginal status of this genre in relation to the practice of 'traditional autobiography' implicitly ascribes to the *testimonio* a superior subversive pedigree. In addition, the direct and documented engagement of testimonial literature with grassroots social and political movements, typically in Latin America, suggests that its subversive status is distinctly culturally specific.[2] However, Beverley also draws attention to the genre's status as a fundamentally 'democratic genre' which provides representation for a broad, perhaps international constituency of marginal subjects including 'the child, the native, the woman, the insane, the criminal'.[3]

According to Beverley, the *testimonio*'s political potential is also expressed as formal resistance to two specific generic conventions that underpin the production of autobiography. First, since the *testimonio* requires the collaboration of testifier, interviewer and, sometimes, translator, it contests the assumption of single author-ship that characterizes the practice of Western autobiography, presenting instead a collaborative, non-hierarchical model of writing.[4] Second, in contrast with auto-biography where the traces of orality are concealed, *testimonios* are often 'punc-tuated by a repeated series of interlocutive and conversational markers', a feature which serves to highlight the ceaseless interplay between the oral and the textual.[5]

The models of reading and authorship that Beverley develops here take for granted a humanist conception of collective voice that could be grounded in a material reality. Indeed, as Beverley notes, while the titles of *testimonios* (which typically contain references to an 'I') may appear to facilitate the affirmation of an individual subject, the *testimonio* can in fact be viewed as enacting a process of contestation by an individual self who is required to be representative of a social class or group:

> *Testimonio* represents an affirmation of the individual subject, even of individual growth and transformation, but in connection with a group or class situation marked by marginalization, oppression and struggle. If it loses this connection, it ceases to be *testimonio* and becomes autobiography [...] and also a means of access to middle- or upper-class status, a sort of documentary *Bildungsroman*.[6]

The role of the author of the *testimonio* is defined along similarly collective lines. Although the author of the *testimonio* is likely to belong to a more privileged social group than the narrator, Beverley suggests that the *testimonio*'s production transforms the role of the traditionally powerful author into that of a 'compiler' or 'activator' whose writing merely provides a reader with unmediated access to the experiences of marginalized groups.[7] It is in the field of reception that the collaborative, non-hierarchical relations that underpin the production of the *testimonio* come to serve as templates for forms of international political solidarity. In effect, by figuring the reader as the ideal interlocutor for the narrator of the *testimonio*, Beverley highlights the centrality of the national and international fields of reception to the realization of the international project of contestation and solidarity that the *testimonio* articulates:

> The complicity a *testimonio* establishes with its readers involves their identification — by engaging their sense of ethics and justice — with a popular cause normally distant, not to say alien, from their immediate experience. *Testimonio* in this sense has been important in maintaining and developing the practice of international human rights and solidarity movements.[8]

This model of agency suggests that there exists an indissoluble and unproblematic connection between the articulation of a collective representative voice and the expectations of a politically responsible field of reception. However, other critics have stressed the potentially negative implications of the unequal power relations that structure the encounter between the author and the testimonial subject as well as between the testimonial text and its Western readerships.

According to Kaplan, the fact that testimonial literature is predominantly read outside of its context of production by 'metropolitan' readers means that 'cross-cultural translation' is inherent to the production of this literature.[9] Kaplan situates the reception of this type of writing within a broader trend towards 'the romanticization and commodification of transnational cultural artefacts'.[10] In spite of the potentially negative implications that derive from the international reception of testimonial writing, Kaplan suggests that it is important (and also implicitly possible) to distinguish these from an 'overarching concern with international intercultural alliances', pointing to the *testimonio*'s capacity to articulate a kind of 'destabilizing resistance'.[11] If she stresses the role of a kind of 'politically responsible' criticism in harnessing the political potential of testimonial writing, arguably, this is underpinned by the assumption that a key aspect of the critic's role is the capacity to make a distinction between reading practices that are based on 'commodification' and those that express what Kaplan refers to as an 'overarching concern with international intercultural alliances'.[12]

In *The Post-colonial Exotic*, Graham Huggan challenges the idea that it is possible to distinguish between the effects of politically responsible readings and those that are 'commodifying'. In his assessment of some of the implications of the international reception for the agency of postcolonial or 'Third World' authors, Huggan uses life-narrative by Aboriginal women as a test case, highlighting the ways in which market-driven demand for exotic products shape both the production and the reception of these texts. In particular, he observes that the growing commercial popularity of such narratives reflects, at least partly, the demand by a mainstream (and presumably white) Australian readership for exotic cultural products, which are also 'preferably in accordance with those tales and images of otherness already possessed'.[13] Nevertheless, Huggan points to the role of a type of 'textual awareness' in problematizing the reception of texts by these authors, an awareness that allows them to provide 'an ironic commentary [...] on the processes by which the book's multiple readerships are constructed'.[14] As part of this, Huggan notes that the ironies that emerge from the interplay between the textual and the paratextual frames have the potential to challenge a range of univocal readings including those that attempt to situate the texts within paradigms of anti-colonial resistance.[15] According to Huggan, this is achieved through a process that brings various culturally constructed notions of authenticity into discursive conflict in such a way as to allow the author to 'reach out to alternative readerships including the people one regards as being one's own'.[16] Following Wendy Waring, Huggan argues that particular attention should be paid to the ways in which the 'paratextual traces' — such as 'cover design, front- and back-cover blurbs, glossary notes, epigraphs, italicised quotations and so on — indicate a tension between what the text says and what its various promoters [...] would have it do.'[17] In the rest of this chapter, I shall read *MTSNS* in the light of these discussions about the relationship between reception, representativity and irony. I shall also examine the ways in which irony influences the nature of the voice that emerges in the text, a feature of the text that is often overlooked in the North American critical readings that I explore in this chapter.[18] In addition, my reading of the text will cast further light on the implications of Huggan's unresolved position as regards both the extent to which textual ironies can be attributed to 'an author' and the likely implications of the text's engagement with its 'multiple readerships'.

The title of *MTSNS*, in presenting an 'I' that identifies itself as both 'black' and 'witch', implies an identification with two supranational collective experiences that are also both at least partly imaginary. In addition, the text is framed by a preface that situates its genesis in an intimate collaborative relationship between a female author, Maryse Condé, and a female subject, Tituba. In keeping with the conventions of realism that govern the production of *testimonios*, the author appears to respond to the expectations of a reading public concerned with her 'true experiences' by confirming the authenticity of the account: 'Tituba et moi avons vécu en étroite intimité pendant un an. C'est au cours de nos interminables conversations qu'elle m'a dit ces choses qu'elle n'avait confiées à personne' [Tituba and I lived for a year on the closest of terms. During our endless conversations she told me things she had confided to nobody else] (Foreword, *MTSNS* & *ITBWS*). The foreword then stages a transition from the voice of an author, Maryse Condé, to that of the first person voice which, in the light of the assurances provided, is presented as Tituba's true voice. The reader is then encouraged to identify with the voice through the revelation of the harrowing conditions of her birth: 'Abena, ma mère, un marin anglais la viola sur le pont du *Christ the King*, un jour de 16★★ alors que le navire faisait voile vers la Barbade. C'est de cette agression que je suis née' [Abena, my mother, was raped by an English sailor on the deck of *Christ the King* one day in the year 16★★ while the ship was sailing for Barbados. I was born from this act of aggression] (*MTSNS*, 13; *ITBWS*, 3).

By highlighting the text's engagement with the official history of the Salem witch trials, and the specific paratextual features that I have outlined above, North American critics have tended to overlook the potential for the ironic use of these features to create a 'reality effect' and have instead situated the text within established paradigms of feminine resistance. In line with the relationship between the traditional author and the female subject defined within the conventions of the *testimonio*, the effacement of the authorial voice is presented as a key precondition for the 'coming to voice' of this marginalized female subject.[19] In an article entitled 'Giving a Voice to Tituba: The Death of the Author', Elisabeth Mudimbé-Boyi reads the epigraph as enacting the transfer of authority and speech from Condé to Tituba, noting that '[w]ith the epigraph, Condé excises herself from the text that follows [...] leaving the entire textual space and a full voice to the character.'[20] Upholding the dominant assumption within paradigms of postcolonial feminine writing that 'voice' is co-extensive with 'agency', Mudimbé-Boyi argues that this act of self-effacement by Condé serves to invest Tituba with 'a full voice' that 'restores her to history' (p. 752).[21]

A certain effacement of authorial voice is one of the most significant effects produced by *MTSNS*. However, the ambiguity that surrounds the authorial voice in the text is not resolved by the transition from Maryse Condé's voice in the preface to the beginning of Tituba's account of her life in 'her true voice'. Instead, this disappearance of the authorial voice serves to intensify the troubling ambiguity of the voice whose story it appears to inaugurate. The ambiguity that the voice holds seems to centre on the very terms in which the self is named and the possibility of attributing this process to a collective experience. This is implied by the structure of the title. While the act of naming herself as a 'sorcière' is undertaken without hesitation, three suspension points separate the protagonist's dual 'naming' of herself as both 'Tituba' and 'sorcière' from the words '*Noire de Salem*' (which is also written in smaller print and italics).[22] Through the distinctive typographical presentation of the title, this process of naming therefore stages an ironic vacillation between the two sets of identities that are articulated in the two sets of names. The appropriateness of reading the title as ironic is apparently confirmed by Condé's comments in interviews although, as I have highlighted in Chapter 1, this medium does not necessarily guarantee the author's intentions. In her interviews with Françoise Pfaff, Condé repeatedly describes the text in terms of 'irony' or 'parody', observing for example: 'Ce que certains critiques n'ont pas compris c'est que le livre est moqueur' [What certain critics didn't understand is that this book is ironic] (*EMC*, 90; *CMC*, 60).

Condé's comments suggest the importance of considering the role of irony in the authorial voices that are produced both within the text and its paratextual frame. In this respect, Celia Britton's discussion of the relationship between Condé s use of irony and the model of authorship that is presented in her fictional texts is pertinent. In an article entitled 'Breaking the Rules: Irrelevance/Irreverence in Maryse Condé's *Traversée de la Mangrove*', Britton underlines the defining role of 'ironic realism' for Condé's writing.[23] Drawing on Barthes's *S/Z*, Britton distinguishes between two types of authorial attitude that arise from the use of irony. Firstly, she presents irony as constitutive of a code that 'is an expression of the author's dominance, asserting her superior intelligence by ridiculing more naïve codes on which it nevertheless depends.'[24] Secondly, she defines a Flaubertian form of irony that does not 'proclaim the author's controlling presence' but rather introduces indeterminacy and uncertainty.[25]

It is noteworthy that the importance of irony in the text has been largely overlooked by Condé's North American critics, including Mudimbé-Boyi, who have tended to emphasize an unambiguous political engagement on the part of Condé and her protagonist, Tituba. The assumption here is that the slave protagonist is representative of a collective experience both in the sense that her experiences are typical of other similar subjects and in the sense that she acts as the political spokesperson for a group to which she is assumed to 'belong'.[26] Such readings rely on the possibility of identifying an authorial figure to which a socially responsible intention could be clearly attributed.

In readings which have highlighted irony, this feature has been attributed to a clearly identifiable author, 'Maryse Condé', and it has also been taken for granted that its target(s) are 'known'. Writing on the presence of parody in the text, Pascale Bécel emphasizes the role of parody in drawing attention to the partial and constructed nature of the official historiographies from which Tituba has been excluded.[27] Lillian Manzor-Coats's reading of the text also assumes that the target of the text's parody can be clearly identified as she argues that the text constitutes 'a parody of feminists' simplistic construction of patriarchy' according to which 'all women are victims of men'.[28] By attributing irony on the basis of the possibility of identifying both an authorial intention and the target(s) of that irony, these readings highlight the presence of a form of irony whose characteristics conform to the first 'ironic code' that Britton defines.

A close reading of the text appears to confirm the existence of a parodic view of both historical and feminist discourses. In the case of the relationship that the text establishes with official 'History', the text's structure is particularly relevant. As Michelle Smith observes, the effect of placing a transcript of the Salem witch trials at the end of the text, after Tituba's account of her life in her 'own voice', is to suggest a re-contextualization of History.[29] Similarly, in support of her reading of the text as a challenge to reductive feminist discourses, Manzor-Coats shows how Tituba's bawdy comments work to undercut the proto-feminist comments made by her cellmate, Hester:[30]

> — Je voudrais écrire un livre, mais hélas! les femmes n'écrivent pas! Ce sont seulement les hommes qui nous assomment de leur prose [...]. Oui, je voudrais écrire un livre où j'exposerais le modèle d'une société gouvernée, administrée par les femmes! Nous donnerions notre nom à nos enfants, nous les élèverions seules...
> Je l'interrompais moqueusement:
> — Nous ne pourrions les faire seules, tout de même! (*MTSNS*, 159–60)
>
> ['I'd like to write a book, but alas, women don't write books! Only men bore us with their prose [...]. Yes, I'd like to write a book where I'd describe a model society governed and run by women! We would give our names to our children, we would raise them alone...'
> I interrupted her, poking fun: 'We couldn't make them alone, even so!' (*ITBWS*, 101)]

The above discussion of proto-feminist ideas in the context of an anachronistic encounter between Hester, the protagonist of *The Scarlet Letter*, and Tituba suggests that *MTSNS* does establish a relationship with both an idea of 'official History' and with certain feminist discourses. This relationship is marked by a disjuncture between what is said and what is meant and the effect of this is to suggest the presence of an ironic intention.[31] However this suggested ironic intention is constantly called into question in the context of the seemingly relentless indeterminacy that characterizes the text. The effect of this is to suggest an ongoing vacillation between the form of irony that Britton associates with an 'ironic code' and the more oblique 'Flaubertian irony'.

The movement between forms of irony thus serves to point to, and also create, the very instability of the authorial presence that marks the text. This instability stems from the proliferation of authorial figures in both the text and its paratext and the resultant impossibility of identifying the authorial voice with any degree of certainty. Indeed, the work and its paratext posit at least four possible authors. The title names Tituba, the witch of Salem as the author of the text; however, a short biography at the start of the book situates the text in the context of Maryse Condé's other work and, with its references to the author's personal trajectory, appears to name Condé as the 'real' author:

> Maryse Condé [...] est née le 11 février à Pointe-à-Pitre (Guadeloupe) d'une famille aisée de huit enfants [...]. Si à Paris, elle obtient en 1987, le Grand Prix Littéraire de la Femme pour *Moi Tituba sorcière...*, en 1993, elle est la première femme à obtenir aux États-Unis le Prix Puterbaugh pour l'ensemble de son œuvre [...].

[Maryse Condé [...] was born on February 11th in Pointe-à-Pitre (Guadeloupe) into a well-to-do family of eight children. In 1987, she obtained the Grand Literary Prize for Women's Writing for *I, Tituba, Black Witch of Salem*. In 1993, she was the first woman to receive the Puterbaugh Award for the body of her work [...].]

A third author, also named 'Maryse Condé', is presented by the preface as the collator of Tituba's testimony. In contrast with the first author who is named 'Maryse Condé', for whom the factual details of the biography serve to guarantee her reality, no information is provided about this second 'Maryse Condé' other than the statement, already quoted, that names her as Tituba's privileged confidante ('Tituba et moi, avons vécu en étroite intimité pendant un an'). This statement may be understood on at least two levels. In addition to a perhaps obvious anthropological reference to the notion that the author lives with her subject with a view to bearing witness to and recounting her story, the statement may also function as a metaphor for the creative process, suggesting that the author's cohabitation with her subject has been imaginary and not actual.[32]

Ambiguity surrounds the degree of equivalence between the 'real' Maryse Condé and this second eponymous author. This ambiguity is reinforced by the transition to the story of Tituba's life in 'her own voice' in which she recounts that she was conceived as the result of the rape of her mother, a female slave, by a British sailor. Tituba claims that the incident occurred 'un jour de 16★★'. This imprecise date simultaneously locates the text in 'real' historical time and presents it as existing outside of 'real' time. The ambiguous quality of the time reference also poses the question of the relationship between the 'real' Condé, whose life is evoked in the author's biography at the start of the text, and this apparently transhistorical and (also possibly) 'fictional' author who collects and transcribes Tituba's story in the seventeenth century and then presents the account for a reading public in the 1980s.

A potential fourth author named 'M.C.' signs the 'Note historique' that is placed at the end of the text in a separate section that appears after the main body of Tituba's account. In the first part of the 'Note historique', the lean, journalistic style suggests an effaced, objective authorial voice. However, in the second part of the account, the objective distance claimed is compromised by the implicit interpellation of 'a reader' through the use of the pronoun 'nous': 'Vers 1693, Tituba, notre heroïne fut vendue pour le prix de sa pension en prison, de ses chaînes et de ses fers' [Around 1693, our heroine was sold for the price of her prison fees and the cost of her chains and shackles'] (*MTSNS*, Note historique, p. 277; *ITBWS*, Historical Note, p. 181). Yet even this apparent shift in the authorial position is ambiguous for the use of the pronoun 'nous' at once evokes a neutral authorial voice and suggests an engagement between reader and writer that is predicated on a shared emotional attachment to 'notre heroïne'. In addition, with the rhetorical question 'A qui?' [To whom?], the voice appears to convey a consternation at Tituba's omission from the historical records which is also implicitly shared by the reader (*MTSNS*, Note historique, p. 278; *ITBWS*, Historical Note, p. 181).

M.C. then offers the following explanation for the absence of historical information on Tituba: 'Le racisme, conscient ou inconscient, des historiens est tel qu'aucun ne s'en soucie' [Such is the conscious or unconscious racism of the historians that we shall never know] (*MTSNS*, Note historique, p. 278; *ITBWS*, Historical Note, p. 181). In common with the author's oblique use of 'nous', this assessment fluctuates between the taking of a position (in this case, political) with regard to Tituba's absence from the historical records (implied by 'le racisme des historiens') and the expression of an objective response to this fact. The emotive potential of the appeal to racism is therefore attenuated (but I would suggest not completely erased) by qualifying this claim with the use of 'psychoanalytical' or 'scientific' language ('conscient ou inconscient') and impersonal verbal structures ('aucun ne s'en soucie'). The distancing effect of these fluctuations is temporarily interrupted by M.C.'s articulation of a resolute authorial presence (marked by 'Je' and 'moi') that claims responsibility for the production of Tituba's story in terms that underscore the fictionality of the account: 'Je lui ai offert quant à moi, une fin de mon choix' [I myself gave her an ending of my own choosing] (*MTSNS*, Note historique, p. 278; *ITBWS*, Historical Note, p. 181). However, this apparent insight into M.C.'s motivations for constructing the text ends abruptly with the return at the end of the note of a curiously distant authorial voice that draws attention to a point of historical detail: 'Il faut noter que le village de Salem se nomme aujourd'hui Danvers et que c'est la ville de Salem où eut lieu la majorité des procès, mais non l'hystérie collective, qui tire sa renommée du souvenir de la sorcellerie' [The reader should note that the village of Salem is now called Danvers. It is the town of Salem — where most of the trials, but not the mass of the hysteria took place — that has become famous for its history of witchcraft] (*MTSNS*, Note historique, p. 278; *ITBWS*, Historical Note, p 181). The effaced quality of this voice is partially mitigated by the reference to 'l'hystérie collective' that suggests the presence of an evaluative authorial attitude. This vacillation between distance and engagement in the final paragraph therefore frustrates any attempts by the reader to establish unambiguously the identity of the author and with it the possibility of assigning political agency.

In view of the unrelentingly ambiguous quality of the authorial presence generated through the interplay between the textual and paratextual frames, the resultant disjuncture of voice and meaning exemplifies the indeterminate 'Flaubertian' irony that Britton identifies in her analysis of the way irony functions in Condé's *Traversée de la Mangrove*. Britton quotes Barthes's argument that: 'Flaubert [...] en maniant une ironie frappée d'incertitude, opère un malaise salutaire de l'écriture: il n'arrête pas le jeu des codes (ou l'arrête mal) en sorte que [...] on ne sait jamais s'il est responsable de ce qu'il écrit' [By using an irony marked by uncertainty, Flaubert deploys the salutary unease that accompanies the practice of writing itself: he does not interrupt (or interrupts only incompletely) the play of textual meaning so that [...] one never knows if he is responsible for what he is writing].[33] In the light of Britton's analysis, I would argue that the irony generated in *MTSNS* is characterized by a polyvalence and an instability that undercut any attempt to read it as representative of 'feminine testimonial literature'. This is because the text posits an ambiguous, disembodied, shifting authorial voice that does not allow for the identification of a writer whose interests could be clearly and *definitively* aligned with that of a specific political group or community. This absence of clear alignment with community interests does not point to a failure to endorse *any* position but rather designates an open-ended, ongoing movement *within* and *between* a number of provisional positions that include the idea of 'feminine testimonial writing'. Central features of *MTSNS* appear to encourage or justify a reading as 'feminine testimonial writing'. Not only does it appeal to the theme of 'giving voice' to a female subject erased from history, it is also structured by a collaboration between the female author 'Maryse Condé' and Tituba. However this apparent endorsement of a feminine position is undercut, for example, by Tituba's challenge to Hester's radical feminist position (based on the exclusion of all men) with the use of bawdy humour.

Nevertheless, at the end of the text, the spirit of the executed Tituba appears to situate herself within a type of female lineage that links her to her mother Abena, her grandmother Man Ya and also to Samantha, the daughter of a female slave whom she names as her descendant and apprentice in the spiritual arts: 'Comme je suis morte sans qu'il ait été possible d'enfanter, les invisibles m'ont autorisée à me choisir une descendante' [As I died without giving birth to a child, the spirits have allowed me to choose a descendant] (*MTSNS*, 269; *ITBWS*, 176). Yet, this final gesture towards an idea of female community is marked by a subtle humour, one that sees Tituba co-opt the evaluative practices applied by slave owners in the selection of the most viable slaves for her own purposes of finding the right descendant: 'J'ai épié dans les cases. J'ai regardé les lavandières donner le sein [...]. J'ai *comparé*, *soupesé*, *tâté* et finalement, je l'ai trouvée, celle qu'il fallait: Samantha' [I spied into every cabin. I looked at the washerwomen breast-feeding [...]. I made comparisons, I fingered and prodded and finally I found her, the one I needed: Samantha] (*MTSNS*, 269; *ITBWS*, 176, my italics). The fact that Tituba's stepfather is also part of this community means that the sense of exclusivity that is potentially implicit in an idea of female community is challenged. This gesture also remains confined to an ephemeral, spiritual plane, thereby rendering it implausible for recuperation as part of a feminist political agenda (such as the one expressed by Hester) capable of producing concrete results in the 'real' world. This movement between positions is in turn mirrored in the comments that Condé makes in her interviews with Pfaff:

> It is believed she was sold to pay for expenses incurred during her incarceration. All this seemed revolting to me, and I wanted to give a life to this obscure and forgotten woman. But since I am not the kind of writer who creates model characters, I quickly destroyed what was exemplary in the story by rendering Tituba rather naïve and sometimes ridiculous.[34]

In the first part of this comment, Condé describes her response to Tituba's disappearance from historical records in terms that suggest that her decision to use her text to 'give a life to this obscure and forgotten woman' reflects a personal engagement which is potentially inflected with a larger political solidarity with other 'forgotten' women'.[35] But this suggestion of political solidarity is shown to be at the very least provisional — if not actually misleading — by Condé's revelation that she intended to undercut what are implicitly 'politically correct' readings of her text by using parody to interrupt the very possibility of reading Tituba as 'exemplary'.

The ambiguous depiction of Tituba is central to this process. For while, as I observed earlier, critical readings have typically presented Tituba as emblematic of an empowered black female subjectivity, Tituba herself is among the targets of the text's diffuse parody. Tituba's self-conscious contemplation of her erasure from history is a pertinent example of the multi-layered workings of this parody. The narrative adopts a mock-serious tone as the witch Tituba is presented as possessing a supernatural presence that enables her to consult the official accounts of the Salem witch trials from which she has been excluded: 'Je cherche mon histoire dans celle des Sorcières de Salem et ne la trouve pas' [I can look for my story among those of the witches of Salem, but it isn't there] (*MTSNS*, 230; *ITBWS*, 149). The demand for representation that she expresses displays none of the collective political consciousness that would enable her story to be read unproblematically in terms of the 'coming to voice' of a representative female subject. Instead, Tituba displays a ridiculous, self-serving vanity as she laments: 'Aucune, aucune biographie attentionnée et inspirée recréant ma vie et ses tourments!' [There would never, ever, be a careful, sensitive biography recreating my life and its suffering!] (*MTSNS*, 173; *ITBWS*, 110). Arguably, then, Tituba's concern with recounting her individual story in a testimonial text undercuts the distinction between 'traditional individualistic autobiography' and 'collective testimony' that I outlined at the start of the chapter. This use of the testimonial text to express an individual demand for representation also potentially satirizes the slightly pious political credentials that are ascribed to this type of text on the basis of its documented commitment to giving expression to a 'collective voice'.

The mock-dramatic quality of Tituba's expression of her desire for representation, cited above, generates yet other levels of irony. Terms such as 'attentionnée' and 'inspirée' are reminiscent of a marketing gloss that might appear on the cover of an actual book about Tituba's life and thus (in line with Huggan's analysis) appear to anticipate the reception of the text as an 'authentic cultural product' by Western readerships. By presenting the potential marketability of Tituba's life in an ironic light, the text raises questions concerning the ability of Western authors or compilers to recuperate the 'true voice' of their Third World subjects. Indeed, it could be argued that the voice that emerges from the testimonial encounter might (as Spivak has highlighted) simply ventriloquize the political beliefs of the authors of the testimonial texts.[36]

Interestingly, Tituba also suggests that there are particular benefits or, at least, an oblique freedom to be had from this exclusion from official history as she asserts proudly that: 'Je n'appartiens pas à la civilisation du Livre et de la Haine. C'est dans leurs cœurs que les miens gardent mon souvenir, sans nul besoin de graphies. C'est dans leurs têtes. Dans leurs cœurs et dans leurs têtes' [I do not belong to the civilization of the Bible and Bigotry. My people will keep my memory in their hearts and have no need for the written word. It's in their hearts and heads] (*MTSNS*, 268–69; *ITBWS*, 176).[37]

The text's use of irony is central to preserving the illegibility of its position in relation to different discourses that are likely to shape its reception. As I suggested earlier, the text's irony cannot be read as a straightforward critique of the idea of a 'feminine coming to voice'. Rather, it generates multiple ironies that work to relativize its engagement with feminist discourses precisely by satirizing a range of other critical and or identitarian positions. While Condé uses irony to critique Tituba's exclusion from official historiographical discourses, her irony is also directed at the world of the Occult, to which Tituba subscribes, and at the discourse of the 'heroic maroon'.[38] In particular, Tituba's fatal involvement with a maroon revolt serves as the context for challenging the dominant and, perhaps, romantic image of maroons as liberators of other slaves. In fact, as Tituba's lover, Iphigene reveals, the maroons' own freedom was reliant on their willingness to denounce other slaves to the planters: 'Il existe entre les maîtres et eux, un pacte tacite. S'ils veulent que ceux-ci les laissent jouir de leur précaire liberté, ils doivent dénoncer tous les préparatifs, toutes les tentatives de révolte dont ils ont vent dans l'île' [There is a tacit agreement between them and the planters. And if they want the planters to let them enjoy their precarious freedom, they have to denounce every plot and every attempt at a slave revolt they hear about on the island] (*MTSNS*, 249; *ITBWS*, 163).

More generally, I would also argue that the novel engages obliquely with the contradictory, competitive identity politics that inform its critical reception in the United States.[39] On the one hand, the story of a 'black' female slave appears to invite a prioritization of political readings that highlight the relevance of the text for engaging with the specific experiences (past and present) of communities that are identified as 'black' and 'female'. On the other hand, the text undercuts its potential co-option within these specific communitarian politics by using Tituba's marriage to John Indian and her subsequent relationship with her Jewish master, Benjamin Cohen d'Azevedo, to draw attention to the shared oppression of the African slaves, the Native American Indians, and the Jewish people. In this way, *MTSNS* articulates a distance from identitarian allegiances that enables it to express a wide-ranging critical consciousness. This process serves as the basis for the text's exploration of the creative possibilities presented by an oblique form of individual agency.[40] Arguably, the text articulates a subtle critique of an over-eager adoption of group identity and, in so doing, highlights the risk that entrenched communitarian interests may scupper any real possibility of political solidarity across cultures. For instance, on entering the household of Cohen d'Azevedo, Tituba appears to link their ignorance of English to a certain cultural insularity that precludes any interest in the experiences of other cultural groups, as she observes that 'cet incessant babil en hébreu ou en portugais donnait la mesure dont cette famille était indifférente à tout ce qui n'était pas son propre malheur, à tout ce qui n'était pas les tribulations des Juifs à travers la terre' [this constant babble in Hebrew and Portuguese showed how indifferent they were to the misfortune of others and to anything that did not concern the tribulations of Jews the world over] (*MTSNS*, 193; *ITBWS*, 123). This leads Tituba to wonder 'si Benjamin Cohen d'Azevedo était au courant des procès des Sorcières de Salem et si ce n'était pas en toute innocence qu'il était entré à la prison' [if Benjamin Cohen d'Azevedo had even heard about the Salem witch trials and whether he hadn't entered the prison by accident] (*MTSNS*, 193; *ITBWS*, 123).

Later in the text, though, Tituba's growing affection for the family and the deepening of her relationship with Cohen d'Azevedo appear to point to the possibility of cross-cultural political and social affiliations.[41] Yet, it is suggested that these affiliations (and the possibilities that accompany them) are provisional, as her relationship with Cohen d'Azevedo comes to an end when his entire family is killed in an arson attack and he grants Tituba her freedom and pays for her passage to Barbados. The provisional nature of this particular relationship serves as a touchstone for the open-ended, fluid nature of the numerous affiliations that Tituba forges throughout the text. In this way, the text suggests a reconfiguration of the idea of 'community' as organic, shifting 'groupings' of individuals. After her death, Tituba alludes to this fluid idea of community with her references to 'les invisibles' who, she notes, are 'outside' the written word. The terms that Tituba uses to describe 'les invisibles' serve as significant pointers to the types of possibility that accompany this type of 'community'. With the references to 'cœurs' and 'têtes' in keeping her 'memory' alive, Tituba alludes to this 'community's' role in maintaining an oral form of 'history' thus implicitly pointing towards an alternative to the written official History from which she is excluded. However, the use of the future tense of 'garderont' suggests that this role has yet to be realized. In addition, the use of the plural form of 'cœurs' and 'têtes' suggests the possibility of different, *individual* versions of this history and the accompanying challenges to the reaching of any form of historical consensus. If this open-endedness and lack of consensus inhibit the recuperation of this potential as a form of politically motivated collective agency, it nevertheless gestures towards an intangible and individually mediated form of 'freedom' to form relations — real or imagined — of one's choosing.

In the final analysis, the text's use of irony to simultaneously address and call into question a range of critical and identitarian discourses suggests that its irony operates in ways similar to those envisaged by Huggan, by effectively pointing up the flawed assumptions that underpin a range of different discourses that are likely to be applied to its reading and putting these into play. Through its shifting affiliations with communitarian politics, this process may be viewed as an individually mediated form of agency that gestures towards an ambiguous space outside established communitarian politics. While this agency presents individuals with the possibility of resisting the imposition of constraining and divisive communitarian identities (those, for example, that define all members of specific cultural groups as 'victims' or others as 'natural enemies'), this potential for a tactical and changeable resistance is not equally accessible to all individuals who are assumed to belong to such groups. Nor is it perhaps even transferable to the 'real' political sphere. *MTSNS* therefore raises and leaves unanswered questions about the relationship between the self, community, writing and agency that I shall explore further in the next chapter.

Notes to Chapter 3

1. Caren Kaplan, 'Resisting Autobiography: Out-Law Genres and Transnational Feminist Subjects', in *De/Colonizing the Subject: The Politics of Gender in Women's Autobiography*, ed. by Sidonie Smith and Julia Watson (Minneapolis: University of Minnesota Press, 1992), pp. 115–38 (p. 122).

2. See for example, George B. Handley, 'It's an Unbelievable Story': Testimony and Truth in the Work of Rosario Ferré and Rigoberta Menchú', in *Violence, Silence, and Anger: Women's Writing as Transgression*, ed. by Deirdre Lashgari (Charlottesville: University Press of Virginia, 1995), pp. 62–79; Jennifer Browdy de Hernandez, 'Of Tortillas and Texts: Postcolonial Dialogues in the Latin American Testimonial', in *Feminist Dialogues on Third World Women's Literature and Film*, ed. by Bishnupriya Ghosh, Brinda Bose and Chandra Talpade Mohanty (New York: Garland, 1997), pp. 163–84; Joanna R. Bartow, *Subject to Change: The Lessons of Latin American Women's Testimonio for Truth, Fiction, and Theory* (Chapel Hill: University of North Carolina Press, 2005).

3. John Beverley, 'The Margin at the Centre: On *Testimonio*', in *De/Colonizing the Subject: The Politics of Gender in Women's Autobiography*, ed. by Sidonie Smith and Julia Watson (Minneapolis: University of Minnesota Press, 1992), pp. 91–114 (p. 93).

4. Beverley, 'The Margin at the Centre', p. 97.

5. Beverley, 'The Margin at the Centre', p. 97.

6. Beverley, 'The Margin at the Centre', p. 103.

7. Beverley, 'The Margin at the Centre', pp. 97–98.

8. Beverley, 'The Margin at the Centre', p. 99.

9. Kaplan, 'Resisting Autobiography', p. 124.

10. Kaplan, 'Resisting Autobiography', pp. 124–25.

11. Kaplan, 'Resisting Autobiography', pp. 124–25.

12. Kaplan, 'Resisting Autobiography', p. 124.

13. Huggan, *The Postcolonial Exotic*, p. 159.

14. Huggan, *The Postcolonial Exotic*, p. 166.

15. Huggan, *The Postcolonial Exotic*, p. 166.

16. Huggan, *The Postcolonial Exotic*, p. 176.

17. Huggan, *The Postcolonial Exotic*, p. 164.

18. In 'Breaking the Rules: Irrelevance/ Irreverence in Maryse Condé's *Traversée de la Mangrove*', *French Cultural Studies*, 15 (2004), 35–47, Celia Britton identifies irony as a characteristic feature of Condé's approach to writing that is typically employed to undermine stereotypes (p. 36).

19. In 'Giving a Voice to Tituba: The Death of the Author', *World Literature Today*, 67 (1993), 751–56. Elisabeth Mudimbé-Boyi links *MTSNS* to the tradition of testimonial literature exemplified by *I, Rigoberta Menchú* (p. 753).

20. Mudimbé-Boyi, 'Giving a Voice to Tituba', p. 752.

21. In 'The (De) Construction of Subjectivity in Daniel Maximin's *L'Ile et une nuit*', *Paragraph*, 24, 3 (2001), 31–44, Britton highlights and questions this assumption (p. 31). See also Lionnet, *Autobiographical Voices* and *Postcolonial Representations: Women, Literature, Identity* (Ithaca, NY, and London: Cornell University Press, 1995); Smith and Watson, eds, *Women, Autobiography, Theory*; Boyce Davies and Savory Fido, eds, *Out of the Kumbla*; Braxton, *Black Women Writing Autobiography*; Green et al., eds, *Postcolonial Subjects*.

22. It should be noted that in the English version of the text this ambiguity is not implied by the structure of the title of the text, which is *I Tituba, Black Witch of Salem*.

23. In 'Breaking the Rules', Britton argues that 'ironic realism refers to the author's tendency to use sardonic humour or irony to comment on social reality' (p. 35).

24. Britton, 'Breaking the Rules', p. 41.

25. Britton, 'Breaking the Rules', p. 41.

26. For further discussion of the text as representing a 'female community', see for example, Patrice J. Proulx, 'Inscriptions of Female Community and Liberation in Maryse Condé's *Moi, Tituba sorcière...*', *Ecrivaines Françaises et Francophones: Europe Plurilingue* (March 1997), 148–61; Pascale Bécel, '*Moi Tituba, sorcière... Noire de Salem*, A Tale of Petite Maronne', *Callaloo*, 18 (1995), 608–15.

27. Bécel, 'Moi Tituba, sorcière', pp. 608–15.

28. Lillian Manzor-Coats 'Of Witches and Other Things: Maryse Condé's Challenges to Feminist Discourse', World Literature Today, 67 (1993), 737–44 (p. 743).

29. Michelle Smith, 'Reading in Circles: Sexuality and/as History in I, Tituba, Black Witch of Salem', Callaloo, 18 (1995), 602–07 (p. 602).

30. Manzor-Coats, 'Of Witches and Other Things', p. 743.

31. In Irony's Edge: The Theory and Politics of Irony (London and New York: Routledge, 1995), Linda Hutcheon defines irony as 'a simple antiphrastic substitution of the unsaid (called the "ironic meaning") for its opposite, the said (called the "literal meaning") — which is then either "set aside" [...] or sometimes only "partially effaced" [...]' (p. 12).

32. Commenting on the writing of MTSNS, Condé observes in EMC: 'L'inspiration "surnaturelle" existe parce qu'on a soudain envie d'écrire à propos d'une créature totalement imaginaire, qu'on n'arrive jamais à rencontrer, qui n'existe pas, que l'on n'a vue nulle part. On ne sait pas très bien pourquoi on a envie d'écrire subitement à propos de tel personnage. L'acte d'écrire est "surnaturel" en lui-même' ['Supernatural' inspiration does exist in a sense, since you suddenly feel like writing about a totally imaginary creature whom you have never seen or met, and who doesn't exist. You don't really know why all of a sudden you want to write about this or that character. The very act of writing is 'supernatural' in itself] (EMC, 89; CMC, 59).

33. Britton, 'Breaking the Rules', p. 41 (my translation of Barthes).

34. Pfaff, Conversations, p. 60.

35. Condé has consistently used her critical writings to highlight and challenge the undervalued role of female authors in the Francophone Caribbean literary tradition. See for example La Parole des femmes: Essais sur des romancières des Antilles de la langue française (Paris: L'Harmattan, 1993); 'Language and Power: Words as Miraculous Weapons', CLA Journal, 39 (1995), 18–25; 'Order, Disorder'; 'The Stealers of Fire'.

36. See Gayatri Chakravorty Spivak, 'Can the Subaltern Speak?', in Colonial Discourse and Post-colonial Theory, ed. by Patrick Williams and Laura Chrisman (Hemel Hempstead: Harvester Wheatsheaf, 1993), pp. 66–111. Spivak argues that critics should resist the temptation to retrieve the voice of the subaltern, firstly, because this voice cannot be retrieved and, secondly, because this approach subscribes to the humanist idea that the voice constitutes an authentic expression of individuality (p. 83).

37. This suggestion of freedom as in some sense 'unreadable' presents a challenge to the totalizing exoticizing terms in which Huggan characterizes the reception of such works.

38. Condé has also challenged the representation of the maroons as heroic in her critical writings and interviews. See for example, Condé, 'The Stealers of Fire', p. 163; Sansavior, 'Entretien avec Maryse Condé', p. 18.

39. See for example Huggan, The Postcolonial Exotic. Huggan draws attention to the dominance of a critical approach to 'Third World Literatures' in the United States that, he argues, is characterized by the tendency to draw on 'broad-based postcolonial methodologies' to press these works into the service of current debates on 'minority cultures within the context of the nation' (p. 241).

40. We are therefore some way from the resolutely ambivalent stance towards the very idea of 'community' that is expressed in ELB.

41. Tituba subsequently highlights her own susceptibility to the exclusive adoption of group identity that she had previously criticized: 'Oui, j'en vins comme les Cohen d'Azevedo à diviser le monde en deux camps: les amis des Juifs et les autres' [Yes, like Benjamin Cohen d'Azevedo, I began to divide the world into two groups: the friends of Jews and others] (MTSNS, 200; ITBWS, 128).

CHAPTER 4

Autobiography and Reading in
Le Cœur à rire et à pleurer:
Contes vrais de mon enfance

The process of calling into question the relationship between self, community and writing that I identified as a key preoccupation in the testimonial text, *MTSNS*, is elaborated further in Condé's account of her childhood, *Le Cœur à rire et à pleurer: Contes vrais de mon enfance*.[1] Published in 1999, when Condé was 62, *LCRP* is structured around a series of vignettes that depict her experiences from birth to age sixteen. While to date the text has attracted relatively little critical attention, the interviews and critical readings that have centred on the text have all tended, to varying extents, to assign it the status of 'autobiography'. *LCRP*'s autobiographical status is defined in terms of a coincidence of form and function. In line with this, a number of critics have read *LCRP* as paradigmatic of 'postcolonial' Caribbean autobiographical writing on the basis of its use of specific literary practices such as the blurring of fact and fiction and intertextual references along with its non-linear narrative structure as a means of giving expression to a distinctive Caribbean subjectivity.[2]

As I highlighted in the Introduction, it is a common critical gesture to align the representative status of 'postcolonial women's writing' with the generic indeterminacy that results from a blurring of fact and fiction. In her article entitled 'The (De) Construction of Subjectivity in Daniel Maximin's *L'Île et une nuit*', Celia Britton argues that the dominant critical approach to texts by postcolonial female subjects takes for granted a 'biographical continuity' between the authors and their female protagonists.[3] Interestingly, Britton implies — and this is certainly exemplified by Condé's work — that such an approach is not entirely unfounded since these texts themselves often problematize any distinction between 'fiction' and 'autobiography', drawing closely on the real-life experiences of their authors and employing the textual conventions of autobiography or *journal intime*.[4] In addition, Britton notes that one of the appeals of this idea of literature as providing the context for 'a coming to voice' of previously marginalized or silenced female subjects is that it offers a straightforward model of agency that reads 'voice' as coterminous with a collective feminine agency.[5] In my reading of Condé's text as 'autobiographical', I shall challenge these critical assumptions through an exploration of the following questions: first, as a corollary to the idea that these texts 'invite' or 'encourage' certain types of 'politically motivated autobiographical readings', can it be suggested that the autobiographical strategies employed by Condé's text demonstrate an awareness of its likely reception? Second, to what extent does the complex relationship between the real-life and fictional experiences in this text create a space for the expression of a form of agency. Third, to what extent do individual and collective concerns coincide in this process?

★ ★ ★ ★ ★

From the outset, *LCRP*'s paratextual frame frustrates any attempt to assign it to a clear generic category. Divided by a colon, the text's title juxtaposes at least two different models of autobiography. The first part with its reference to the emotional states 'laughter' and 'tears' appears to situate the text within a model of 'feminine confessional writing' that is ambiguously coded. Indeed, this first part of the title contains cues both to an idea of feminine emotionalism and to the model of postcolonial women's writing as resistance, critical paradigms that I identified earlier as those that would be typically applied to the text.[6] In the second part of the title, the reference to the individual experiences of Condé's childhood with 'mon enfance' problematizes the collective focus that is assumed to subtend both models of 'female writing'. The expression 'contes vrais' is ambiguous.[7] It casts doubt on the idea that *LCRP* is anchored in a material reality that guarantees its authentic status while also suggesting an ironic reference to the tendency (that Condé identifies in her interviews) by French critics to read Francophone Caribbean literature as 'stories'.[8]

As I argued in my discussion of *MTSNS*, the multiplicity of potential reading cues contained in *LCRP*'s title generates various levels of irony that work to undercut the different readings of the text that are offered by the critical paradigms that I discussed above.[9] The first level of reading with which the text engages is present on the 'blurb' on the text's back cover: 'Dans la Guadeloupe des années cinquante, on tient son rang en se gardant de parler créole; on méprise plus noir et moins instruit que soi. Les conventions priment les sentiments' [In 1950s Guadeloupe, you maintain your social standing by avoiding speaking Creole; you view with contempt those who are of a darker complexion and less well educated than yourself. Social conventions are more important than feelings].[10] The content and phrasing of this blurb suggests that its function is what Graham Huggan refers to as the 'interpellation of a "globalized market reader"', who is constructed as a kind of "anthropological tourist" of the unfamiliar worlds represented in the text.'[11] Apparently offering tantalizing 'secrets' from this unfamiliar world, the blurb thus packages the text as an exotic performance intended for the enjoyment of an 'homogenized' metropolitan French 'market reader'.[12]

The term 'contes vrais' therefore acts as an ironic reference to the 'exoticizing' nature of the French codes of authenticity that are likely to inform the reception of *LCRP* and this in turn potentially undermines the reading of the text invited by the publisher's blurb. The epigraph further undercuts the blurb's translation of the text as conveying a distinctly Caribbean reality described in exotic terms as 'la nostalgie de l'âme caraïbe' [the nostalgia for the Caribbean soul]. The epigraph is a quotation drawn from Proust's first work *Contre Sainte-Beuve*, a work which is generally considered to be the avant-texte for *A la recherche du temps perdu*: 'Ce que l'intelligence nous rend sous le nom du passé n'est pas lui' [Remembrance of things past is not what we retrieve from the mind].

The use of this epigraph to this specific text by Proust to inaugurate Condé's autobiographical project is certainly significant. The quotation is taken from a critical essay written as a response to — and a warning against — Sainte-Beuve's injunction to read literary texts for the biographical information that they provide about their author. This is a particularly suggestive quotation in light of what I have argued is Condé's insistent and well-documented defence of the literary qualities of her writing against the instrumentalist reading practices typically endorsed by politicized critical approaches. Through its slightly cryptic terms, the quotation encourages caution. By figuring the past as a (false) construction of 'intelligence' or 'the mind', there is thus an implicit questioning of the authenticity of the experiences that are represented in the text and this process of questioning undermines the assumptions of veracity attached to the use of the adjective 'vrais' in Condé's title. If the reader is put on guard against such constructions, this reference to an important but lesser-known work by a canonical French writer also serves to signal Condé's intellectual pedigree and to position her culturally as a French 'insider'.[13]

The reference to this most canonical of French autobiographers at the start of *LCRP* suggests the potential for an especially productive type of individual authorial agency that is paradigmatically readerly. On one level, it signals Condé's intention and also her ability to situate her autobiographical project within a French literary tradition that she constructs herself. This intertextual gesture therefore disrupts the text's implicit positioning within a Francophone Caribbean oral tradition, opening it up instead to a plurality of possible readings that necessarily include an established idea of 'the French literary tradition'.[14]

On another level, the potential disruption of reductive French readings of the text can also be extended to its reception within politically motivated paradigms of reading. If the first part of the text's title appears to endorse an idea of 'women's writing', the assumption that the narrative subject is representative of a larger female community, grounded in a material reality is undercut by the individualistic and fictional inflections of the second part of the title. In addition, the text's epigraph, which appears to align it with the Proustian autobiographical project, can be read as subtly questioning the dominant conception of postcolonial women's autobio-graphical writing as written against masculine and colonial models of subjectivity.[15]

Although *LCRP* explores the complex and difficult relationship between Condé and her mother, the depiction of this relationship does not provide the context for the claiming of a clearly articulated political stance. Instead, the shifting authorial voice that Condé deploys in the text generates an irresolvable uncertainty that unsettles certain accepted feminist political positions. As in *MTSNS*, this voice has a vacillating quality that continuously defers both the possibility of assigning a stable meaning to these comments and that of attributing responsibility for them to 'an author'. The destabilizing potential of this vacillating voice is conveyed with great effectiveness in the chapter 'Ma Naissance' where Condé's birth is narrated from a number of fluidly shifting points of view. Condé uses her mother's pregnancy to contrast the generous maternity benefits enjoyed by today's women with the modest ones to which her mother's generation had access: 'En ces temps-là, on ne connaissait pas ces scandaleux congés de maternité; quatre semaines avant l'accouchement, six semaines après; ou vice versa. Les femmes travaillaient jusqu'à la veille de leur délivrance' [At this time, there was no such thing as this [scandalous] maternity leave we have nowadays: four weeks before delivery, six weeks after or vice versa. Women worked right up to the day before giving birth] (*LCRP*, 20; *TFTH*, 12).[16] On the one hand, the comments appear to express, in transparent terms, Condé's disapproval of what she suggests are excessively generous maternity leave. But, on the other hand, the complex layering of narrative points of view that structure this chapter subtly undercuts a univocal reading of this comment as unambiguously 'anti-feminist' in its implied opposition to benefits that have accrued to women largely as a result of feminist political advocacy.

   In a modern context where women's rights to a certain level of maternity benefits is broadly taken for granted, the reference to maternity leave as 'scandaleux' suggests that the comment is 'knowingly' controversial. The apparent seriousness of this *prise de position* is however undercut by the mischievous tone of an extended description of her mother's pregnancy that frames this comment (that is itself also not clearly attributed). For example, her mother's surprise at becoming pregnant at a relatively advanced age is depicted with irreverence: 'Passé la honte d'avoir été prise, à son âge respectable, en flagrant délit d'œuvre de chair, ma mère ressentit une grande joie de son état' [Once she had gotten over the shame of being caught *in flagrante delicto* of the pleasures of the flesh at her respectable age, my mother was overjoyed at her condition] (*LCRP*, 19; *TFTH*, 11). The effect of the multiple shifts of point of view is to defer any clear identification of anti-feminist intention. Arguably, this playful switching from one narrative point of view to another is also productive of diffuse ironies that work to call into question a range of representative critical positions that are likely to 'originate' in these.

   One of the key 'yardsticks' of an author's representativity is the extent to which she and, by extension, the protagonists that she creates are required to serve as exemplary 'witnesses', a requirement that as I noted in Chapter 3, typically involves a conflation of the text's status as political intervention and exotic product. Condé's text responds to this imperative with humour and ambivalence in the chapter entitled, 'Chemin d'école', providing instances of witnessing that foreground the tensions between her conservative familial context, the schooling that she receives in France, and the Francophone Caribbean literary tradition in relation to which she implicitly situates her memoir.[17] A close reading of three scenes of witnessing in this chapter will allow for an analysis of the ways in which Condé translates their ambiguously creative potential as forms of performance. The chapter begins with an apparently unmediated act of witnessing that is situated in a 'real' temporal plane through a reference to the protagonist's age. With the use of the modal form of the verb 'devais', Condé makes a perhaps typically autobiographical concession to the unreliability of memory: 'Je devais avoir treize ans' [I must have been thirteen] (*LCRP*, 97; *TFTH*, 105). In the course of the chapter, this conventionally sanctioned uncertainty extends progressively to the comments that are represented.

The difficulties surrounding the attribution of comments find a particularly suggestive structural and dramatic articulation in the different types of experiential and textual quotations or 'borrowings' that accompany the various shifts in narrative point of view in this chapter. Although the first paragraph begins with Condé's point of view, this fades into what is implicitly the point of the view of the autobiographical protagonist's parents. Condé's musings on her stay in post-war Paris begin with 'Je devais avoir treize ans' [I must have been thirteen] and end with 'seule distraction qui nous soit permise jusqu'à six heures du soir' [the only distraction we were allowed at home] (*LCRP*, 97; *TFTH*, 105). These reflections are followed immediately by a parodic reproduction of her parents' warning that she should avoid going out after six o'clock in the evening in Paris since 'des nègres au sexe vorace pouvaient s'approcher des vierges de bonne famille et les désrespecter avec des paroles et des gestes obscènes' [[black] males hungry for sex might solicit us virgins from respectable families and taunt us with obscene words or gestures] (*LCRP*, 97; *TFTH*, 105).[18] The phrase 'd'après mes parents' appears to mark clearly the transition from Condé's 'voice' to that of her parents and to distinguish these comments from the rest of her observations in this chapter. The use of the verb 'désrespecter' means though that the process of assigning the above comments to her parents is far from clear-cut, conveying as it does an ambiguous sense of 'received wisdom' that makes it difficult to distinguish not only the young Condé's opinions from those of her parents but also perhaps from a wider, if diffuse, social acceptance of these ideas. The possibility of attributing the comments to her parents is further complicated by the troubling quality of the humour that is generated by Condé's reproduction of the racist language that, it is implied, is used by her parents: 'des nègres au sexe vorace'[[black] men hungry for sex]. This humour is troubling precisely because it raises questions about the identity and the intention of any speaker(s).

The sense of uncertainty generated by the above comments is intensified by the reproduction of the following scene punctuated by visual markers (the dash that is used to identify spoken language) of direct speech: ' — Elle est mignonne, la petite négresse!' ['Isn't she adorable the little Negro girl!'] (*LCRP*, 97; *TFTH*, 105). While the speakers are not explicitly identified, it is implied that they are the white French passengers with whom Condé comes into contact on the Parisian metro and buses: 'Paris pour moi, était une ville sans soleil, […] un enchevêtrement de métro et d'autobus où les gens commentaient sans se gêner sur ma personne' [Paris for me was a sunless city […] a maze of Metros and buses where people commented on my person with a complete lack of consideration] (*LCRP*, 97; *TFTH*, 105).

The construction of this scene is suggestive both of experiential quotations and 'textual borrowings' as it mirrors almost exactly a similar one depicted in *PNMB* where Fanon transcribes one of the numerous objectifying comments to which he is subjected by 'le Blanc':

> — Regarde, il est beau ce nègre...[19] ['Look how handsome that Negro is! ...']
> (*PNMB*, 92; *BSWM*, 86)

Condé's apparent reprise of this scene appears to constitute an instance of 'bearing witness' to her individual experience of racialized objectification that draws on the (literary) model provided by Fanon's *PNMB*. In the context of this intertextual reference to Fanon's text, it is significant that the objectifying effects of 'looks' are foregrounded. However, in contrast with the unremittingly oppressive inflections assigned to the gaze in *PNMB*, this scene in Condé's memoir takes this racially objectifying look as the starting point for a complex and productive dialogic process that reflects on the nature and uses of the objectifying gaze itself.

The juxtaposition in this chapter of an ironic reworking of the stereotype of black 'male hypersexuality' that is debunked in *PNMB*[20] with an act of witnessing of racial objectification that takes Fanon's text as its model serves as a pointer to the ways in which Condé's readings of other texts dramatize the ambiguously creative potential of 'the objectifying look'. The creative charge of these types of look is released through the process of reading, one that confronts the protagonist's experiences with two autobiographical Francophone Caribbean texts: Joseph Zobel's *La Rue Cases-Nègres* and Fanon's *PNMB*.

When, as a student in France, Condé is asked to present a Francophone Caribbean text to her white French classmates, the discovery of Joseph Zobel's semi-autobiographical novel *LRCN* provides her with an essential insight into the socio-historical dynamics that had shaped her native Guadeloupe: 'D'un seul coup tombait sur mes épaules le poids de l'esclavage, de la Traite, de l'oppression coloniale, de l'exploitation de l'homme par l'homme, des préjugés de couleur dont personne, à part quelquefois Sandrino, ne me parlait jamais' [In one go, I was saddled with slavery, the slave trade, colonial oppression, the exploitation of man by man, and color prejudice, which nobody except occasionally Sandrino ever mentioned to me] (*LCRP*, 101; *TFTH*, 109).

Condé finds therefore that she is required to downplay her privileged background and present herself in a way that conforms to the stereotypical expectations of her French teacher and classmates: '*Aux yeux* de ce professeur communiste, *aux yeux* de la classe entière, les vraies Antilles, c'étaient celles que j'étais coupable de ne pas connaître' [In the eyes of my Communist teacher, in the eyes of the entire class, the real Caribbean was the one that I was guilty of not knowing] (*LCRP*, 102; *TFTH*, 110, my emphasis). This experience provides Condé with an illuminating insight into the provisional and also the strategic potential presented by all identities as types of ill-fitting, 'hand-me-down garments': 'Je commençai par me révolter en pensant que l'identité est comme un vêtement qu'il faut enfiler bon gré, mal gré, qu'il vous siée ou non. Puis, je cédai à la pression et enfilai la défroque qui m'était offerte' [At first I rebelled, believing that identity is something you have to accept whether you like it or not, whether it suits you or doesn't. Then I gave in to outside pressure and slipped into the old clothes I was being handed] (*LCRP*, 102–03; *TFTH*, 110).

While Condé represents her response to her French teachers' and classmates questions as a form of capitulation, her response also suggests that the demands for certain kinds of stereotypical 'representations' or 'performances' encoded in this 'regard' may rely on a certain complicity on the part of the object of the look. This would mean that the effects of such demands are not wholly disabling or constraining. The possibilities presented by this complicity are shown to be realized in the fictional sphere, in the interstitial spaces between the real and the imaginary, and the readerly identifications with the 'figures' of the real that are produced in literature.

In order to construct the image of Guadeloupe required by her French classmates, the young Maryse consults not a factual work but a semi-autobiographical novel by the Martinican author Joseph Zobel. Both acts — the decision to respond to her classmates' demand for a presentation about Guadeloupe and the text that she consults — are shown to be choices, and to that extent, expressions, albeit partly circumscribed ones, of her individual freedom. It is in her reading of Zobel's novel that we see the fullest articulation of this freedom. The young Condé's intense imaginary identification with Zobel's protagonist, José, creates the conditions for her realization of a type of *engagement politique* that is essentially literary, one that is also claimed with hindsight by Condé: 'Aujourd'hui tout me porte à croire que ce que j'appelais plus tard un peu pompeusement "mon engagement politique" est né de ce moment-là [...]' [Today, I am convinced that what I later called somewhat pretentiously my "political commitment" was born at that very moment[...]] (*LCRP*, 103; *TFTH*, 110–11). It is certainly significant, then, that the protagonist's sense of political engagement occurs in the context of a double choice to submit to a demand for information and to bring her full self — physical, emotional and imaginary — to the process of reading so that she effectively takes on the role of the fictional character in much the same way as a method actor:

> Quelques semaines plus tard, je fis devant la classe suspendue à mes lèvres un brillant exposé. Depuis des jours, mon ventre traversé des gargouillis de la faim s'était ballonné. Mes jambes s'étaient arquées. Mon nez s'était empli de morve. La tignasse grenée de mes cheveux s'était roussie sur ma tête sous l'effet du soleil. J'étais devenue Josélita, sœur ou cousine de mon héros. (*LCRP*, 103)[21]

> [A few weeks later, I gave a dazzling presentation in front of the whole class, leaving them spellbound. For days, my pot belly had rumbled with hunger. My legs were bowed. My nose was filled with snot. My mop of kinky hair had reddened from the effects of the sun. I had been transformed into Joselita, the sister or cousin of my hero. (*TFTH*, 110)]

The above experience suggests that reading may be viewed as form of agency that potentially allows for a reformulation of the programmatic inflections of the term 'engagement politique' (along with a certain pompous high-mindedness at which Condé balks with hindsight) as a series of open-ended imaginary and emotionally charged identifications with a range of textual 'others'.[22] At the same time, reading serves as a space for rehearsing politically committed gestures that perhaps (as Sartre envisages) also translate into actions in the 'real' world.

The possibilities presented by these emotionally charged engagements with textual others are illustrated in the distinctly circular structure of the individual chapter and, more broadly, in terms of the overtly intertextual patterning of this memoir. The chapter ends as it begins under the sign of Fanon's *PNMB* with the protagonist's assertion that: 'J'étais "peau noire, masque blanc" et c'est pour moi que Fanon allait écrire' [I was a 'black skin white mask' and Fanon was going to write his book with me in mind] (*LCRP*, 103; *TFTH*, 111). By identifying herself as "peau noire, masque blanc", Condé also suggests an oblique identification with Mayotte Capécia, the female author whom Fanon characterizes in this text as epitomizing the desire for 'lactification', or self-whitening.[23] Such a representative reading is nevertheless complicated both by the oblique confession of individual guilt and by the positive intentions that Condé appears to ascribe to Fanon's thesis. Fanon writes not 'contre' but 'pour elle' — an act of feminist-defined 'literary aggression' is transformed in the space of reading into an expression of a type of altruistic 'fondness'.[24] On the one hand, the juxtaposition of remembered readings of *LRCN* and *PNMB* in this scene suggests that the imaginary filial identification with *LRCN* works to nuance the aggressive charge of Fanon's reading of Capécia and clears the way for a type of three-way identification between the author-figures Condé, Capécia and Fanon at the end of the chapter. On the other hand, the suggestion of irony that hangs over this double assertion of identity and guilt means that the resolution of this process remains continuously, and perhaps also necessarily, *deferred*. If this deferral renders the text incompatible with the programmatic concerns of representative feminist readings, this incompatibility gestures towards a type of self-conscious dialogue between Condé's and Fanon's œuvre as well as between the range of cultural discourses in which their work is located. This specific ambiguous reference may be viewed then as an intertextual instance that simultaneously anticipates and undermines the selective use of Fanon's discourse to censure inauthentic cultural performances by female writers such as Capécia and Condé.[25] Through ironic repetition, Condé is able to reclaim such cultural symbols for the purposes of her own ambiguously open-ended self-construction. An empathetic practice of reading that accommodates or even includes antithetical positions is therefore suggested: all positions are usable, open to readings and (re)writings. Indeed, it is ultimately such inclusive reading practices that allow for the inherent literariness of works such as *PNMB* to the released as material for the writer's life, condensed as infinitely productive images, constantly re-worked as part of the writer's ongoing creative practice of self-construction.[26]

More broadly, the creative potential of these inclusive practices of reading is represented in the text through the complex web of intertextual references that structure the narrative. Re-workings of key scenes in Condé's first novel, *Heremakhonon* (itself a highly intertextual work) are combined with references to foundational texts within a Francophone Caribbean tradition (that draws together Fanon's *PNMB*, Césaire's *CRPN*, Zobel's *LRCN*, Chamoiseau's *Chemin d'école* and the Haitian author Jacques Roumain's *Gouverneur de la rosée*) along with references to African-American cultural texts such as the magazine *Ebony* and Toni Morrison's novel *The Bluest Eye*, and to canonical authors of English literature (Shakespeare, Keats, Austen and Woolf). The eclectic quality of the reading that is performed in the narrative can also be viewed as responding strategically to various forms of *scopic* regulation of Condé's identity (symbolized by the objectifying looks that are represented and reworked in the narrative). By pointing to the construction of her identity from a range of cultural texts that both include and extend beyond the French and Francophone Caribbean literary traditions, this reading provides an enlarged cultural matrix as the context for this strategic process. Through its combination of a range of cultural references in a non-hierarchical manner, *LCRP* points to the potential for a continuous re-negotiation of its author's subject position in relation to these discourses.

The protagonist's critical reflection upon, and questioning of, various cultural texts is intrinsic to the project of self-definition that she develops in the text. Through this critical process, she charts a map of engagement with these texts that moves with fluidity between an increasing awareness of their role in structuring her sense of identity, their rejection, strategic imitation, and transformation. This is achieved by putting these texts in relation to those of other 'types' and from other cultural contexts in ways that problematize the very question of the origin of both these texts and narrative subject that 'refers' to them.

The contours of this particular map of cultural engagement are sketched out in the first chapter, 'Portrait de famille'. The chapter begins with a reflection on her parents' fervent belief in their Frenchness: 'Pour eux, la France n'était nullement le siège du pouvoir colonial. C'était véritablement la mère patrie et Paris, La Ville Lumière qui seule donnait de l'éclat à leur existence' [For them France was in no way the seat of colonial power. It was truly the Mother Country and Paris was the City of Light that lit up their lives] (*LCRP*, 11; *TFTH*, 3). Condé attempts to make sense of her parents' value system by consulting texts from different traditions. The first one that she consults, *Le Petit Larousse illustré*, although useful for deciphering the esoteric Latin phrases with which her father embroidered his conversation is of little use when the author and her family are confronted in a Parisian restaurant by the 'exoticizing' readings of the waiters who compliment them on their command of the French language:

> — Qu'est-ce vous parlez bien le français!
> Mes parents recevaient le compliment sans broncher ni sourire et se bornaient à hocher du chef. (*LCRP*, 15)

> ['You speak excellent French, you know!' My parents bore the compliment without turning a hair or smiling, merely a nod of the head. (*TFTH*, 4)]

The limitations of this cultural text are underscored by her parents' attempt to resist this reading as 'accomplished exotics' by drawing attention to their own cultural sophistication and education evidenced by their familiarity with a range of luxury tourist destinations that include la Côte d'Azur. However, these attempts at resistance are impotent since they are undertaken 'only after the waiters' backs are turned' and remain mired in references to 'civilization' that are constitutive of the very French cultural codes that mark them as 'foreign':

> — Pourtant, nous sommes aussi français qu'eux, soupirait mon père.
> — Plus français, renchérissait ma mère avec violence [...]. Nous sommes plus instruits. Nous avons de meilleures manières. Nous lisons davantage. Certains d'eux n'ont jamais quitté Paris alors que nous connaissons le Mont-Saint-Michel, la Côte d'Azur et la Côte basque. (*LCRP*, 13)

> ['Yet we are as much French as they are,' my father sighed. 'Even more so,' my mother continued vehemently [...]. 'We are more educated. We have better

manners. We read more. Some of them have never left Paris, whereas we have
visited Mont Saint-Michel, the Riviera, and the Basque coast.' (*TFTH*, 5)]

The above enumeration by the protagonist's parents of the list of coastal sites to
support their claim to a French identity, serves to convey their anxieties about
the extent of their 'Frenchness'. It is perhaps significant, therefore, that the spatial
dynamics that structure these anxieties is insistently 'coastal' as this implies an idea
of 'Francophone' identity as constructed on the periphery of 'real' Frenchness.[27]
In a sense then, the damaging effects of this French cultural model are subjected
to a critical 'reading' by her politically aware brother Sandrino who characterizes
their parents as 'des aliénés' [alienated people] 'qui n'éprouvaient aucun orgueil de
leur héritage africain' [(who) took no pride in their African ancestry] (*LCRP*, 15;
TFTH, 8).

  If Sandrino's comments appear to endorse the adoption of an Afrocentric identity
as a more appropriate or authentic choice for the protagonist and her family, this
assumption is itself challenged by Condé's readings of African-American texts.
Condé recalls with irony her mother's attempts to encourage her and her siblings to
emulate the model of successful black families celebrated in the African-American
magazine *Ebony* by sticking up pictures from the magazine above her bed. One such
photo, Condé remembers, was of an African-American family made up, like her
own, of eight children, all of whom, however, were 'médecins, avocats, ingénieurs,
architectes' [doctors, lawyers, engineers and architects] (*LCRP*, 15; *TFTH*, 6). Thus,
while the reading of the French and African-American texts serves to highlight
the limitations of the cultural codes that underlie these texts, the very process
of gaining critical awareness of their limitations is constitutive of 'the identity in
process' of this young protagonist.

  But the uses of this critical practice of reading are not simply a matter of recognizing and rejecting inappropriate texts. As the protagonist's reading of *LRCN* and
PNMB would perhaps lead us to expect, some of cultural texts cited as part of this
broad intertextual practice are also shown to be open to a creative transformation
and re-working. While as a student in Paris the protagonist discovers that she
is required to conform to a stereotypical reading of identity, the context of this
experience proves, as I argued earlier, to be highly productive for her ongoing self-
construction. It is in this chapter entitled 'Chemin d'école' that Condé describes
her introduction to communist ideology through the newspaper *L'Humanité* by this
same teacher at her Parisian high school. While she admits that her understanding
of this ideology was at that time still very superficial, the protagonist appears to
intuit that this body of ideas constituted a potentially effective counter-discourse,
observing that 'nous la devinions en complète contradiction avec les valeurs
bourgeoises que le lycée Fénelon incarnait à nos yeux' [we guessed that it was a
complete contradiction of the bourgeois values embodied, as we saw it, by the Lycée
Fénelon] (*LCRP*, 99; *TFTH*, 107). Indeed, the class consciousness conveyed by this
body of ideas would provide Condé with a particularly fertile critical discourse
for her ongoing representation (in both her fictional and non-fictional œuvre) of
her own ambiguous, mobile positionings in relation to the social class that she
refers to as the 'négro-bourgeoisie'. So, if at times in the text Condé parodies the

pretensions of this class with a view to distancing herself from this social group, she also underscores, via an unflinching depiction of her own class-based prejudices, the extent to which her very identity is intimately bound up with this group.[28] It is ironic that it is a communist teacher who requires that the young Maryse conform to a stereotype of 'proletarian blackness', an assumption that reflects the simplifying tendencies of communist discourses that defined all people of the 'Third World' as 'proletarian'. However, Condé's representation of the black bourgeoisie in the text and in her broader œuvre is revelatory of her own creative reading and adaptation of this communist ideology to take account of the social realities of Guadeloupe. In this context, class identity as defined within a traditionally dominant communist discourse is fractured and complicated by multiple racial identities.

The centrality of the creative reading and adaptation of French texts to Condé's project and the ways in which this process is allied to an ongoing disruption of the French 'origins' of such texts is illustrated by the complex play of transformations and associations set up by the title of the final chapter of this memoir, 'Olnel ou la vraie vie'. The title of this chapter points to a transformative association with Claire Etcherelli's *Elise ou la vraie vie*, a novel that depicts the coming to class consciousness of a French female protagonist through her work in a car factory and her relationship with an Arab man. While, in common with Etcherelli's text, this last chapter traces Condé's growing class and political consciousness in part through her relationship with a man (in this case, the Haitian, Olnel) the title problematizes a reading of this experience as representative of a feminist political sensibility by replacing the female first name in Etcherelli's title with that of Condé's boyfriend 'Olnel'.[29] The French context of this coming to consciousness is also relativized by a proliferation of references that link Condé's culturally eclectic readings (Césaire's *CRPN*, Keats, Austen, Plato, etc.) to a romantic identification with the model of political independence of Haiti represented in *CRPN*: 'Ah, être née dans un vrai pays, un pays indépendant et non un krazur de terre départementale!' [Oh how I would have liked to be have been born in a real country, in an independent country — and not this speck of an overseas country] (*LCRP*, 134; *TFTH*, 145).

The possibilities for the expression of authorial agency that are suggested by *LCRP*'s references to other texts can also be potentially extended to the *types* of connections that are forged between these cited texts. It is significant that a number of the texts which it references may be classified as at least 'semi-autobiographical' and, as a result, they feature narratives that are structured by a fluid relationship between 'fact' and 'fiction' (these include Zobel's *LRCN* and Proust's *CSB* and *Combray*, Fanon's *PNMB* and Césaire's *CRPN* and Chamoiseau's *Chemin d'école*). The apparent preoccupation of *LCRP* with reading other texts in which the boundaries between 'the fictional' and 'the real' are blurred serves to echo and intensify this work's own process of casting doubt on the 'reality' of both the subject and the experiences that it depicts. Indeed, the narrative is structured by an accumulation of devices that generate the kind of diffuse wide-ranging uncertainty that appears to pose and leave unanswered questions concerning the very referentiality of the text. These include the liberal use of *style indirect libre*, which, as I indicated earlier, inhibit the clear identification of a representative voice and the boundaries of individual subjectivities. Further uncertainty is generated by the dream-like, or even supernatural, quality of some of the protagonist's recollections. For example, in the chapter entitled 'Leçon d'histoire' [History Lesson], the young Condé recalls her abusive relationship with a white girl in the context of which she submitted to being beaten and treated as the girl's servant. At the end of the chapter, Condé's reflections highlight her own uncertainty as to the extent to which her memory is in fact 'real' or 'supernatural' (*LCRP*, 44; *TFTH*, 58).[30]

This implied rapprochement of the positions of the author and the reader is, however, revealed as unstable in the final chapter which ends with a reference to Etcherelli's *Elise ou la vraie vie*. In the final paragraph of *LCRP*, Condé's ambiguous reading of Etcherelli's text serves to place the next stage of her life beyond the vision of her potential readers. This reference to Etcherelli's formulation 'la vraie vie' at this point gestures towards an illuminating recasting of the uses of Condé's identification with the literary creations of other authors. While Condé draws on Etcherelli's text to close her memoir, in contrast to her readings of *LRCN* and *PNMB*, she does so without offering any critical reflection on her textual borrowing, so as to suggest an oblique blending of authorial voices: 'Je venais de la rencontrer, la vraie vie, avec son cortège de deuils, de ratages, de souffrances indicibles, et bonheurs trop tardifs [...]. Mais moi, ingrate, je ne la regardai même pas tandis que j'avançais faussement éblouie vers l'avenir' [I had just met the real world with its long procession of tribulations, failures, unspeakable sufferings, and belated happiness [...]. I, however, in my ingratitude did not even look at her as I walked in a daze of illusions toward my future] (*LCRP*, 136; *TFTH*, 147).[31] By closing her memoir in the presence of the voice of another author whose text is, like her own, ambivalently placed between fact and fiction, Condé raises not only the tantalizing question of the (generic) ambivalence of her own text but also that of the subject that it represents.[32]

What emerges therefore from this readerly autobiography is an irreducible undermining, a putting into doubt of the process of identification that would typically guarantee the referentiality of texts assumed to belong to the generic category of 'autobiography'. Featuring an authorial figure constituted by various practices of reading — from textual quotations, to identification with fictional protagonists and, finally, an emulative incorporation of the voice of another author — *LCRP* situates itself at odds with politicized conceptions of autobiography as a realm for the expression of a collective voice and of action. In this context, the text's self-conscious awareness of, and ambiguous responses to, these and other expectations of representativity serve to articulate a form of agency that protects its status as a 'literary autobiography'. This form of 'literature' is therefore presented not so much as a realm of political agency that 'represents' an individual in relationship to a community; rather, it is presented as a multi-layered textual space in which individual readers offer a multiplicity of possible and necessarily subjective readings that are perhaps also based on the types of imaginary identifications with the various autobiographical and fictional subjects that are mobilized within *LCRP*. However, such readings and identifications are optional and, as in the case of the author, the potential for agency that is expressed by this creative process is a 'singular' one.[33]

Notes to Chapter 4

1. A second edition of the text was published in 2002 under the title 'Le Cœur à rire et à pleurer: Souvenirs de mon enfance'.

2. See Nick F. Nesbitt, 'Le Sujet de l'histoire: Mémoires troublées dans *Traversée de la mangrove* et *Le Cœur à rire et à pleurer*', in *Maryse Condé: Une nomade inconvenante: Mélanges offerts à Maryse Condé*, ed. by Madeleine Cottenet-Hage and Lydie Moudileno (Petit Bourg, Guadeloupe: Ibis Rouge Editions, 2002), pp. 113–19; Leah Hewitt, 'Vérités des fictions autobiographiques', in Cottenet-Hage and Moudileno, eds, pp. 163–68; Françoise Vergès, 'Labyrinthes', in Cottenet-Hage and Moudileno, eds, pp. 185–90; Erica L. Johnson, 'Departures and Arrivals: Home in Maryse Condé's *Le Cœur à rire et à pleurer*', in *Gender and Displacement: Home in Contemporary Francophone Women's Autobiography*, ed. by Natalie Edwards and Christopher Hogarth (Newcastle: Cambridge Scholars Publishing, 2008), pp. 15–33.

3. Britton, 'The (De) Construction of Subjectivity', p. 44.

4. Britton, 'The (De) Construction of Subjectivity', p. 44.

5. Britton, 'The (De) Construction of Subjectivity', p. 45.

6. In *Beyond Feminist Aesthetics: Feminist Literature and Social Change* (London: Hutchinson Radius, 1989), Rita Felski points to the risk that female confession simply generates an 'illusion of a "natural" female self', that is 'both aesthetically and politically naïve, confirming the existing prejudices of readers rather than challenging them' (p. 118).

7. In contrast, the title of the 2002 edition 'souvenirs de mon enfance' foregrounds the role of individual memories.

8. In *Entretiens*, Condé highlights the tendency by French readers and critics to take for granted that texts by Francophone Caribbean writers are implicitly devoid of serious subject matter and merely objects of entertainment or 'divertissement' (p. 106).

9. Huggan, *The Postcolonial Exotic*, p. 168.

10. This blurb is not reproduced on the cover of the English translation for this text, 'Tales from the Heart: True Stories from my Childhood', and the translation of this passage is my own.

11. Huggan, *The Postcolonial Exotic*, pp. 164–65.

12. Huggan, *The Postcolonial Exotic*, p. 165.

13. Genette, *Paratexts*, pp. 156–60. Writing on the function of the epigraph, Genette observes: 'the epigraph itself is a signal (intended as a sign) of culture, a password of intellectuality. While the author awaits hypothetical newspaper reviews [...] and other official recognitions, the epigraph is already, a bit, his consecration. With it, he chooses his peers and thus his place in the pantheon' (p. 160).

14. In this respect, Barthes's comments on reading as characterized by a predisposition to acknowledging the plurality of the text in *S/Z* are particularly illuminating: 'Interpréter un texte, ce n'est pas lui donner un sens [...] c'est au contraire apprécier de quel pluriel il est fait' [To interpret a text is not to give it meaning [...]. On the contrary, it is to appreciate the plurality of meanings that make it up] (*S/Z*, p. 11).

15. See Smith and Watson, 'De/colonization', pp. xiii–xxxi and my discussion of this in the introduction.

16. I would argue that as a judgement of the maternity benefits is clearly implied in original French text, the translation into English would be enhanced by translating (rather than suppressing, as it does) the modifier 'scandaleux' as 'scandalous' or 'excessively generous'.

17. The chapter shares its title with Patrick Chamoiseau's 1994 memoir 'Chemin d'école' (republished under the new title *Une enfance créole II*).

18. Although the English translation omits the explicit reference to the men as 'black' or 'Negro' men, it is essential to the full subversive effect of the scene that this detail be included in the English translation of the text.

19. Fanon, *PNMB*, 92.

20. See Fanon, *PNMB*, 134–35.

21. This engaged reading predicated on choice is detailed in Jean-Paul Sartre, *Qu'est-ce que la littérature*? 'Ainsi, la lecture est-elle exercice de générosité et ce que l'écrivain réclame du lecteur n'est pas l'application abstraite, mais le don de toute sa personne, avec ses passions, ses

préventions, ses sympathies, son tempérament sexuel, son échelle de valeurs' [Thus reading is an exercise of generosity, and what the writer requires of the reader is not the application of abstract freedom but the gift of his whole person, with his passions, his prepossessions, his sympathies, his sexual temperament, and his scale of values] (*QQL*, 57; *WIL*, 37).

22. This process of emulation also extends to a kind of literary cannibalism that according to Nicole Simek in *Eating Well* allows one author to fuse with the protagonists of another author (p. 169). The end of Condé's account of her identification with the autobiographical hero of *LRCN* points to this practice: 'C'était la première fois que je dévorais une vie. J'allais bientôt y prendre goût' [It was the first time I had cannibalized a life. Something I would soon take a liking to] (*LCRP*, 103; *TFTH*, 110).

23. Although Condé does not explicitly name Mayotte Capécia in the text, this association is implied by her earlier critique of Fanon's depiction of Capécia in one of her essays. For example, in 'Parlez-moi d'amour...?', *Autrement*, 9 (1983), 206–12, Condé challenges Fanon's differential treatment of Mayotte Capécia and Jean Veneuse.

24. Fanon's dismissal of the female Martinican writer Mayotte Capécia has attracted a significant amount of feminist criticism. See for example Gwen Bergner, 'Who Is That Masked Woman? or, The Role of Gender in Fanon's *Black Skin, White Masks*', *Publications of the Modern Language Association*, 110 (1995), 75–88; Lola Young, 'Missing Persons: Fantasising Black Women in *Black Skin, White Masks*', in *The Fact of Blackness: Frantz Fanon and Visual Representation*, ed. by Alan Read (Seattle, WA, Bay Press; London: Institute of Contemporary Arts, 1996), pp. 86–101; Rey Chow, 'The Politics of Admittance: Female Sexual Agency, Miscegenation, and the Formation of Community in Frantz Fanon', in *Frantz Fanon: Critical Perspectives*, ed. by Anthony C. Alessandrini (London and New York: Routledge, 1999), pp. 34–56; Denean Sharpley-Whiting, 'Fanon and Capécia', in Alessandrini, ed., *Frantz Fanon*, pp. 57–74; Clarisse Zimra, 'Daughters of Mayotte, Sons of Frantz: The Unrequited Self in Caribbean Literature', in *An Introduction to Caribbean Francophone Writing: Guadeloupe and Martinique*, ed. by Sam Haigh (Oxford and New York: Berg, 1999), pp. 177–94.

25. See my discussion of this in Chapter 1.

26. In *Entretiens avec Maryse Condé*, Condé appears to apply literary criteria to her assessment of Fanon's *Les Damnés de la terre*, characterizing it as 'beautiful writing': 'J'aime beaucoup Fanon. D'abord parce qu'il écrit magnifiquement. Je trouve *Les Damnés de la terre* un des plus beaux textes en langue française que j'aie jamais lu [...]' [I like Fanon a lot, especially because he is a wonderfully good writer. *The Wretched of the Earth* is one of the most beautiful texts I have ever read in the French language] (*EMC*, 93; *CMC*, 62).

27. For a discussion of this idea in terms of the use of the term 'francophone', see Harrison, *Postcolonial Criticism*, pp. 103–05; David Murphy, 'Choosing a Framework: The Limits of French Studies/Francophone Studies/Postcolonial Studies', *Francophone Postcolonial Studies*, 1 (2003), 72–80 (pp. 73–74); Forsdick, 'État Présent: Between "French" and "Francophone": French Studies and the Postcolonial Turn', *French Studies*, 59 (2005), 523–30 (pp. 526–30).

28. In my interview with her, Condé represents this identification with ambivalence: 'Je crois que quand je dis par exemple, en Guadeloupe, que j'étais un enfant de la bourgeoisie noire, je m'aligne aux trois quarts du pays. La bourgeoisie chez nous, comme partout d'ailleurs, est absolument détestable. [...]. Je pense que là aussi, ce n'est pas l'authenticité que je cherche. C'est une authenticité personnelle' [I think that when I say for example that I was a black middle-class child. I am aligning myself with three-quarters of the country. The black middle class in Guadeloupe, like everywhere else, is absolutely detestable. I don't think I am seeking to be authentic by saying that. It is a personal authenticity] (pp. 32–33).

29. A feminist reading of Etcherelli's work is confirmed by its reception. See for example, Paul Roach, 'Introduction', *Elise ou la vraie vie* (London: Routledge, 1987), pp. 1–50. Roach notes that the novel was awarded the Prix Feminina in 1967 and was hailed by the *Elle* critic Claude Lanzman and Simone de Beauvoir as a work of 'feminist interest' (pp. 2–3).

30. For a reading of the repression of the memory of slavery as a type of 'haunting' of the Francophone Caribbean collective consciousness, see Maeve McCusker, 'Troubler l'ordre de l'oubli: Memory and Forgetting in French Caribbean Literature', *Forum for Modern Languages Studies*, 40 (2004), 438–50 (p. 443).

31. There is a striking similarity between Etcherelli's depiction of her future as marked by an almost palpable sense of foreboding and Condé's retrospective vision of the future. However, the protagonists' attitudes to the future can also be contrasted: Etcherelli's protagonist expresses an unsentimental clear-sightedness and an intention to 'defend herself' while Condé's autobiographical protagonist is presented as 'éblouie' or bewildered, reflecting with hindsight and with a certain sentimentality on the future. In the final paragraph of *Elise ou la vraie vie*, the protagonist muses: 'La douleur me guette, tapie dans mon futur, camouflée dans mes souvenirs, elle m'attend pour me frapper, mais je la contournerai et je me défendrai hardiment' [Pain is lying in wait for me, lurking in my future, camouflaged in my memories, it is waiting to strike me, but I will get around it and defend myself vigorously] (pp. 280–81).

32. For an analysis of the debates surrounding the reception of *Elise ou la vraie vie* as 'documentary' or 'fiction', see, Roach, 'Introduction', pp. 1–50; Sara Poole, *Elise ou la vraie vie*, Critical Guides to French Texts (London: Grant & Cutler, 1994).

33. In using this term I am thinking of works such as Peter Hallward, *Absolutely Postcolonial*; Derek Attridge, *The Singularity of Literature* (London and New York: Routledge, 2004); and Harrison, ed., 'The Idea of the Literary'.

CHAPTER 5

Literature, Art and Identity Politics in *Les Derniers Rois mages*

With her eighth novel, *Les Derniers Rois mages*, Condé returns to her preoccupation with the idea of origin in the definition of identity. But she does so in ways that allow her to account for how this process is shaped by race and gender as forms of identity politics. *DRM* has one key feature which distinguishes it from the other four novels that I have considered thus far: its protagonist is male. The novel's protagonist is Spéro Jules-Juliette, a failed Guadeloupean painter now living in a small Southern American town, Charleston, and married for the last twenty-five years to an African-American woman, Debbie. The novel charts Spéro's musings on his life over the course of one Sunday 10th December, the date that commemorates the death of the family's founding ancestor, an African king exiled in Martinique at the end of the nineteenth century. Spéro recalls his attempts to trace his lineage back to this exiled African king with the aid of a text 'Les Cahiers de Djéré' purportedly written by his great-grandfather Djéré. By way of exploring the novel's particular treatment of ideas of origins and identity in this chapter, I will explore three significant narrative features of the text that have thus far not attracted any significant critical attention: first, the fact that the main character's claim to identity is based on a reputedly 'real' story written down by Spéro's great-grandfather Djéré and presented in the form of an unpublished text called 'Les Cahiers de Djéré' (and of which excerpts are presented in the novel); second, the fact that Spéro, the protagonist, is a commercially unsuccessful artist; third, the conception of politics in the text based on African-American identity politics. What I hope to demonstrate is that by placing the story of origins at its centre, the novel explores the relationship between literature, art, and identity politics as forms of representation that rely on the conflation of notions of 'politics' and 'artistic creation'. It is also through a reflection on these sets of relationships, I will argue, that the novel engages with the ways in which specific French and North American intellectual cultures create differing conditions of possibility for artistic practice and freedom.

Given its central concern with a quest for origins, *DRM* invites comparison with Condé's first novel, *ELB*, which is structured around a similar preoccupation. But there are important differences between the two novels. The role assigned to the journey is a key source of difference between the two works. In *ELB*, Véronica seeks to anchor her identity in a literal journey to Africa — a journey whose failure leads her to conclude that she has found the 'wrong' ancestors. In contrast, in *DRM*, the literal journey to Africa is marginalized from the main narrative focus of the novel. Only three relatively minor characters make this journey: Spéro and Debbie's daughter, Anita, Debbie's cousin, Jeanne, and her friend, Jim. In common with *ELB*, the protagonist is of Guadeloupean origin and the novel therefore appears to express a desire to explore the factors that shape this specific identity. However, by situating the narrative in the context of a marriage between a Guadeloupean man, Spéro, and an African-American woman, Debbie, who are living in America, *DRM* exemplifies Condé's concern to take account in her fiction of the increasing emigration of Francophone Caribbean people towards countries such as the United States. For Condé, literature plays a key role in giving expression to, and also reflecting critically on, these exchanges while also serving as a space for engaging creatively with the specificities — historical, cultural, and political — of Francophone Caribbean and African-American experience.[1] In addition, by anchoring the narrative around the series of engagements on the part of a male artist figure, Spéro, with the story of origins on the one hand and African-American identity politics on the other, the novel is concerned to examine the potential for the conjunction of art and literature to serve as space outside or beyond such specificities.

The story at the centre of Spéro's identity quest has characteristics that align it with the 'permanent questioning of text and context' that Condé attributes to literature.[2] With the ambiguity characteristic of Condé's discourse, this turn of phrase evokes and undercuts a distinction between the fluid ideas of 'text' (literary work and physical text) and 'context' as the framework for writing, reading and reception. The title 'Les "Cahiers" de Djéré' suggests that one way in which the relationship between writing and reception can be configured is through a distinction between an individual or subjective creation and a collective critical or objective practice. And this distinction is implicit to the title. On one level, the title appears to emphasize a single author's responsibility for the creation of the work and implies that it has something specific or unique to say about his experiences. At the same time, the title bears the traces of a dialogic or collaborative relationship between an author and a group of readers or critics. The use of inverted commas around the title 'Les "Cahiers"' points to the assignation of a provisional title by someone other than the author (although the person or persons responsible for the naming are never explicitly identified). In addition, reading the term *cahiers* as 'journal' underlines the work's status as collaborative in the sense of having being the result of an oblique process of critical selection. It is perhaps such a process of selection that accounts for the odd number of *cahiers* that is discovered: while there are supposedly ten notebooks, only three, the odd numbered 1, 3 and 7, are presented in the novel, while the whereabouts of the other seven *cahiers* are never revealed.

This interplay between an individual creation and a broader process of collective intervention is shown to be the defining feature of attempts to resolve the uncertainty surrounding the sources of the *cahiers* and to fill their literal and metaphorical gaps. However, from the very beginning Spéro's attempts to claim his ancestry on the basis of the *cahiers* are frustrated. Early in the novel, we are informed, in mysterious terms, that the *cahiers* have been the object of a failed attempt at authentication by Spéro, who had sought the expert opinion of a former administrator of the Colonies, M. Bodriol, in Paris: 'Pour des raisons qu'il garda secrètes, cette visite ne fut pas un succès' [For reasons he kept secret this visit was not a success] (*DRM*, 23; *LAK*, 10).

Initially, the narrative appears to hold out the tantalizing possibility of recovering the actual conditions in which the text was written. But drawing together Spéro's individual and familial memories and those of the local community, this process is shown to be necessarily subjective and perhaps also *impossible*.[3] What is emphasized instead is the role of an oblique collaborative creative model in the *cahier*'s genesis. Through the use of flashback and *style indirect libre*, the narrative links the memories of Spéro with those of his maternal and paternal ancestors (including those of the text's author Djéré). At the same time, the narrator questions the very possibility of establishing Spéro's claim to royal African ancestry as attempts to verify the authenticity of the text serves only to highlight the fallibility of its various sources.

It is suggested that the *cahiers* are a synthesis of a number of other texts that may include Djéré's reputedly substantial collection of journals and books on the history of Africa and the Dahomey region that were destroyed during the 1928 hurricane. In addition, the accuracy of both the author's personal memory and that of collective memory is cast into doubt. The omniscient narrator raises questions about the accuracy of Djéré's memories of this father, believed to be an African king, noting that 'Djéré n'avait que cinq ans quand son père avait quitté la Martinique, et pourtant il croyait avoir en mémoire chaque détail de son apparence et chaque parole de sa bouche' [Djéré was only five when his father left Martinique and yet he thought he could recall every detail of his appearance and every word he had spoken] (*DRM*, 70; *LAK*, 42).

Collective memory is itself shown to be inevitably tainted or defective and subject, like all memory, to an oblique process of editing or cleaning up that is associated with deliberate forgetting and a related process of re-imagining:

> L'oubli fait la toilette du souvenir, c'est connu. [...]. Tout le monde croyait avoir vu, de ses yeux vu, le vieillard déambuler sous un parasol tenu au-dessus de sa tête par une de ses femmes, au côté de son *honton* [...]. Avec un luxe de détails, les gens décrivaient le sabre à large lame ouvragée qu'il portait au côté et surtout la frange de perles bleues qui cachait sa figure. (*DRM*, 53)

> [Oblivion scrubs the memory clean, they say. [...]. Everybody was sure they had seen with their own two eyes the old man amble beside his *honton* [...].With a wealth of detail, people described the sabre with the wide engraved blade he wore on one side and especially the fringe of blue pearls that veiled his face. (*LAK*, 30)]

Crucially, the ambiguity surrounding the accuracy of the memory is presented as having a creative potential that enables the people to re-imagine the story and invest it with an almost mythical quality that is characterized by a painterly celebration of detail, 'un luxe de détails' [a wealth of detail] (*DRM*, 53; *LAK*, 30).[4]

Illuminating parallels can be drawn between Spéro's artistic practice and the painterly quality of the attempts by collective memory to reconstruct the past. It is undoubtedly significant that Spéro is a painter whose first engagements with the story at the start of the novel take the form of a painted representation of the photograph that is assumed to depict his grandfather Djéré in the arms of his father: 'Il ouvrit les yeux sur le portrait de son arrière-grand-père qu'il avait peint lui-même à 14 ans à partir de la photographie qui depuis trois générations s'étalait sur la cloison de la salle à manger de la maison familiale' [He opened his eyes on the portrait of his great-grandfather that he himself had painted at the age of fourteen from the photograph that for three generations had adorned the dining-room wall of the family home] (*DRM*, 15–16; *LAK*, 5). Arguably, Spéro's reworking of this photograph points to the possibility for a broadening of the specific questionings concerning his identity to a consideration of art as both a creative and a critical practice that questions the notion of a single origin.

The connections between pictorial and written representation symbolized by the artist Spéro's ruminations on the written text, "Les Cahiers de Djéré", provide the backdrop against which the novel undertakes a self-reflexive process of questioning. In the first instance, the narrative draws attention to a value common to both art and literature as a detachment or freedom from the concerns of daily life but it does so in order to stress the ambiguity of this view. Detachment is linked to the potential to overcome personal trauma as Djéré begins to write after his stepfather Romulus is murdered during an altercation at a cock fight: 'En écrivant, peu à peu, il atteignait un grand calme, un parfait détachement' [By writing he gradually attained a great serenity and a perfect detachment] (*DRM*, 82; *LAK*, 51). Spéro experiences a similar sense of freedom in the practice of painting that enables him to resist pressure to support his parents financially by taking work as a school teacher: 'Quand il se plantait devant son chevalet, des ailes lui poussaient aux épaules. Il ne pensait à rien. A rien de ce qui fait qu'on a tant de mal à passer le temps qu'on doit passer sur cette terre' [When he stood in front of his easel, wings grew on his shoulders. He thought of nothing. Nothing that would make him think about how to spend the time we have on this earth] (*DRM*, 26; *LAK*, 12).

This detachment is in turn linked to a form of intellectual independence expressed in the critical predisposition that Spéro adopts in relation to the complex codes of representation that shape African-American identity politics. Through Spéro's internal discourse, a distinction is drawn between the prescriptions of identity politics and the possibilities presented by a type of critical detachment associated with art. The attempt to prescribe a politically relevant role for art is one of the key targets of this process of questioning. Spéro's experience of teaching drawing classes at a desegregated college serves to illustrate the stakes of this process as he is removed from his post after students complain that he uses only models taken from European art to the exclusion of black or African art. Yet this experience is the context for his assertion of art as a universal practice for which only a culturally transcendent set of aesthetic values can be applied: 'Pour lui, ce n'était que des chefs-d'œuvre de l'art. Avait-il tort? N'était-il en réalité qu'un aliéné, comme le soutenaient les enfants? L'art a-t-il aussi une couleur?' [For him they were masterpieces of art. Was he wrong? Was he in fact alienated as the students claimed? Does art have a colour as well?] (*DRM*, 221; *LAK*, 148).

Spéro's preference for teaching art with a view to highlighting its universal value evokes an association between art and some notion of universal human experience. This view of art provides the context for the exploration of characteristics of French and North American intellectual cultures that may be viewed as incommensurable. In this respect, Spéro's expressed attachment to the idea of the universal or transcendent value of art is, arguably, testament to the shaping role of the distinctly modern French intellectual culture that I outlined in the introduction for his thinking on art. At the same time, the students' negative reaction towards his choice of artists points to the perhaps culturally specific censure that may be attached to any attempts to claim an autonomous status for art.[5] By placing this resistance in the context of a middle-class African-American community, DRM therefore gestures towards the role of the political priorities of a specific North American intellectual culture in limiting the possibilities for artistic freedom by effectively casting any appeal to the universal status of art as politically irresponsible.[6] The particular susceptibility of the 'Third World' or 'black' artist to such attempts to subordinate art or literature to politics is the target of a form of double-edged irony in the novel. For example, one of Spéro's lovers, Paquita, the Mexican artist (herself a type of pastiche artist-figure) laments 'en très mauvais anglais que les créateurs des pays du tiers-monde ne sont pas libres, car le monde auquel ils appartiennent entend contrôler leur vision. Pas de place pour l'artiste baladin qui aime l'amour, les fleurs et le chant des oiseaux [in very bad English that artists from the Third World had their hands tied because their societies were intent on controlling their vision of things. No room here for the artist enamoured of love, flowers and birdsong] (DRM, 124 ; LAK, 80).[7]

A contrasting view of the possibilities presented by an art unconstrained by political concerns is suggested by the cahiers. Spéro's reading of the cahiers provides him with a set of critically viable metaphorical frameworks that enable him to question both his own assumptions and those of the world around him. This process in turn feeds his ongoing critique of the imprisoning effects of identity politics. Notebook number one "Les origines" is characterized by a proliferation of images that associate 'roots' with imprisonment and contains, for example, the following cryptic warning: 'La forêt est forteresse. Derrière ses murailles, elle emprisonne les perroquets macaw à tête de plumes rouges et bleues [...]. La forêt est labyrinthe. Le python vert et le serpent-chat y perdent leur chemin' [The forest is a fortress. Behind its walls it cages the red-and-blue-crested macaws [...].The forest is a labyrinth. The green python and the cat-eyed snake lose their sense of direction] (DRM, 89–90; LAK, 57). The mythological structure of the cahiers is therefore richly suggestive of the imprisoning effects of politics, a recurring theme in the novel.

Throughout DRM, Spéro associates politics with various types of imprisonment of the individual and the community. His personal life provides him with fertile territory for these reflections. Spéro observes that the Debbie he had met and married in Guadeloupe had, on her return to Charleston, retreated to 'la prison de la race' [the prison of race] (DRM, 108; LAK, 69). In line with this idea of imprisonment, Debbie's investment in racial politics is associated with a fetishistic relationship to identity that is characterized by the collecting and displaying of a range of visual symbols that she keeps behind the closed doors of her bedroom:

> Debbie referma sur elle la porte de sa chambre où il n'entrait jamais [...] avec ses photos de Paul Robeson [...], de Mahalia Jackson en bouclettes et robe de concert, de Martin Luther King Jr devant le Lincoln Monument à Washington [la chambre] ressemblait à un musée de la déesse 'Black Americana'. (*DRM*, 40)

> [Debbie closed the door behind her. A place where Spero never set foot, her room resembled a museum dedicated to the goddess 'Black Americana': photos of Paul Robeson, Mahalia Jackson in curls and concert dress, Martin Luther King in front of the Lincoln Memorial [...]. (*LAK*, 21)]

With this emphasis on collecting works of art such as photos and literature, the African-Americans are figured as 'curators' of unchanging or frozen symbols of identity.

This tendency to fetishize identity has implications for the types of engagement with contemporary Africa that are made possible for people who subscribe to African-American identity politics and this is one of the themes that is explored in the novel. Three characters connected to Debbie and Spéro go to Africa: Jeanne (Debbie's cousin), her friend Jim, and their daughter Anita. Arguably, the experiences of Jeanne and Jim are programmed by the idealized representations of Africa and blackness to which they have been exposed. Jeanne consequently experiences a sense of disillusionment when she goes to live in various African countries with her diplomat husband and finds that the stark political realities of these countries do not match the romantic expectations of 'Africa' instilled in her by her particular African-American background: 'L'Afrique n'était plus l'Afrique [...]. Les leaders charismatiques avaient perdu leur charisme et du nord au sud, de l'est à l'ouest, la paix des soudards commençait de régner' [Africa was no longer Africa [...]. The charismatic leaders had lost their charisma and from north to south, and from east to west, the work of thugs had started] (*DRM*, 258; *LAK*, 174). In contrast, it is implied that it is partly Jim's limited and now distant contact with Africa that enables him to uphold and celebrate an idealized view of Africa. It is significant too that this view of Africa is presented as supported by a taste for its ceremonial features which can be worn like costumes in what are effectively 'performances' of African identity. This preoccupation is the object of the narrator's criticism who observes: 'Ils avaient fait de l'Afrique leur carnaval, leur défilé de mardi gras dont ils pillaient les oripeaux. Ils ne cherchaient à comprendre ni son sens ni sa signification [...]' [They had made Africa into their carnival, their Mardi Gras procession whose rags they had looted. They did not attempt to understand either its sense or meaning] (*DRM*, 172; *LAK*, 115).[8]

The focus on the external performance of such fetishized identities is also shown to be a form of fakery since it projects an image of successful blackness which glosses over the complex causes of the difficulties that confront individuals.[9] The novel highlights the role of the media and the intelligentsia in generating a self-reinforcing script for a quasi-official black identity and in upholding an idealized view of blackness for public consumption. An ironic contrast is drawn between the substantial coverage of Malcolm X's assassination in the newspaper *The Black Sentinel* despite the fact that 'la bourgeoisie haïssait ses idées à Charleston [...]' [the middle class in Charleston hated his ideas [...]], and its downplaying of Major Dennis's arrest for fraud (*DRM*, 232; *LAK*, 155). The narrative thus suggests that the politically prescribed representations of reality produced by this newspaper may be viewed as another form of fakery aimed at presenting the community in a positive light.

A similar preoccupation with generating politically viable scripts is pointed up in relation to the writing of history. Spéro's reflections on Debbie's collaboration with the black historian Isaac Jamieson to record the history of the Middleton family highlights the ways in which the exigencies of identity politics prescribe certain kinds of idealized representations that flatten out the complexities of reality: 'Spéro aurait aimé coller l'oreille à la porte du bureau de Debbie pour entendre comment ils travestissaient une époque complexe et ambiguë en chapitre d'histoire édifiant' [Spero would have liked to listen at Debbie's study door to hear how they travestied a complex and ambiguous period into an edifying chapter of history] (*DRM*, 289–90; *LAK*, 195).[10]

In addition, the novel points out that it is through the emphasis on idealized representations of past and present realities that identity politics effectively limits the capacity of individuals to view their place or contributions in history as well as to envision their current and future realities. Spéro's reflections highlight the narrow separatist conception of history that is propagated by African-American identity politics in Charleston. The following comments by W. E. B. Du Bois on Charleston (recounted to him by Debbie) epitomize this tendency to view history in terms of oppressors and oppressed: 'Elle lui raconta la visite que W. Du Bois avait rendue à Charleston quand il avait refusé d'admirer les réalisations des esclavagistes, mais avait exhorté ses frères à bâtir leur Charleston à eux' [Debbie told him of W. Du Bois's visit to Charleston, when he had refused to admire the accomplishments of the slave owners and urged his brothers to build their own Charleston] (*DRM*, 103; *LAK*, 66).

The polarized reasoning that underpins this type of thinking is challenged by Spéro: 'Pouvoir noir, pouvoir blanc, cela ne signifiait plus rien. De même que l'argent n'a pas d'odeur, le pouvoir n'a pas de couleur. Il n'est pas blanc. Il n'est pas noir' [Black power, white power, it no longer meant anything. Just as money had no smell to it, power had no colour to it. It's not white. It's not black] (*DRM*, 258; *LAK*, 175). In line with this, it is implied that the effect of encouraging African-Americans to view themselves as eternal victims is fundamentally disempowering and leaves them ill-equipped to make a mark on current economic realities. Anita's decision to choose a minor black university, instead of aiming for a more prestigious mainstream university such as Yale or Princeton, suggests that viewing oneself as a victim potentially translates into a narrowing of one's ambitions (and leads Debbie to the shameful but private admission that her daughter's apparent preoccupation with race is out of step with economic realities):

> Pourtant sans jamais vouloir l'admettre publiquement, elle [Debbie] comprenait bien que ce temps-là était révolu maintenant que brillait le soleil des *yuppies* et qu'en cette fin des années 80 la race ne faisait plus du tout recette. Plus du tout! Alors, elle rêvait de Yale, Harvard, Princeton [...] comme tant d'autres mères.
> (*DRM*, 123)

> [Without ever admitting it publicly, nevertheless she realized that those times
> were over, now that the yuppies had made a place for themselves in the sun, and
> it was the end of the eighties when the concept of race was no longer a winning
> ticket. Far from it! So she had dreamed of Yale, Harvard and Princeton [...] like
> so many other mothers. (*LAK*, 79)]

Debbie's awareness that her assessment of her daughter's decision may be viewed as
politically unpalatable amongst her black middle-class peers points to a key negative
outcome of this type of politics: economic and social success are figured as forms of
cultural treachery or inauthenticity.[11]

The focus on external displays of politically appropriate identity is in turn
shown to consistent with an exclusionary type of politics that limits the capacity of
individuals to forge relationships outside the prescribed community. Spéro's French
accent is a source of suspicion, as he observes wryly when he comments that 'ces
gens-là n'avaient aucune confiance dans un nègre qui parlait l'anglais avec un accent
français [...]' [these people didn't trust a nigger speaking English with a French
accent [...]] (*DRM*, 42; *LAK*, 22). This suspicion acts as a pointer to the exclusionary
tenor of an identity politics whose legitimacy is built on the definition and rejection
of outsiders. Perhaps unsurprisingly, Jesse Jackson's Rainbow Coalition is also
greeted with distrust: 'Ils n'éprouvaient que méfiance pour sa coalition arc-en-ciel.
Depuis que le monde est le monde, les individus à peau claire détestent les individus
à peau noire. Alors pourquoi essayer de les lier les uns aux autres?' [They did not
trust the Rainbow Coalition. Ever since the beginning of time, light-skinned
individuals have detested dark-skinned individuals. So why try to make them get
along?] (*DRM*, 291; *LAK*, 196). With the reference to 'depuis que le monde est le
monde' [since the beginning of time] the narrative highlights the static a-historical
view of identity politics that such suspicion legitimates.

What these accounts of various types of exclusion highlight therefore is the role of
identity politics in forging a sense of individual identity that is built on the exclusion
of strangers and certain parts of the community as well as perhaps parts of the self
(or personal history) that are considered to be undesirable. The ways in which such
thinking leads to the editing out of undesirable aspects of one's personal history are
suggested by Debbie, who stops recording the story of her father George Middleton
when she learns that his story contains elements that potentially undermine
her political ambition to represent black history in an exclusively positive light
(*DRM*, 100).

★   ★   ★   ★   ★

The critical distance that the novel establishes in relation into identity politics
(and the racial identities defined by these) is extended to a broader questioning
of the assumptions that underpin gender-based identities. The narrative succeeds
in unsettling accepted identity positions along with the power relationships that
they entail and the critical readings that they authorize.[12] Additionally, a marked
preoccupation with the stereotypes of male–female relationships and family
dynamics within the Francophone Caribbean serves as the context for creative
interchanges between literature and criticism. In particular, the novel's engagement

with Fanon's representation of Mayotte Capécia in *PNMB* has an oblique, playful quality that exemplifies the ways in which literature can not only read and critique critical theory, but also release and tap into its creative charge (and, in so doing, unsettle the distinction between critical theory or criticism and literature).[13] The novel reverses Fanon's image of Capécia as a literal and symbolic 'blanchisseuse' (through her relationship with a white man) by naming one of the characters Mayotte, and making her not a 'blanchisseuse' [washerwoman] but a 'charbonnière' [coal woman] (*DRM*, 77).[14] In contrast with *PNMB*, the novel never makes an explicit connection between Mayotte's occupation and her attitude towards black men.[15] But in a subtly ironic reversal of Fanon's reasoning, it does suggest that by entering into a relationship with the African king (whose blackness leads the Martinicans to comment on his 'blueness') she may be considered to be implicated in a process of 'blackening'.

The novel's presentation of the 'blanchisseuses' also works to provide a social context for this role and thus potentially presents an oblique challenge to the straightforwardly symbolic value that Fanon attributes to the work of the 'blanchisseuse':[16] This challenge to Fanon's representation of Mayotte Capécia is represented spatially, since both 'blanchisseuses' and 'charbonnières' are depicted on the same dock providing their services to large transatlantic ships during the visit of the royal African family to Saint-Pierre:

> Là, Ouanilo, sa joie éteinte, regarda avec désespoir les navires de la Compagnie générale transatlantique venus de Nantes, Bordeaux, Le Havre, Marseille, dont aucun ne pouvait le ramener vers l'Afrique. Les 'charbonnières', montrant leur jambes droites comme des fûts de palmier, leurs paniers en équilibre sur la tête, remplissaient déjà les soutes des paquebots tandis que les blanchisseuses, pimpantes et couvertes de bijoux, quant à elles, rapportaient dans de grands *trays* le linge des passagers qu'elles avaient lavé blanc comme coton. Tout le monde s'installa tant bien que mal dans le vapeur de la compagnie Girard. (*DRM*, 139–40)

> [There, the dejected Ouanilo looked in despair at the ships of the Compagnie Générale Transatlantique from Nantes, Bordeaux, Le Havre, and Marseilles, none of them could take him back to Africa. The coal women, their skirts hitched over legs as straight as palm trunks, their baskets balanced on their heads, were already filling the bunkers of the steamships, while the washerwomen, elegantly turned out and bedecked with jewels, were bringing back in large trays the passengers' laundry they had washed as white as cotton. Everybody settled down as best they could in the steamer belonging to the Girard Company. (*LAK*, 90–91)]

The presentation of this scene is significant for, on one level, it evokes a purposeful, everyday bustle. The effect of placing the 'blanchisseuses' in the midst of the scene is to situate this occupation in a material social reality and this acts as a counterpoint to the de-contextualized symbolic value that Fanon's analysis assigns to this type of work.[17] However, there is also a staged quality to the scene that is conveyed by the detailed description of the 'charbonnières' and the 'blanchisseuses' in motion. These descriptions work to construct a lingering (perhaps male) gaze that experiences the women as visually exotic:[18] The 'charbonnières' are described as 'montrant leur jambes droites comme des fûts de palmier' [(showing) legs as straight as palm trunks] while the blanchisseuses are 'pimpantes et couvertes de bijoux' [elegantly turned out and bedecked with jewels] [(*DRM*, 139; *LAK*, 91). While the source of the gaze is never clearly identified, the image of the transatlantic ships from large French ports suggests that they may provide the vantage point from which the women are being observed. The juxtaposition of Ouanilo's melancholy reflection on Africa with this image of transatlantic ships works to establish another symbolic framework for the scene: the role of the transatlantic slave trade in setting up a backdrop or a stage on which the 'blanchisseuses' and the 'charbonnières' are merely actors.

The novel's questioning stance with regard to Fanon's depiction of Mayotte Capécia is extended to dominant and implicitly stereotypical representations of family dynamics in the Francophone Caribbean based around the idea of paternal irresponsibility. While *DRM* highlights the tragic effects of the departure of Djéré's father, it also undercuts an assumption of generalized paternal irresponsibility through the use of irony and cliché. For example, in the following quotation, the narrator comments disparagingly on the departure of Djéré's father: 'Roi africain ou pas, le papa de Djéré s'était comporté comme tous les autres nègres de la terre. Il ne s'était pas occupé de son enfant. Il l'avait laissé derrière lui à la charge de sa seule pauvre maman' [African king or not, Djéré's father had behaved like all other African papas on this earth, he neglected his child. He left him behind in the care of his poor single mother] (*DRM*, 20; *LAK*, 8) The ironic tone of the comment which generalizes the departure of Djéré's father to 'tous les nègres' suggests that it is the stereotyping behind this reasoning that is also being criticized. In addition, the idea that all black males are absent or irresponsible fathers is challenged by the seriousness with which Romulus takes the responsibility for providing for his stepson Djéré, extending the house and creating a furnished room just for him (*DRM*, 284).

Nevertheless, the novel does draw attention to the impact of the departure of Djéré's father on the Jules-Juliette family with the observation: 'Cet abandon avait bouleversé toute l'existence de Djéré et de ses descendants' [This abandonment would drastically affect Djéré's entire existence and that of his descendants] (*DRM*, 16; *LAK*, 5). The implied argument here is that the departure of Djéré's father sets in motion a tragic pattern of paternal absenteeism in the Jules-Juliette family. Djéré himself, for example, neglects his son Justin initially because of his preoccupation with the *cahiers* and, later, as a result of his alcoholism (*DRM*, 49–50). The absenteeism of fathers also has a negative impact on the women of the family, in this case Hosannah, who is required to look after both her adult son and her grandson until her death (*DRM*, 86).

The role of mothers and grandmothers in taking responsibility for their children is emphasized. But the novel avoids an idealization of the maternal role by pointing, for example, to a link between overindulgent mothering and the drunken irresponsibility of Djéré as well as the uncaring selfishness of Justin (who follows Hosannah's funeral cortège 'les yeux secs' [without a tear]) (*DRM*, 120; *LAK*, 76). The omniscient narrator notes: 'Certains ne se gênaient pas pour blâmer Hosannah qui, après avoir gâté pourri son enfant, faisait à présent de même avec l'enfant de son enfant' [Some people were only too quick to blame Hosannah, who after having spoiled and mollycoddled her own son was now doing the same with her grandson] (*DRM*, 50; *LAK*, 28).

The dismantling of stereotypes of women as powerless victims that the novel undertakes in relation to Caribbean women is extended in its characterization of African–American women. African–American women are presented both as victims of irresponsible male behaviour and as contributing to such behaviour. The narrator reflects ironically on the ease with which Spéro is able to have affairs with black women, including his wife's best friend Paule, attributing his success to 'cette grande solitude des femmes noires qui fait l'objet de tant d'articles d'*Ebony*, ou de revues plus sérieuses' [the great solitude of black women, the constant subject of articles in *Ebony* and more serious magazines] (*DRM*, 68; *LAK*, 40). Spéro's numerous conquests are presented as 'willing victims' of different forms of neglect at the hands of a generalized category of 'black men'. These forms of neglect attributed to black men are portrayed variously in black print culture in terms of 'abandonment', 'imprisonment', 'abominations' such as having a relationship with another man, or 'betrayal of the race' through having an affair with a white woman (*DRM*, 68). In this way, the novel draws attention to the role of the media in providing a type of mythology for these women's sense of victimhood.

In a further development of this idea of willing victimhood, it is implied that Debbie tolerates and tacitly encourages Spéro's infidelities (going so far as to give subtle encouragement to the affair between Spéro and her best friend, Paule): 'En privé, elle se comparait à la *bara muso* d'un polygame, s'accommodant de coépouses pour le plaisir de la couche de son mari, mais dirigeant l'économie du foyer' [In private, she likened herself to a *bara muso*, a first wife sharing her husband's bed with co-wives yet managing the household finances] (*DRM*, 44; *LAK*, 24). The ironic tone of this description of Debbie's complacent attitude to Spéro's affairs highlights the fact that her attitude is, along with control over the finances, a means to gaining the upper hand in the marital relationship. Indeed, this pursuit of power by middle-class African–American women such as Debbie is linked to the exclusion of their male partners from their lives so that, for example, Spéro complains that he is denied the opportunity to play an active role in his daughter's life and is also banished from the marital bed after her birth (*DRM*, 33–34).

The exclusion of men is echoed in the academic context. Spéro reflects with irony and some outrage on the work of a black female author from Alabama 'dont on se demandait si elle ne voulait pas tout simplement faire disparaître les hommes de la surface de la terre' [who gave the impression that she wanted to banish men from the face of the earth] and whose latest work was dedicated to the exclusive celebration of 'toute une généalogie de femmes qui semblaient venues sur terre par l'opération du Saint-Esprit' [a whole generation of women who seemed to have appeared on this Earth through the operation of the Holy Spirit] (*DRM*, 146; *LAK*, 95). Through this marginalisation of the masculine perspective in their pursuit of recognition of their identity as women, female writers and academics therefore repeat the very process that their work is aimed at combating.[19] The culmination of this exclusion of men from their lives is presented as a symbolic castration depicted in one of only two paintings by Spéro to attract the interest of potential buyers but which he refuses to sell:

> Son Erzulie Dantor à lui, prétendue déesse de l'Amour, était en réalité une redoutable mégère que personne ne pouvait apprivoiser. Elle tenait dans ses mains multiples un couteau pour castrer les mâles, un fouet pour les fouetter et un Livre grand ouvert pour les apprendre à respecter ses Commandements. (*DRM*, 304)

> [His own portrayal of Erzulie Dantor, supposedly the Goddess of Love, was in fact a formidable shrew whom nobody and nothing could tame. She held in her many hands a knife to castrate men, a whip to lash them, and an open book to teach them to respect her commandments. (*LAK*, 205)]

By harnessing the symbolic potential of this artwork, the novel challenges the traditional way of figuring male and female relationships that portray men as dominant and women as powerless and under-represented. Indeed, at the end, the novel appears to express a certain sympathy for men who are presented as ineffectual and generally less well equipped than women to face life's challenges:[20]

> Le bon Dieu était un très mauvais metteur en scène. Dans le théâtre de la vie, aux femmes, il avait distribué la force, le courage, l'ambition. Aux hommes il n'avait donné que le besoin éperdu d'être entourés d'amour comme un fœtus dans le ventre de sa mère. (*DRM*, 307)

> [The good Lord was a terrible director of humankind. On the stage of life, he had cast women with strength, courage and ambition. Men had to make do with the frantic need to be steeped in love like a foetus. (*LAK*, 207)]

This oblique expression of sympathy for the male perspective is significant in light of the ambiguous view of the idea of 'women's writing' that emerges in Condé's œuvre.[21] In my interview with Condé, she observes: 'Je m'efforce de ne pas être une "écrivaine-femme". Je suis une femme *mais* qui écrit' [I try not to be a 'woman writer'. I am woman who writes] (my emphasis).[22] If this comment conveys Condé's acknowledgement of the determinants that shape her identity, the second part of the comment ('mais qui écrit) points to the sense of freedom from her identity as a woman that she negotiates in writing. This freedom that Condé has consistently associated with literature can therefore be viewed as the examination and critique of such determinations. It is also the projection beyond such determinations so that, ultimately, the very role of the (female) author is dissolved.[23]

★ ★ ★ ★ ★

The wide-ranging questioning and critique of various representations of identity — whether based on skin colour or gender — undertaken in the novel does not translate into an oblique argument in favour of literature or art as a simple alternative. Indeed, this emphasis on questioning extends a broader challenge to the very idea that art or literature may constitute some unique or privileged position. The fact that the novel features a number of failed artists is significant because it admits the possibility of failure as characterizing — and indeed as necessary to — the production of art. Failure takes various forms: not only do artistic projects remain unfinished or incomplete, as in the case of the *cahiers*; but artists, such as Spéro, also fail to make a living by selling their work. These failures are nevertheless associated with a form of autonomy that enables Spéro, for example, freed from economic pressures, to take on projects that genuinely interest him such as painting the teenager Roshawn and making a satirical painting of Debbie and Paule.[24] It is certainly significant that questions from Roshawn (while she is being painted) provide the context for Spéro's reflection on the ways in which the process of representation itself exposes the limits of language and the ever-present temptation to resort to clichés: 'Comment parler en vrai de vrai de la Guadeloupe? Soit! Le pays n'est plus l'enfer du tan lontan' [What can you really say about Guadeloupe? OK! The island is no longer the hell it once was] (*DRM*, 208; *LAK*, 139).

The idea of art as unique or original is shown to be as illusory as the quest for origins. In the course of reflecting on his preparations for his failed artistic debut in Charleston, Spéro initially appears to take it for granted that it is possible to distinguish between copying and being inspired by other sources or artists as he recalls: 'Il s'etait inspiré — sans jamais les copier purement et simplement — des maîtres chers à Debbie et avait produit en un temps record trente-six toiles' [His inspiration came from the masters dear to Debbie, and without ever copying them purely and simply, he had produced thirty-six canvasses in record time] (*DRM*, 103–04; *LAK*, 64). However, he later undercuts this distinction when he is asked by Major Dennis, the black mercenary, to produce some forgeries of major Haitian paintings. Finding he is unable to distinguish between his own work and that of the Haitian painters, he begins to wonder whether he is in fact just a forger (*DRM*, 230).

While the novel challenges the idea that literature or art and indeed the author her- or himself may occupy some privileged position, there is nevertheless an implicit exploration of the value of art or literature in terms of the personal or subjective effects that it produces, and of the possibilities that these present for the shifting process of constructing an identity. If art is shown to possess a transformative capacity that enables Spéro for example 'to grow wings' as he paints, these are realizable only in the context of a necessary irresponsibility in relation to social and political prescriptions.[25]

The limited scope attributed to art and literature is also suggested by the depiction of music:

> Parfois, Linton prenait son saxo et la noirceur du Montego Bay devenait moins noire [...] et les clients, même les plus désabusés, s'arrêtaient de boire, de se chamailler [...] pour se tourner vers l'endroit d'où venait la parole magique. Pendant un moment, Spéro lui-même oubliait qui il était et il se croyait redevenu un fils de panthère. Quand Linton déposait son instrument cependant, il redevenait lui-même. (*DRM*, 107)

> [Sometimes Linton took up his saxophone and the Montego Bay became less dark [...] and even the most jaded customers stopped drinking, bickering [...] to turn toward the spot where the magic was coming from. For a moment even Spero forgot who he was and became the son of the Leopard. When Linton put down his instrument, however, he became himself again. (*LAK*, 68–69)]

Music is assigned an inspirational quality that enables Spéro and the patrons in the bar to momentarily transcend their current realities and, in Spéro's case, to imagine himself differently. Such effects are however fleeting and, as a result, not transferable to the political plane. At the same time, by gesturing towards literature's capacity to allow individuals to transcend their immediate experiences, it is suggested that this in itself has a value which may require another set of criteria other than political and purely instrumentalist ones.[26]

Spéro appears to grope towards such criteria as he wonders whether finally the value of the *cahiers* consisted in feeding his imagination:

> Est-ce que tout cela n'avait pas simplement alimenté son imagination d'enfant, puis d'adolescent? Peut-être. Mais l'imagination est la souveraine. C'est elle qui nourrit les rêves qui à leur tour nourrissent le cœur et guident la vie. Si elle dépérit, la vie aussi dépérit. (*DRM*, 192)

> [Hadn't all that merely fostered his childish and then his adolescent imagination? Perhaps. But imagination is sovereign. It nurtures dreams that in turn nurture the heart and guide one's life. If imagination perishes, life perishes too. (*LAK*, 128)]

The particular value of 'nourishing the heart' that Spéro attributes here to *les cahiers* is also significant. In effect, the novel points to literature's role as a humanizing space for readers in which they are able to explore their feelings and thereby gain some form of self-knowledge. With this reading of the function of literature, *DRM* thus situates itself implicitly within the long-standing French tradition of literature (that extends from the Romantics to the *nouveaux romanciers*) as a realm for the representation and cultivation of the imagination and all forms of subjective human experience. At the same time, the novel marks its distance from the narrowly circumscribed politicized role assigned to literature within the dominant North American postcolonial studies paradigm that I have defined in the Introduction. In *La Parole des femmes*, Condé identifies novels by women writers as a context for this humanizing function:

> Tous ces romans féminins qui n'abordent pas les problèmes politiques, qui ne font qu'effleurer quelques tensions, qui ne prétendent pas donner de leçons, n'en sont pas moins précieux pour la connaissance que nous avons de nous-mêmes.[27]

> [All these novels by women which do not address political problems, which only touch on a few tensions and which make no claim to give us lessons, are no less precious for the self-knowledge that we gain from them.]

In addition, the idea that literature 'feeds one's dreams' points to Condé's view of literature as providing a utopian space for dreaming that takes readers and the writer beyond reality and allows for the exploration of alternative and unique possibilities for, among other things, constructing a sense of identity. In her article 'Language and Power: Words as Miraculous Weapons', Condé emphasizes the centrality of 'writing' for the construction of authorial identity:

> For each and every writer, writing is both a constructive and destructive urge, a possibility for growth and for change. We write to build ourselves word by

word, to forge our unique identity. With the help of our imagination and our mastery of the word, we replace the world we live in with a utopia.[28]

In another essay 'Notes sur un retour au pays natal', Condé underscores, through the use of the pronoun 'nous', the essential link between the possibilities for imaginative self-construction available to both author and readers: 'Vous le voyez, la littérature antillaise, si nous voulons l'écrire au présent de façon valable, cela nous entraîne dans des sphères auxquelles nous n'avions pas pensé' [You see, if we want to write Caribbean literature in a way that is in step with contemporary realities and is also worthwhile, that leads us into areas that we had never envisaged].[29] The proliferation of unanswered questions in the novel also implies that this is a potential that is actualized through a process of individual questing. In this way, literature may be considered to guide life not in the sense of giving lessons which is subtly critiqued in *La Parole des femmes* but rather in the sense of providing a heuristic space in which readers find their own truths.[30]

Crucially, literature and art are also presented as extending beyond such provisional, individual truths by connecting human beings to universal truths that transcend not only politics but ultimately art itself. For example, in what appears to be a cautionary note to readers to make the best of their lives, the novel contains a number of references to mortality, and near the end of the novel, the ancestor now installed in the afterlife *Kutome* finds that he misses his former life: 'Les tourments de sa vie de vivant lui manquèrent [...]. Il se rappelait aussi le bonheur que lui donnaient les femmes et à présent, esprit sans sentiments, il comprenait qu'il n'avait pas su savourer l'existence' [He missed the torments of his life as a mortal [...]. He remembered too the happiness women gave him, and now a spirit devoid of feeling, he realized he had not gotten the most out of life] (*DRM*, 296–97; *LAK*, 200). The fact that the old king's spirit misses his 'torments' points to another key value that is potentially transmitted by literature — that of enabling readers to accommodate the experience of being troubled.[31]

In conclusion, the novel explores the possibilities provided by the conjunction of literature and art to nuance, through a process of questioning, a range of individual and collective determinations that are taken for granted within North American postcolonial critical paradigms. These include notions of identity, culture, politics and history, along with the accompanying expectations of representativity that are commonly attached to the literature and art produced by members of minority groups. While hinting at the possibilities for creative freedom that this process of questioning provides for the reader as well as for the author or artist, the novel avoids the trap of idealizing the role of art or literature by representing the artist figures as flawed and ineffectual and imbuing the artistic process with an almost irresolvable sense of frustration and futility. Indeed, the novel ends with an acknowledgement of the limitations of art. At the novel's close, Spéro appears to have exhausted the possibilities of ethnic, cultural and professional identities (he has given up on art and the possibility of returning to the place he once imagined as home), but he is nevertheless preoccupied with the possibility of restarting his relationship with his wife and, finally, with his own death as he sits symbolically at the end of the pier. In this way, the novel ends with a reflection on the things that make us human: our human relationships, our feelings and our mortality. Notions of art, literature and identities themselves appear as transcended by these ultimate realities. In a sense, this final privileging of the intimate sphere of individual relationships as the source of a form of transcendent value is a measure of the limitations that *DRM* ascribes to the representative function of identity politics, the dominant form of politics in the novel. Identity politics is finally presented as types of degraded performances that are ultimately dissatisfying for the individual. In the final chapter, I examine the implications of the extension of this critique to the representative viability of all forms of politics in the context of globalization.

Notes to Chapter 5

1. See for example Condé, 'O Brave New World'.
2. Quoted in Leah D. Hewitt, 'Condé's Critical Seesaw', *Callaloo*, 18 (1995), 641–51 (p. 642).
3. For a reading of Spéro's failure to authenticate the text as a 'testimony of exile and dispossession', see Mildred Mortimer, 'A Sense of Space and Place in Maryse Condé's *Les Derniers Rois mages*', *World Literature Today* (Focus on Maryse Condé), 67, 4 (1993), 757–62 (p. 759).
4. See Condé, 'The Stealers of Fire'. Condé quotes Glissant's comment in *Caribbean Discourse* that 'Myth is the first state of still-naïve historical consciousness, and the raw material for the project of a literature' (p. 164).
5. Harrison, *Postcolonial Criticism*. The following observations by Harrison about literature are also relevant to 'art': 'Evidently, the currency of any notion of literary or authorial "autonomy", or any model of the capabilities and responsibilities of "literature" is culturally and historically limited' (p. 144). For an examination of the issues of censorship raised by such limitations also see Nicholas Harrison, *Circles of Censorship: Censorship and its Metaphors in French Literature, History and Theory* (Oxford: Oxford University Press, 1995).
6. See Harrison, 'Who Needs an Idea of the Literary?', pp. 1–17.
7. Condé in 'Order, Disorder', also links this focus to the exclusion of the exotic tradition in Francophone Caribbean literature: 'Therefore, the pictures of individual love and psychological turmoil were banished. Any description of nature was forbidden. Lyrical outbursts about the mountains or sea and the sky were left to so-called "exotic poets" writing at the beginning of the century, who had been sentenced to literary death' (p. 123).
8. Anita's engagement with Africa appears to be along more practical lines (although it is partly shaped by a didactic relationship, seemingly taken for granted, with the community in which she works) as her father's enquiries reveals that she is not only involved in development work but also in teaching development theory in Benin (*DRM*, 259).
9. Lydie Moudileno and Francis Higginson, 'Portrait of the Artist as a Deamer', *Callaloo*, 18 (1995), 626–40. Moudileno points to Spéro's role as a 'cynical non-American' in pointing up the 'collective fantasy' that 'girds the apparent cohesion' of this community (p. 630).
10. For a more detailed discussion of Debbie's simplifying approach to recording history see Ann Smock, 'Marsye Condé's *Les Derniers Rois mages*', *Callaloo*, 18 (1995), 668–80.
11. This in turn creates the conditions for the schism between external displays of prescribed blackness and culturally uplifting behaviours (such as voluntary work in black charities, the production of black dance etc.) and the fear of less privileged African-Americans: 'Sous leurs belles phrases et leurs discours, se cachaient la honte et la peur de leurs frères du ghetto et de la drogue dont le nombre chaque jour croissant leur prouvait que leurs grands combats n'ont servi qu'au mieux-être d'une poignée de chanceux' [Under their flowery language and speeches was hidden the shame and fear of their brothers hooked on drugs, whose growing numbers proved their magnificent struggles had only bettered the lucky few] (*DRM*, 289; *LAK*, 195).
12. Leah D. Hewitt, 'Condé's Critical Seesaw'. Hewitt highlights the novel's questioning of positions that carry 'a certain moral weight' (p. 642).
13. For an insightful discussion of the distinctive relationship between literature and criticism in the works of postcolonial authors see Harrison, *Postcolonial Criticism*.

14. 'Alors, ne pouvant plus noircir, ne pouvant plus négrifier le monde, elle va tenter dans son corps et dans sa pensée de le blanchir. D'abord, elle se fera blanchisseuse: [...]' [Since she could no longer try to blacken, to negrify the world, she was going to try in her own body and mind, to bleach it. To start, she would become a laundress [...] (*PNMB*, 37; *BSWM*, 31).

15. Fanon generalizes Capécia's predisposition towards self-whitening to 'all Martinican women' and then later in his analysis to 'all black women': 'Nous sommes avertis, c'est vers la lactification que tend Mayotte. Car enfin il faut blanchir la race; cela *toutes* les Martiniquaises le savent, le disent, le répètent' (my emphasis) [We are thus put on notice that what Mayotte wants is a kind of lactification. For in a word, the race must be whitened; every woman in Martinique knows this, says it, repeats it] (*PNMB*, 38; *BSWM*, 33).

16. Fanon's analysis of *Je suis Martiniquaise* has attracted a significant amount of feminist criticism. See for example Gwen Bergner, 'Who Is That Masked Woman?'; Lola Young, 'Missing Persons'; Rey Chow, 'The Politics of Admittance'; Denean Sharpley-Whiting, 'Fanon and Capécia'; Clarisse Zimra, 'Daughters of Mayotte, Sons of Frantz'.

17. See Bergner, 'Who Is That Masked Woman?'. Bergner argues that Fanon's representation of the black woman is abstracted from the relevant social context as he appears to 'overlook the ways in which colonial society perpetuates racial inequality through structures of sexual difference' (p. 83).

18. For a discussion of the history and evolution of the usage of the term 'exotic' see Charles Forsdick, *Victor Segalen and the Aesthetics of Diversity: Journeys between Cultures* (Oxford and New York: Oxford University Press, 2000).

19. In contrast, it is a male author, Djéré who is ascribed an artistic vision that is concerned with representing both sides of the gender divide in 'Les Cahiers de Djéré': 'Là-dessus, il avait essayé de raconter qui était son père et aussi qui était sa mère' [In them he had attempted to recount who his father was and who his mother was as well] (*DRM*, 21; *LAK*, 9). It is also his grandson, Spéro, who appears open to the possibility that his maternal ancestry is as important as his paternal one: 'Peut-être l'ascendance maternelle est-elle aussi importante que la paternelle?' [Perhaps one's mother's family tree is as important as one's father's?] (*DRM*, 179; *LAK*, 119).

20. On the author's relationship to an idea of 'female writing' Hewitt ('Condé's Critical Seesaw') observes: 'The leitmotif of a female genealogy appears throughout Condé's novels, but in *Les Derniers Rois mages*, it is voiced by a man whose dealings with women are certainly less than ideal [...]. It is as if *Les Derniers Rois mages* is meant to correct any (false) impression that Condé is a writer who promotes a feminist stance over and against men's concerns' (p. 649).

21. For examples of Condé's shifting position to the idea of women's writing see 'Language and Power'; *La Parole*; 'Order, Disorder'; 'The Stealers of Fire'; Sansavior, 'Entretien avec Maryse Condé'.

22. Sansavior, 'Entretien avec Maryse Condé', p. 31.

23. For a discussion of the ways in which writing by women brings about a 'pyrrhic victory' that is characterized in terms of the dissolution of the role of the female author, see Condé, 'The Stealers of Fire'.

24. Ironically, although Spéro had previously sold numerous tourist paintings in his native Guadeloupe, these are the only two paintings produced in Charleston which attract buyers. But Spéro refuses to sell them.

25. For a discussion of this idea of 'necessary irresponsibility' of literature, see Harrison, 'Who Needs an Idea of the Literary?'.

26. For a critique of literary instrumentalism in critical approaches to literature see for example Bahri, *Native Intelligence*; Attridge, *The Singularity of Literature*; Harrison, 'Who Needs an Idea of the Literary?'.

27. Condé, *La Parole*, p. 77.

28. Condé, 'Language and Power', p. 19.

29. Condé, 'Notes sur un retour au pays natal', p. 21.

30. See Condé, 'Chercher nos vérités', in *Penser la Créolité*, ed. by Maryse Condé and Madeleine Cottenet-Hage (Paris: Karthala, 1995), pp. 301–05.

31. Condé has often associated literature with 'troubling' her readers. See for example *La Parole*, p. 77; Sourieau, 'Entretien avec Maryse Condé', p. 1097.

CHAPTER 6

On the Creative Uses of Gaps: (Re)-imagining Identity in *Desirada*

'A part le bonheur, il n'est rien d'essentiel' [Happiness is all there is]

Chanson martiniquaise [*Song from Martinique*] — preface to *Desirada*

All four novels that I have considered thus far have taken as their starting point the 'identity quests' of various protagonists of Caribbean origin and have cast light on certain culturally and historically informed assumptions concerning identity. In light of this focus, Condé has expressed an ongoing preoccupation with the ways in which the cultural encounters and exchanges that accompany the process of globalization have led to a continual redefinition of what it means to be 'Caribbean' or 'black'.[1] In *Desirada*, Condé's eleventh novel, she extends this process of reflection by placing three generation of women of Francophone Caribbean origin at the centre of the diverse affiliations and interactions between immigrants in the United States and France. The novel's protagonist, Marie-Noëlle, was born in Guadeloupe to a teenage mother, Reynalda. After trying to drown herself while pregnant, Reynalda had been rescued by a local woman, Ranélise, who then took care of the girl while Reynalda came to France on her own. There, she had enjoyed a relatively rapid social ascension, rising from her position as a maid to gain a doctorate and becoming a respected and sought-after expert on the abuse of women from ethnic minority groups. Having spent the first ten years of her life in Guadeloupe, Marie-Noëlle is then reunited with her mother and her mother's new partner Ludovic in Paris, and she eventually goes to live in Boston, in the United States. However, Marie-Noëlle is haunted by unresolved feelings of pain and abandonment that stem from her difficult childhood in which she has suffered as a result of a lack of closeness and affection with her mother Reynalda along with feelings of exclusion in the new family that her mother had built with Ludovic. These feelings become indistinguishable from her unanswered questions about the identity of her father. When Ranélise dies, Marie-Noëlle travels to Guadeloupe in the hope that she will solve the mystery of her father's identity. However, her visit to Guadeloupe and her meeting with her grand-mother Nina provide her with no clear answers as to the identity of her father, only a suspicion that her father is likely to be the priest to whom her mother had been close. In disappointment, she returns to Boston to finish her doctorate and finds permanent work as a university lecturer. The novel ends with the protagonist claiming a 'monstrous identity'.

While *Desirada* has thus far attracted relatively little critical attention, placing the narrative features that I have outlined above in the context of one of Condé's essays will allow for an illuminating discussion of the implications of the protagonist's 'monstrous identity'. As I noted in the introduction, a distinctive characteristic of Condé's œuvre is the ongoing dialogue that it constructs between her essays and her novels on key concerns: a historical account of the various attempts to define an idealized Francophone Caribbean identity and a related discussion about the creative possibilities generated by the confrontation of such idealized representations with the actual experiences of people of Francophone Caribbean origin in the context of immigration and the increasing trend towards globalization. These possibilities are the subject of Condé's essay 'O Brave New World', published in 1998, one year after the publication of *Desirada*.[2] The essay takes as its starting point a number of negative readings of globalization as 'homogenization' and 'the effacement of difference', and considers its implications for Caribbean societies which lack political and economic power.[3]

Condé's concern with globalization suggests parallels with the work of Édouard Glissant. These parallels are evident at the level of the generic choices of both authors: the novel-essay pair of *Desirada* and 'O Brave New World' is matched by Glissant's *Tout-Monde* and *Traité du Tout-Monde* published in 1993 and 1997 respectively. In addition, in the course of 'O Brave New World' Condé situates, in passing, her approach to thinking about globalization in relation to Glissant's definition of creolization in *Traité du Tout-Monde*. There are structural similarities too: in support of their vision of globalization both Condé and Glissant construct highly intertextual works. However, I think that in spite of these similarities what characterizes Condé's approach to defining globalization is precisely the range of intellectual and cultural influences on which it draws, influences that extend beyond Glissant's specific framework. Glissant's creolization is just one of the influences that Condé cites (influences that include major Caribbean or black writers and theorists such as Caryl Phillips and Stuart Hall).[4] In addition, there is one key difference between Glissant's and Condé's approaches to defining globalization in the novel-essay pairs which, in my view, point to the need to consider *in their own right* both the content and discursive structure of Condé's arguments on globalization. Perhaps the most significant difference is in terms of the two authors' commitment to what may be characterized as 'theoretical rigour'. The highly theoretical definitions of terms such as *globalité*, *chaos-monde* and *relation* that underpin Glissant's *Traité du Tout-Monde* (and his broader œuvre) is matched by the narrative complexity of the novel *Tout-Monde* which features a multiplicity of locations and narrative perspectives. In contrast, *Desirada* tracks the experience of three generations of women across three locations and its structure is relatively simple featuring three main narrative frameworks: the omniscient narrator, the protagonist, and the account of Nina, Marie-Noëlle's grandmother. In addition, as I shall seek to demonstrate, Condé's discussion of globalization in 'O Brave New World' privileges not theoretical rigour but rather a concern to locate the trend of globalization within the historically situated experiences and encounters of the 'black diaspora'. And, in marked contrast to Glissant, Condé employs a style that is distinctly conversational and aphoristic. (What Chris Bongie has characterized as the 'middlebrow' status of Condé's œuvre may thus be viewed as intrinsic to her definition of globalization.)

Condé argues for the role of peoples of the black diaspora from the Caribbean, Africa and North America in shaping the process of globalization. She links this contemporary politico-economic and cultural phenomenon to a form of proto-globalization that she sees as having emerged in the context of the international black-consciousness movements that arose in Paris in the early to mid-twentieth century:

> A certain measure of globalization was in fact initiated after the Second World War when black America, Africa and the Caribbean came into close contact in Paris. [...] Paris had become the ideal place for exchange and communication.

These contacts are shown to serve as the context for a rediscovery of Africa, one that is facilitated by Paris's role as the centre of France's colonial administration.[5] Crucially, through the complexity of the historically situated intellectual map that it constructs, the essay highlights the ways in which these movements made inter-ventions in the political and cultural spheres. This map may also be understood as representing a form of global and essentially politicized black identity. Such a yoking of culture or literature to politics would make their interventions broadly congruent with the model of Sartrean *engagement* that I developed in the intro-duction. However, the reformulation of a fundamental tenet of Marxism (one upheld by Sartre in *Qu'est-ce que la littérature*), the idea that class was the only legitimate basis for political claims would also be central to this process as Condé observes:

> [...] Marxism embraced enthusiastically by the majority of the black intellectuals, was little else but the dream of a world without borders, whose foundation was no longer Race but Class. [...] So during the first quarter of the 20th century, the minds of the black intellectuals, Caribbean, African, and American alike, were haunted by dreams of internationalization and globalization, based first on color, then on a common exploitation of their people.[6]

These contacts between black intellectuals are thus the context for the forging of a form of global political imaginary that also produces a common identity for these diverse peoples based on the concept of race and the experiences of shared oppression. Yet these contacts are also the site of *actual* political failure, a failure to achieve political consensus that Condé calls 'a shattered dream of unity'.[7] In effect, this politicized black identity did not succeed in marshalling the interests of different constituencies — divided by language, culture and national identities — into the creation of a viable global political culture.

The trajectory of globalization offered by Condé's essay can be read as follows: the failed politicized model of proto-globalization associated with black-consciousness movements is superseded by a contemporary model characterized not by a privileging of a quest for a common or universal political goal but rather by forms of what I will call the 'particularized experiential'. These actual experiences of migration, although realized in common, are motivated by such diverse reasons so as to not be fully recuperable as 'collective' or 'universal' in a political (or even 'theoretical') sense. In this respect, Condé observes: 'The causes of this mass phenomenon are multiple. Some flee dictatorship and genocide at home. Others, poverty and starvation. Yet others, religious fanaticism'.[8] Given the distinguishing particularity of this contemporary experience of globalization, it is perhaps fitting that Condé should identify the Francophone Caribbean family, an institution that is both particular and universal, as exemplifying the changes that accompany globalization as she points to the 'major increase in the number of families being formed on foreign soils'.[9] Furthermore, it is literature and not politics, Condé argues, that is best equipped to account for and give expression to these changes. For Condé, literature is uniquely capable of responding to the imperative which she characterizes in strikingly theoretical terms as a quest for 'new definitions of human collectivities'.[10]

She ascribes a decisive role to the literature produced by second-generation (black) writers, 'brought up outside of the country of their parents', who succeed in capturing the particularity of this experience and responding to the challenge to find these new definitions. According to Condé, the literature produced by these writers exemplifies 'cultural mixing' or 'métissage culturel', often featuring a diversity of geographical settings and characters which are not necessarily of the same ethnicity as their authors (or as Condé notes explicitly, 'not even black').[11] Interestingly, through her brief reference to *Desirada*, Condé suggests that her own literature is guided by similar representational imperatives. And she cites *Desirada* as a type of literary test case for this quest for new definitions, noting that the novel's portrayal of three generations of women reflects 'the evolution of the Caribbean people: from a secluded, easily classifiable community to a nomadic people, creating a world of its own wherever it finds itself'.[12] Condé conceives of literature as being profoundly implicated in a culturally diverse and complex social reality that necessarily extends an author's representational responsibility beyond his or her natural constituencies as defined by notions such as 'home country', 'race' and 'language' (although in Condé's case, her starting point is a constituency that may be viewed as 'natural' to her: women of Guadeloupean origin). The enlarged ethic of responsibility (or what Sartre called the writer's responsibility to all men) to which it gestures may be read as a realization of the inclusive, universalist ideals that underpins Sartrean *engagement*.[13] But this estrangement from any presumed origins also leads to a questioning of the very notion of 'authentic literature' in ways that problematize the Sartrean appeal to precisely this idea in *QQL*.[14] Reflecting on this idea of authentic literature, Condé muses:

> Maybe all fictions are authentic since they are a reflection of the author's inner self [...]. One wonders if an identity is not simply a matter of choice, of a personal decision based on the possession of certain individual values; a certain image of women, a belief in the family, a certain relationship to oneself and to others, and to the invisible world around as well as an attitude towards death.[15]

Through this questioning of the nature of authentic literature, Condé thus points to a type of identity mediated by individual choice and a diffuse idea of personal belief. It is a similar conjunction of choice and belief that is the basis for a utopian form of *engagement* as a clear-sighted facing up to the 'conflicts and tensions' that bedevil global societies.[16] Condé imagines this as a future-orientated project that unites politicians and various types of artists in perhaps necessarily impressionistic terms at the end of the essay. Yet this is a hybrid project, which, while situated within the realm of the arts, draws its sense of urgency and conviction from a traditional idea of politics (and indeed as is suggested by the imagined alliance between artists and politicians) maintains a belief in the future viability of a new form of politics. Condé asserts: 'However, I am convinced that with the help of creators, writers, musicians, and dancers, backed by a new generation of politicians, it will be possible to overcome the challenge of the future'.[17] In the light of the above discussion, I shall explore the extent to which *Desirada* offers new possibilities for re-imagining the terms of the questions that recur in Condé's theoretical and literary work concerning the relationship between an evolving Francophone Caribbean identity and conceptions of politics and literature, family and home.

★ ★ ★ ★ ★

Featuring a protagonist who attempts to fill the gaps in her personal history through sojourns of varying lengths in Guadeloupe, France and the United States, *Desirada* is undoubtedly shaped by a preoccupation with new possibilities for defining identity in an increasingly globalized world. This process is indistinguishable from a critical engagement with existing, dominant categories for defining identity, together with their cultural and ideological underpinnings. In particular, the failure of the universalizing category of 'the political' emerges as a counterpoint to Marie-Noëlle's individual quest. Condé's conception in 'O Brave New World' of the evolution of globalization from the proto-globalization based on an essentialized black identity towards a more experiential model better suited to the creative practice of fiction writing thus finds its literary articulation in *Desirada*. Politics appears in the novel not as an overarching system of organized representation centred around the building of consensus but rather but as a series of fragmented and ultimately ineffectual practices, perhaps symptomatic of an increasingly atomized postmodern public sphere. In keeping with Condé's reading of the political in 'O Brave New World', this traditional notion of politics in *Desirada* is marked by a *belatedness*, a sense that what Chris Bongie (drawing on Peter Hallward) has called the 'properly political' has already failed. It is a failure that the omniscient narrator presents in a matter of fact tone that alternates with a type of bored irony.[18]

    That politics can only aspire to a theoretical universality is implied by its treatment in the narrative as both physical trace and narrative device. Politics is presented thus as mere ideas evoked materially in horizontal lists suggesting an idea of empty words that merely *sit on* the surface of reality, a presentation that recalls the Barthesian conception of myth as a form of 'depoliticized speech'.[19] In a development of this idea of speech, it is also suggested that such myths may possess an almost sacred quality expressed through the recitation of political buzz words, like secular acts of faith, in which 'la conversation [...] d'un jour sur l'autre ne variait pas beaucoup' [the conversation [...] did not vary from one day to the next] (*Desirada*, 55; *DesiradaE*, 44) The narrator's ironic attitude towards this traditional idea of politics is revealed to be at odds with the reverential nostalgia with which it is invested by some characters in the novel. Politics in the different forms in which it is remembered by various characters is bathed in a nostalgic glow, part of a longed-for past. When Ludovic and his friend Rodrigue meet up to reminisce about their youth, memories of childhood escapades are intermingled with those of their politicized youth. These memories are the subject of nostalgic remembrance and the context for passionate political discussions that take for granted a universal anti-colonial black consciousness:

> Rappel des bêtises enfantines de Ludovic et Rodrigue. Anecdotes carabines du temps où Rodrigue était interne dans un hôpital de Moscou. Récits illustrant la détresse des Africains. Diatribes contre le néo-colonialisme qui prenait la relève du colonialisme et, pour finir, discussions passionnées. Sur la révolution cubaine. (*Desirada*, 55–56)

> [Memories of childhood pranks by Rodrigue and Ludovic. Medical student stories from the time when Rodrigue was an intern at a hospital in Moscow. Stories describing the misery of Africans. Diatribes against neocolonialism, which was replacing colonialism. Finally, heated discussions about the Cuban revolution. (*DesiradaE*, 44–45)]

This idea of an endlessly 'repeated discourse' is accorded a more creative inflection in the novel's treatment of identity politics in the context of the regular meetings between Anthea and her African-American female friends. At these meetings each recounts what are implicitly well-worn tales of their victimization at the hands of white people: 'Pourtant [...] elles s'assombrissaient et la conversation en venait immanquablement au racisme. Chacun d'entre elles y allait de sa triste histoire sur le refus des Blancs, des Caucasiens à reconnaître la valeur de ceux qui ont une autre couleur de peau qu'eux [...]' [Yet [...] their mood darkened, and the conversation unfailingly turned to racism. Each of them had their own sad story to tell about the refusal of whites, the Caucasians, to recognize the value of those with a different skin colour] (*Desirada*, 112; *DesiradaE*, 98).

The effort invested in the construction of such tales of victimization is, in a sense, testament to the essentially imaginary territory occupied by this form of identity politics and by the community whose interests it would seek to defend. In contrast to *DRM*, there is no homogeneous African-American community in the culturally diverse universe constructed in *Desirada* around which a legitimizing consensus for this form of politics might be built. Politics is thus relegated to the intimate sphere, present only in the fleeting mythology of identity politics re-enacted by Anthea and her friends during their social gatherings, a ritualization of politics that is richly suggestive of its status as a form of instrumentalized myth that works to script, what is in this case, a victimized black identity for Anthea and her friends.

The confrontation of these representations with Marie-Noëlle's experiences is shown to have a demystifying value. If Marie-Noëlle responds with scepticism to the advice of Anthea and her friends it is because she is unable to find any evidence in support of their polarized views on identity in her lived experience:[20]

> Marie-Noëlle n'était pas émue. [...] où était-il ce monde des Blancs, des Caucasiens qu'on voulait qu'elle redoute? Pas vraisemblable. Irréel comme celui des loups-garous. Elle allait et venait dans un tout autre monde. Parmi des

Noirs, des basanés, des métis, des métèques, des exilés, des transplantés, des déracinés. La majorité de ceux qu'elle côtoyait savaient à peine l'américain, ne lisaient pas les journaux, ne regardaient que les programmes de télévision en langue étrangère. (*Desirada*, 112)

[Marie-Noëlle was not moved. [...] where was this world of white folk, Caucasians they warned her about? Quite unreal. As unreal as the world of werewolves. She was used to a very different world. A world of blacks, half-castes, mixed-bloods, and the exiled, the displaced, and the uprooted. Most of these could hardly speak English, did not read newspapers, and only watched TV programmes in their own language. (*DesiradaE*, 99)]

The implication of Marie-Noëlle's ironic characterization of the whites as 'loups-garous' [werewolves], mythical monsters is that both sets of polarized identities — 'whites' and 'victimized blacks' are possibly mythological categories. Barthes's reading of myth as unproductive or limiting would lead us to expect that Marie-Noëlle's rejection of these categories is definitive. In fact, Marie-Noëlle's scepticism towards such ready-made, identitarian myths provides the basis for her own reformulation of these very categories. The alternative universe that Marie-Noëlle describes is based on a contrast between the fictions provided by Anthea and her friends and her own lived experience. Although centred around a list of identities which starts with 'des Noirs', this universe does not assign to this identity a fixed, victimized status (*Desirada*, 112–13). Instead, with this list, Marie-Noëlle situates 'des Noirs' in a context that appears to privilege mixed origins and a state of immigration or exile. There is therefore an implicit equation of the term 'des Noirs' with ideas of 'mixed' origins, or 'a belonging to elsewhere'. The effect of this is to suggest that the category 'des Noirs' is not in any real sense 'separate' but is necessarily mixed because its meaning is reliant on the other categories of exclusion in this system. In addition, as Marie-Noëlle observes, these categories of identity are predicated on a certain absence of access to the cultural life in the United States (reading newspapers, being able to speak the language) and crucially, the groups defined by such identities also maintain a pragmatic economic relationship to the United States. What is invoked therefore is an idea of inequality that is founded not on race but on economic power.[21] In this way, it is implied that it is economic rather than racial equality which may provide a viable basis for a more inclusive form of political action or politics although this possibility is not explored explicitly in the novel.

Cultural politics is another form of politics present in the novel. However, there is no sense in which cultural politics is held up as an alternative to the exhaustion or the impoverishment of politics as a collectively configured activity. Various collective political initiatives in the cultural sphere end in failure: the attempt by Marie-Noëlle's husband Stanley to create an orchestra, the M.N.A., that aimed to 'traduire l'apport des migrants' [translate the contribution of immigrants] founders as the creative energy that he sought to translate in his music becomes mired in a hectoring, ineffectual political rhetoric that does not succeed in capturing the public imagination (*Desirada*, 117–18). A similar fate befalls Muntu, the organization run by Ludovic, which aims to provide a mentoring and support structure for young immigrant males; the narrative traces its evolution from a viable social project that makes a difference (*Desirada*, 233) to a project that is out of step with the values of its constituency. In common with the treatment of political ideas in the novel, the organization's failure although narrated from Ludovic's perspective, suggests a divided response: Ludovic's almost palpable sense of disappointment is undermined by the omniscient narrator's obliquely ironic tone. This account of Muntu's failure does, however, also provide a useful condensed history of transformations that have shaped the cultural field and its relationship to consensual politics:

> D'ailleurs, Muntu mourait de sa belle mort. Les jeunes [...] n'avaient en tête que les filles et la frime. Aucun projet sérieux. Les seuls mots de révolution ou de marxisme les faisaient bâiller. l'Afrique, Cuba, Fidel Castro, Sékou Touré les intéressaient beaucoup moins que Stevie Wonder ou Marvin Gaye. (*Desirada*, 100)

> [Furthermore Muntu had died a natural death. The young guys [...] were only interested in girls and showing off. Nothing serious was planned. The mere words 'Revolution' or 'Marxism' made them yawn: Africa, Fidel Castro, Sékou Touré interested them far less than Stevie Wonder or Marvin Gaye. (*Desirada*E, 86)]

An era of Marxist, pan-Africanist collective cultural projects that drew their legitimacy from some form of imaginary consensus around great revolutionary leaders such as Fidel Castro or Sékou Touré has given way to one in which 'culture' has become untethered from any idea of revolutionary politics. What has emerged in the wake of this change is a profound reformulation of the idea of consensus, as a shared taste for the type of partially politicized black global cultural products embodied by the music of the iconic African-American singers Stevie Wonder and Marvin Gaye. This is a type of cultural consensus that is directed not necessarily towards any concrete political action, but rather towards the generation of templates for forms of individual self-definition. Politics, in this case, is not, as it is traditionally understood, a system that is capable of mobilizing a group that is somehow concrete, but a type of cultural commodity, viable only in so far as it provides opportunities for expressing individuals' personal style.

★ ★ ★ ★ ★

The novel's depiction of the family allows for a more extensive treatment of the possibilities offered by identity and cultural politics for engaging with identity as a form of myth or fiction that is *productive* in the sense of being open to a process of individually mediated re-imaginings. By making the lack or absence of a father figure — and the attempt to fill it by an imaginary reconstruction of her mother's life — the determining characteristics of Marie-Noëlle's identity, *Desirada* suggests a Lacanian conception of the subject as forged in division or lack and structured initially by imaginary constructions. Before I consider in detail how the relationship between the protagonist's familial context and the imaginary shapes her identity quest, it is necessary to provide a brief account of the Lacanian model of subjectivity.

In the Lacanian model of subjectivity outlined in *Ecrits I*, the infant is born into the Imaginary Order, a state in which the infant is unable to distinguish between itself and the outside world and in which it experiences an imaginary merging of itself and the maternal body.[22] This in turn generates a fantasized sense of wholeness and plenitude.[23] In the Mirror Stage the infant maintains this fantasized sense of self-unity by identifying with the idealized image of himself in the mirror. As Anthony Elliott observes, the imaginary misrecognition on which this infantile image of self-unity is based serves as the template for an ongoing relation to subjectivity, shaping both individual self-perception and the 'fantasy-generated images of others'.[24] The imaginary is, then, essentially an alienation of subjectivity with the small child experiencing itself as 'other' in the process of looking into the mirror.[25] Celia Britton's reading of the Lacanian model highlights the fact that it is in the Symbolic Order that the child learns to speak. It is also here that the father intervenes symbolically in the imaginary mother/child couple thereby disrupting the child's imaginary unity with his mother.[26] The symbolic order is the domain of received social meanings and the wider social network that pre-exists the child governing amongst other things the rules of kinships and the language system. As Britton observes, it is the insertion of the child within this pre-existing matrix of social meaning that produces the child as a subject.[27] Therefore, if it is assumed that subjectivity is imagined, then the series of ongoing identifications that produce it are taken to be outside of the subject's control.

In keeping with the Lacanian model of subjectivity, the family in *Desirada* is the context for the primary lack that shapes the protagonist's quest for identity (the separation from mother). However, the experiences of the majority of families depicted in the novel do not match Lacan's normative model. While Lacan's reading of subjectivity appears to take for granted the existence of a stable, culturally uniform nuclear family bound by ties of blood as the framework for the development of subjectivity, the familial context in which Marie-Noëlle finds herself is characterized instead by separation, instability and cultural heterogeneity.[28] Marie-Noëlle has spent the first years of her life haunted by an acute awareness of the risk of separation from her surrogate mother, Ranélise (*Desirada*, 21). At the age of ten, her biological mother, Reynalda, sends for her and she finds herself relocated to Paris and becomes part of a new family that comprises her unmarried biological mother Reynalda, her mother's partner, Ludovic, and a half-brother, Garvey. The roles are also reversed in the family, with Ludovic acting as 'le poto-mitan de la maison' [the mainstay of the home] and providing Marie-Noëlle with nurturing that may be characterized as 'maternal' (*Desirada*, 39). It is Ludovic, not her mother, for instance, who helps Marie-Noëlle with her first period (*Desirada*, 39). In contrast, Reynalda is emotionally unavailable to her daughter and is instead preoccupied with her research and with the abused women whom she represents (*Desirada*, 39, 40, 42). Indeed, the family is presented as the framework for the transmission of a dysfunctional model of motherhood from Nina to Reynalda and then to Marie-Noëlle, a framework that inhibits rather than facilitates the imaginary identification with the mother figure as envisaged in the Lacanian Mirror Stage.

Marked by the spatial and cultural disruption brought about by immigration and the formation of alternative families, the family is presented as isolated or irredeemably cut off from an original, 'native land', as well as from a new social network; there are no visitors and no stories from home (*Desirada*, 41). The family is also the bearer of multiple 'social orders' (Ludovic has lived in many countries and is multi-lingual), and therefore does not allow Marie-Noëlle access to the idealized, 'natural' Francophone Caribbean identity that, as Condé argues, is implicitly endorsed by the Créolité school.[29]

In common with the questioning of an ideal family, the notion of home as a place to which one has a 'natural right' is also called into question by Marie-Noëlle's journey to Guadeloupe. Marie-Noëlle's return to Guadeloupe does not allow her to 'remonter le temps' [go back in time] as she had hoped and she discovers instead that the past is effectively 'another country' (*Desirada*, 108). The Guadeloupe that she finds as an adult differs markedly from the one that she had imagined as a child. Instead of the postcard images conjured up by her imagination 'pour lui tenir chaud' [to keep her warm], she is confronted by 'pauvreté, laideur' [poverty and ugliness] (*Desirada*, 139, *DesiradaE*, 125).

She also finds that she does not fit in in Guadeloupe as she is unable to play by the unwritten social rules or 'perform' convincingly the social rituals that serve to unite the community. During Ranélise's funeral, she does not cry and drinks too much (*Desirada*, 137–38). The other mourners' attitudes confirm her feeling of not belonging as they hold her at a fearful distance sensing that 'elle venait d'ailleurs' [she came from elsewhere] and has thus had experiences that lay beyond their horizon of understanding (*Desirada*, 138; *DesiradaE*, 124).

The resolution of the mystery of her identity also proves elusive, as the clues that she seeks have been erased by the passage of time. She learns that her putative father, Gian Carlo Coppini, is dead, that the business no longer exists and (with the exception of her mother's childhood friend Fiorella who is abroad at the time of her visit) that the family has returned to Italy (*Desirada*, 171–74). She is only able to collect contradictory, fragmented testimonies, none of which enables her to confirm the identity of her father. For example, just before her departure from Guadeloupe she learns from Claire-Alta that her heavily pregnant mother, with whom Claire-Alta had shared a room while they were teenagers, had received a mysterious letter one day which she had kept to herself and also that one of her mother's most treasured possessions had been a bible (although the significance of this last clue only becomes apparent to her with hindsight) (*Desirada*, 256). Meanwhile, Marie-Noëlle's meeting with Fiorella's husband reveals the unsuccessful attempt by his father (on the basis of Fiorella's testimony) to bring a case against Gian Carlo Coppini for his alleged involvement in the disappearance of Reynalda (*Desirada*, 173).

Indeed, it is in Guadeloupe that the idea that the protagonist may have some natural right to a Guadeloupean identity is challenged implicitly (during the wake in which she does not behave according to local expectations of propriety) and also explicitly by Fiorella's husband who remarks: 'L'identité, ce n'est pas un vêtement égaré que l'on retrouve et que l'on endosse avec plus ou moins de grâce. Elle pourrait faire ce qu'elle voulait, elle ne serait jamais une vraie Guadeloupéenne' [Identity is not like some piece of clothing that is lost and found and then slipped on hoping it will fit. Whatever she did she would never be a true Guadeloupean] (*Desirada*, 172; *DesiradaE*, 158).

Marie-Noëlle's return to Guadeloupe is also the context in which the novel underscores the limitations of collective memory as a means of anchoring the protagonist's identity. There is an oral dimension to identity formation in this traditional context that is articulated through the telling of stories that situate individuals in the narrative of the community's development. Bonne-Maman, Judes Anozie's grandmother, functions as a guardian of collective memory and its oral transmission through her ability to remember and effectively commemorate the lives of members of the community and history from the perspective of the community:

> De sa voix flûtée, Bonne-Maman [...] racontait le jour du cyclone 1928 qui, elle en était fière, était aussi celui de sa naissance [...]. Elle gardait serré dans sa commode un journal jauni, soigneusement préservé, *Le Nouvelliste* [...], il avait donné la liste des nouveau-nés qui avaient, pour connaître la lumière du monde, bravé les fureurs de la nature [...]. (*Desirada*, 161–62)

> [In her flutelike voice Granny [...] was describing the day the hurricane of 1928 struck — which, she was proud to say, was also the date of her birth [...]. Carefully locked away in her chest of drawers she kept a yellowed copy of *Le Nouvelliste* [...] , it listed the names of the babies who braved the wrath of nature to emerge into the light of this world [...]. (*DesiradaE*, 147)]

But through this emphasis on the orality of collective memory this account also foregrounds Marie-Noëlle's exclusion from the communitarian narrative of identity.[30]

Marie-Noëlle's absence from the unofficial records of collective memory would seem to assign a privileged role to familial memory in securing the protagonist's sense of identity. In fact, this familial memory can only provide the protagonist with more questions about her identity. Marie-Noëlle's meeting with her own grandmother does not bring her any closer to confirming her identity as the daughter of Gian Carlo Coppini. Confronted only with a proliferation of unanswered questions concerning her origins, the protagonist attempts to ground her identity in a genealogy that is witnessed and validated by her grandmother:

> C'était la première fois qu'elle déclinait sa généalogie, qu'elle nommait au grand jour le nom de ceux qui l'avaient engendrée. Et c'était comme si enfin, elle prenait possession d'elle-même et qu'elle marquât sa trace sur la terre. (*Desirada*, 180)

> [It was the first time she had stated her lineage, that she had openly named the name of those who had begotten her. And it was as if at last she had taken possession of herself and made her mark on this earth. (*DesiradaE*, 165)]

But her grandmother's 'rire sans fin' [never-ending laughter] shatters her attempts to construct her genealogy (*Desirada*, 180; *DesiradaE*, 165).[31]

In addition, her meeting with her grandmother confronts her with the impossibility of bridging the gap between her imagination (implicitly fed by her mother's stories) and an oblique reality as her grandmother observes:

> Tu as l'air déçue toute chagrinée. Ce n'est pas cette histoire-là que tu avais envie d'entendre, pas vré? [...] Tu avais envisagé des tas d'autres choses dans ta tête et tu étais venue jusqu'ici, tu avais enjambé l'eau pour trouver un fondement à tes imaginations. (*Desirada*, 202)

[You look disappointed, all upset. It wasn't this story you wanted to hear, was it? You dreamed of something else. You busied your head with a lot of other things and you came as far as here, crossed the ocean to find some justification for what you imagined. (*DesiradaE*, 183–84)]

Instead, Nina's testimony contradicts that of her mother Reynalda as she suggests an alternative 'truth': that Gian Carlo Coppini is not her father (*Desirada*, 202). Nina concludes by telling Marie-Noëlle that she does not belong in Guadeloupe where '[c]hacun depuis la naissance connaît le chemin dans lequel il doit marcher et la place où, à la fin, il faudra qu'il se couche' [everyone knows the path he must tread from cradle to grave] and advises her to return to America and live her life (*Desirada*, 202–03; *DesiradaE*, 184).

In emphasizing the failure of both communitarian and familial memory to ground the protagonist's identity, the novel therefore marks an important shift in Condé's position on the role of collective forms of memory in the constitution of individual identity. Individual memory, imagination and choice emerge as central to the process of self-construction.[32] The ambiguous outcome of the protagonist's meeting with her grandmother acts as a pointer to the process of self-construction that is undertaken in the novel: gaps and failure serve as the starting point for a circular process of self-construction that one imagines oneself, but also in relation to a range of collective and individual myths or 'stories'. Nina's injunction to Marie-Noëlle to forget her mother's stories implies that this process of self-construction also involves recognizing and perhaps discarding various forms of collective fictions and imagining new ones. I now consider briefly the construction of what I will call the 'imaginary-imagination' in the novel.

The novel is structured by two conceptions of the imaginary which, although different in principle, are not antagonistic but overlapping and interdependent with one creating the conditions for the emergence of the other. The first, named in the novel from the start as 'souvenirs imaginaires', is broadly associated with the protagonist's conscious and unconscious recourse to ready-made images of identity in an ultimately abortive attempt to recuperate a sense of the past and, with it, an idealized complete identity. The second, although not named, is linked to an idea of 'imagination' or 'creative identifications', and is concerned with the ways in which the protagonist is able to use her imagination to strategically marshal conscious and unconscious material to re-create an ambiguous, fluid identity in the context of 'gaps' and 'absence' and identifications with people 'other' than herself.

In the opening scene of the novel, the protagonist stages her own birth:

Ranélise lui avait tant de fois raconté sa naissance qu'elle croyait y avoir tenu un rôle; non pas celui d'un bébé terrorisé et passif [...] mais celui d'un témoin lucide; d'un acteur essentiel, voire de sa mère, l'accouchée, Reynalda elle-même [...]. (*Desirada*, 13)

[Ranelise had described her birth so many times that she believed she had actually played a part — not that of a terrorized and submissive baby [...] but that of clear-sighted witness, her very mother, the mother in labour, Reynalda herself [...]. (*DesiradaE*, 3)]

If this scene suggests an idea of 'souvenirs imaginaries', it is never identified explicitly as such. Instead its status as 'un souvenir imaginaire' is implied by association to a second imaginary memory relating to Marie-Noëlle's christening which is explicitly named as '[l]e deuxième souvenir imaginaire' [the second thing [...] imagined] (*Desirada*, 17; *DesiradaE*, 7). With the conjunction in 'souvenirs imaginaires' of the terms 'memories' and 'imaginary', there is the suggestion here of both a Lacanian notion of 'constituted subjectivity' and the open-ended possibility for reflecting upon, reworking and situating in an entirely new imaginary context these ready-made symbolic frameworks. In the above description of the memory of Marie-Noëlle's birth, family memories serve as the starting point for a process of creative reworking. The two contrasting images, 'bébé terrorisé et passif [terrorized and submissive baby]' and 'un acteur essentiel, voire de sa mère, l'accouchée' [a major role, her very mother, the mother in labor], are richly suggestive of the movement between two poles of subjectivity that is implicit to this process: one constituted and structured by unconscious identifications and 'myths' and the other characterized by a capacity for conscious reflection and self-construction. The fact that it is in the protagonist's imagination that these two conceptions of subjectivity are dramatized is significant since it points to the role of individual imagination as a reflective and creative space that both hosts and transcends the Lacanian unconscious realm of the imaginary and of literature as I have defined it. In the following section, I consider the possibilities presented by individual imagination for reconfiguring mythical representations of family, home and identity itself.

★   ★   ★   ★   ★

The confrontation of the idealized view of the family with Marie-Noëlle's experiences points to the family's status as a myth which is open to re-imagining.[33] The gap between the protagonist's expectations (shaped implicitly by mythical representations of the family) and her own experiences prompts a re-imagining of the family. In place of an ideal of the natural family, predicated on ties of blood, the novel explores the enriching potential of elective families so that, for example, Marie-Noëlle's friend, Anthea, adopts and raises a Ghanaian girl, Molara, who thrives in her care.[34] In line with this, the omniscient narrator muses: 'Enfant biologique, ou adoptée qu'importe?' [Biological or adopted child, it did not really matter] (*Desirada*, 109; *DesiradaE*, 95). More broadly, the narrative draws a contrast between this nurturing mother–daughter relationship and the traumatic ones that stem from natural families, and highlights through the positive portrayal of Molara's adoption that natural families do not necessarily look after the well-being of children more effectively than elective ones.

Friendships play a key role in the novel providing the characters with an evolving support network. Marie-Noëlle forges a number of friendships throughout the novel, many of which, although transient and circumstantial, are of great value to her (such as her relationship with Leïla and Araxie in the sanatorium and with Saran, a young Guinean girl). Indeed, implicitly there is a sense in which Marie-Noëlle's various friendships all have equal value for her (a value that is independent of their longevity) and this is reflected in the fact that, as Britton observes, even

Marie-Noëlle's relatively minor friendships are described in detail in the novel (*Desirada*, 138–39).[35]

The various friendships presented in the novel also function to a certain extent as surrogate families in which the roles that are fulfilled by members are not 'pre-ordained' or taken for granted but negotiated *intuitively* in response to the needs of the individuals involved. For example, Mme Esmondas, the childless medium who befriends Marie-Noëlle, acts as much-needed mother figure for a girl who feels unable to connect with her own mother: 'Mme Esmondas, maternelle comme ma mère ne l'était pas [...]'[Mme Esmondas, motherly in a way her mother never was [...]] (*Desirada*, 49; *DesiradaE*, 38). The fact that Mme Esmondas welcomes her without demands suggests that these surrogate families may be in fact more nurturing and more respectful of individual needs than natural families.[36] In contrast, it is Marie-Noëlle who fulfils the nurturing, maternal role in her friendship with the Argentinean medium, Arelis Di Ferrari — for example, by undressing her and putting her to bed after she drinks too much (130).

The capacity to empathize with and be open to individuals who are different from themselves is a key ability developed by friendship and, in this sense, friendship can be viewed as enabling individuals to develop and expand their capacity for empathy and for accommodating 'difference'. Marie-Noëlle's friendship with Anthea, an African-American academic with whom she has, on the face of it, very little in common, highlights the predisposition of openness to difference that is potentially cultivated in the context of friendship: 'Les seuls moments plaisants étaient ceux qu'elle passait chez Anthea à partager une existence tellement différente de la sienne' [The only pleasant moments were those spent at Anthea's partaking of a life so different from her own] (*Desirada*, 116; *DesiradaE*, 101).[37]

Friendships also provide an interactive space in which individuals swap stories, providing 'material' which stimulates and feeds the imaginary process of identity construction. Therefore, Marie-Noëlle collects stories of 'belonging' and of family from Mme Esmondas (*Desirada*, 47) and from her friends Leïla and Araxie (*Desirada*, 75). In addition, her discussions with Anthea and Arelis Di Ferrari raise questions about her genealogy, in response to which she invents answers, such as when she confides to Arelis that her father may be Italian (*Desirada*, 127). The stories shared and questions posed in the context of these friendships thus enable Marie-Noëlle to refine her quest (by deciding to focus on the identity of her father) and provide the creative stimulus for the construction of her own stories of identity. In this way, identity is presented as a form of interactive and perhaps collaborative fiction that one constructs in relation to people that one chooses as friends and also one's imagined or real family history.[38]

While an idea of choice is central to the re-imagining of 'home' in the novel, the role of chance in framing an individual's choice is a key consideration. In the following conversation with Bonne-Maman the protagonist realizes that she considers the United States to be her home:

> Marie-Noëlle ne savait pas comment parler de l'Amérique, en dehors des mythes qu'elle secrète: rapports Blancs/Noirs, Puritanisme, Sexualité, Violence. Elle ne savait pas parler de son vécu ni expliquer son attachement pour un pays

qu'elle avait abordé par hasard [...], mais qui la retenait fermement. (*Desirada*, 162–63)

[Marie-Noëlle didn't know how to talk about America apart from the myths it secreted: race relations, puritanism, sexuality, and violence. She did not know how to speak of her experience nor explain her attachment to a country that she had accosted by chance [...] but that nevertheless kept a firm hold on her. (*DesiradaE*, 148)]

Interestingly, the protagonist gains an awareness of America as her home in a relational context, during her discussion with Bonne-Maman. Marie-Noëlle's reflections suggest that home may be viewed and, in a sense, also experienced as a space with which one develops an affective link perhaps in spite of oneself and that one chooses, one that is also characterized by an estrangement from an idea of origins.[39] It is significant, however, that the protagonist is unable to find the words to describe her particular connection to the United States and must instead rely on tired myths. This reliance implies that the possibilities for explaining one's identity are circumscribed by existing myths. Moreover, by pointing to the gap between these recycled myths and her own oblique connection to America, Marie-Noëlle alludes to the irreducible nature of an identity that cannot be translated into words.

This idea of home as serving as a gap from 'origins' allows for an exploration of the broader possibilities for re-imagining identity in terms of storytelling or mythmaking that is subject to individual choice. The different types of identities that are presented by the novel are structured by choice in distinctive ways. While the identities of Marie-Noëlle, Garvey and Anthea rely on an imaginary relationship with existing myths or stories, there are marked differences in the choices that they make in the context of this relationship. In Garvey's case, a pragmatic, syncretic approach to constructing his identity is conveyed symbolically through his creative reformulation of (Francophone) Caribbean mythology whereby the new baby's placenta is buried in the leaves of a banana tree:[40] 'Il était Européen. Un Antillais de l'immigration [...]. Son placenta était enterré sous un des platanes de Savigny-sur-Orge' [He was a West Indian from an immigrant family [...]. His placenta was buried under one of the plane trees in Savigny-sur-Orge] (*Desirada*, 231; *DesiradaE*, 211).[41] In contrast, Anthea's identity is based on an apparently wholesale and uncritical appropriation of the myth of a glorious Africa on which Marie-Noëlle reflects at the end of the novel:

Bientôt, Anthea, elle, reviendra du Ghana, la tête toute farcie de ce qu'elle aura imaginé. Je l'entends déjà. Elle me racontera par le menu l'histoire d'Efua. Elle me répétera les histoires cent fois rêvées du Paradis d'autrefois. Du Middle Passage, ce terrible voyage que nous avons tous effectué avant même d'être nés. De notre dispersion aux quatre coins du globe et de nos souffrances. En échange, je n'aurai que mes petites misères à moi, la véritable raison de mon voyage en Europe, les circonstances de mon nouvel échec. Ma dépression. Le début de ma guérison. Honteuse, je me tairai donc en attendant qu'à mon tour j'apprenne à inventer des vies. (*Desirada*, 281)

[Soon Anthea will return from Ghana, her head full of her imaginings. I can already hear her. She'll repeat the stories dreamed a hundred times of the lost paradise. Of the Middle Passage, the terrible journey we all took before we

> were even born. Of our scattering to the four corners of the earth and of our
> suffering. In exchange, I shall have my own little tales of misfortune to tell her,
> the real reason for my journey to Europe, and the circumstances of yet another
> failure. My nervous breakdown. The beginning of my recovery. Ashamed, I
> shall keep silent until I learn to invent a life. (*DesiradaE*, 259–60)]

The sarcastic pleasure with which Marie-Noëlle imagines Anthea recounting
her African experiences underscores the possibility that the appeal of traditional
politicized approaches to defining one's identity may lie in the opportunity that
they offer for participating in a kind of human mythology — for anchoring our
individual lives in a mythological structure that allows it to seem more significant
than it perhaps is. While such a mythology draws its sense of conviction and creative
energy from the imaginary structures of the black-consciousness movements
discussed earlier, here their political energy is transmuted as colourful stories that
allow for a kind of individual 'happiness', or 'reassurance'. A contrast is suggested
between the grand mythological stories that Anthea constructs, and in a sense also
re-enacts, and the personal stories marked by failure and a certain concern with
individual truth or authenticity ('la véritable raison de mon voyage en Europe') [the
real reason for my trip to Europe]). What is implied by the use of sparse, seemingly
objective language is that this truth is also unadorned and, as a result, unlikely to
deliver 'un certain bonheur' [a certain kind of happiness] (*Desirada*, 281; *DesiradaE*,
259). If Marie-Noëlle points to the fact that Anthea's approach to constructing a
sense of identity represents a more colourful or inventive approach, the protagonist's
assertion that she intends [to] 'inventer des vies' suggests that her starting point is
one of a necessary detachment from such life stories. Crucially, by linking this
identity to a form of critical estrangement figured in terms of 'inventing lives', the
novel also places the protagonist's identity beyond the process of fictionalization
that is presented as intrinsic to defining human identity. This process of self-
fictionalization is necessarily relational occurring in the context of (and, in some
sense, also for the benefit of) 'others' and their stories.[42] Interestingly, it is following
Marie-Noëlle's inconclusive meeting with Mme Duparc (when she accepts that
she will never know the truth concerning her mother's story) that the protagonist
articulates an idea of identity 'in space' or 'in gaps'. Such an identity simultaneously
takes as its starting point and is *in excess* of the fictional impulse. The protagonist's
acknowledgement that she is product of her mother's 'brilliant intellect' is thus
accompanied by her awareness that all is to be reinterpreted:

> Désormais, il me faudra tout simplement vivre avec cet inconnu, ce noir
> derrière moi. Je suis sortie du noir [...]. Dans le fond, elle est un écrivain, ma
> mère, et elle a bâti sa fiction. Moi qui vis, je dois chercher la vérité autre part.
> Où? Il faudrait tout réinterpréter, tout recommencer depuis le commencement.
> (*Desirada*, 252)

> [From now on, I shall simply have to live with the unknown, this area of
> darkness behind me. I came out of the dark [...]. She's basically a writer, my
> mother, and she has constructed her fiction. I'm living it and must search for
> the truth elsewhere. Where? It needs a new reading, starting all over again from
> the beginning [...]. (*DesiradaE*, p 231)][43]

However, by pointing to a process of 'reading' or 'reinterpretation', the protagonist also suggests that this identity is at once a type of radically inventive critical consciousness as well as a ceaselessly evolving point of departure ('Moi qui vis, je dois chercher la vérité autre part. Où? Il faudrait tout réinterpréter, tout recommencer depuis le commencement [...]' [Where? It needs a new reading, starting all over again from the beginning [...]).[44] That this realization inaugurates a new phase of self-assertion for Marie-Noëlle is expressed in the narrative by the shift for the first time from the third to the first person, a pronominal shift that continues until the end of the novel.

In the final analysis, the novel's ending serves to highlight the ambiguous relationship that this identity articulates in relation to existing stories of identity:

> Ludovic s'irritait quand je parlais de ma monstruosité [...]. Il ne comprenait pas qu'en fin de compte, réelle ou imaginaire, cette identité-là avait fini par me plaire. D'une certaine manière, ma monstruosité me rend unique. Grâce à elle, je ne possède ni nationalité, ni pays ni langue. Je peux rejeter ces tracasseries qui tracassent tellement les humains. (*Desirada*, 280–81)

> [Ludovic got annoyed when I talked about my monstrosity theory. [...]. In the end, he didn't realize that I ended up liking this identity, real or imaginary. In some way or other my monstrosity makes me unique. Thanks to it I have no nationality, no country, no language. I can shrug off those tiresome bedevilments that bedevil human beings. (*DesiradaE*, 259)]

In pointing to her separation from the concerns that 'tracassent' other human beings, Marie-Noëlle evokes an ambiguous place 'beyond identity' or an identity that is defined precisely by an absence of 'identification' or an identification with a kind of irreducible otherness: 'Grâce à elle, je ne possède ni nationalité ni pays ni langue' [Thanks to it, I have no nationality, no country, no language] (*Desirada*, 281; *DesiradaE*, 259). But by defining her identity in terms of what she does not possess she implies that this otherness is only possible in the context of these very fictional factors of identity, thereby gesturing towards an identity that is characterized by an oblique relationship of deferral of these very factors.

In conclusion, the novel marks an important development in the relationship between literature, identity and the imagination, themes integral to Condé's œuvre. The ambivalent relationship between 'fact' and 'fiction' or 'fiction' and 'autobiography' that I have explored throughout this book emerges once again in this novel, but this time as a form of philosophical-critical consciousness as well as a practice that is enacted through lived experience and a process that is indistinguishable from and indeed intrinsic to the process of identity formation. This suggests a move beyond a conception of literature as a creative act that 'represents' the individual or a community towards an exploration of literature as a realm of individual imagination in which the individual constructs a 'singular' identity in relation.[45] In placing identity and literature itself at the intersection of individual imagination and experience, the novel moves both notions beyond a Lacanian position of subjection to the imaginary. Identity and literature are instead situated within an ambiguous individually mediated space characterized by a relationship of deferral to real and imaginary representations. With this refiguring of identity and literature, the novel simultaneously raises questions about the status of politics. The novel's ending points to the unresolved status of politics and the ways in which it continues to maintain a powerful claim on the individual imaginations that it represents. Indeed, in *Desirada* politics persists as a sign that is radically divided. On the one hand, the novel appears to proclaim the lack of viability of traditional politics. On the other hand, it is haunted by an oblique nostalgia for the passionate conviction of traditional politics, a nostalgia that is evident in Marie-Noëlle's imagined conversation with Anthea about her trip to Africa which draws heavily on the rhetorical energy of the grand narratives of black-consciousness movements that I described at the start of the chapter. In this irresolution, *Desirada*'s final position diverges from the more clearly optimist reading of the possibilities for political action endorsed at the end of the essay 'O Brave New World'. This divergence may perhaps point to the necessary 'political irresponsibility' that Condé has consistently arrogated to literature. Yet the sense of non-identity that the protagonist claims at the end of the novel may also offer another option (one not necessarily incompatible with the notion of 'political irresponsibility'): the potential to re-imagine the very idea of 'the political' and its future forms.

Notes to Chapter 6

1. See, for example Condé, 'The Role of the Writer'; 'Language and Power'; 'Chercher nos vérités'; 'O Brave New World'; 'Order, Disorder'.
2. This essay is the published version of a keynote address given by Condé at a joint meeting of the Comparative Literature Association and the African Literature Association in 1998.
3. Condé, 'O Brave New World', p. 1.
4. Condé, 'O Brave New World', p. 5.
5. Condé, 'O Brave New World', p. 1.
6. Condé, 'O Brave New World', p. 3.
7. Condé, 'O Brave New World', p. 3.
8. Condé, 'O Brave New World', p. 3.
9. Condé, 'O Brave New World', p. 4.
10. Condé, 'O Brave New World', p. 5.
11. Condé, 'O Brave New World', pp. 4–5.
12. Condé, 'O Brave New World', p. 5.
13. See Sartre, *Qu'est-ce que la littérature?*, p. 75.
14. See for example, Sartre, *Qu'est-ce que la littérature?*, Chapter 1, 'Qu'est-ce qu'écrire?', pp. 13–44.
15. Condé, 'O Brave New World', p. 6.
16. Condé, 'O Brave New World', p. 6.
17. Condé, 'O Brave New World', p. 7.
18. Bongie, *Friends and Enemies*, p. xiii.
19. Roland Barthes, *Mythologies* (selected and translated from French by Annette Lavers) (London: Vintage, 2000), pp. 143–48.
20. For a reading of Marie-Noëlle's response to this advice as pointing to '[une] inadéquation de l'espace urbain aux récits qui tentent de le rendre habitable' [an incompatibility between the urban space and the narratives which attempt to make it habitable] see Dominique Licops, 'Expériences diasporiques et migratoires des villes dans *La Vie scélérate* and *Desirada* de Maryse Condé', *Nottingham French Studies*, 39 (2000), 110–20 (p. 118).
21. Fanon, *PNMB*. Fanon argues that construction of the black is intimately linked to the operation of specific power relations, relations that are produced and reinforced by the capitalist system:

> S'il y a complexe d'infériorité, c'est à la suite d'un double processus:
> — économique d'abord

— par intériorisation ou, mieux, épidermisation de cette infériorité, ensuite. (*PNMB*, 8)
— [If there is an inferiority complex, it is the outcome of a double process:
— primarily economic
— subsequently, the internalization — or better, the epidermalization — of this inferiority.]
(*BSWM*, 4)]

22. Jacques Lacan, 'Le Stade du miroir comme formateur de la fonction du Je telle qu'elle nous est révélée dans l'expérience psychanalytique', in *Ecrits I* (Paris: Seuil, 1966), pp. 89–97.

23. Lacan, *Ecrits I*, pp. 90–91.

24. Anthony Elliott, *Psychoanalytical Theory: An Introduction* (Basingstoke: Palgrave, 2000), p. 104.

25. In *Ecrits I*, Lacan observes: 'Il y suffit de comprendre le stade du miroir *comme une identification* au sens plein que l'analyse donne à ce terme: à savoir la transformation produite chez le sujet quand il assume une image [...]' [The Mirror Stage should be understood as an identification, in the full sense that the analysis gives to this term: that is, the transformation created in the subject when he assumes an image] (*Ecrits I*, p. 90, my translation).

26. Celia Britton, 'Structuralist and Post-Structuralist Psychoanalytic and Marxist Theories', in *The Cambridge History of Literary Criticism*, vol. VIII ('From Formalism to Post-Structuralism'), ed. by Raman Selden (Cambridge: Cambridge University Press, 1995), pp. 197–252 (pp. 104–05).

27. Britton, 'Structuralist and Post-Structuralist', pp. 104–05.

28. For a provocative account of the impact of instability and changes to the traditional social and cultural systems (brought about by capitalism) on individual subjectivities see Gilles Deleuze and Félix Guattari, *L'Anti-Œdipe: Capitalisme et schizophrénie* (Paris: Minuit, 1972).

29. See Condé, 'Chercher nos vérités'.

30. Celia Britton, *The Sense of Community in French Caribbean Fiction* (Liverpool: Liverpool University Press, 2008). Britton notes that the novel does nevertheless evoke a diffuse idea of community based on exclusion or 'not belonging' (p. 135). For example, the protagonist's meeting with a taxi driver who recounts his own experience of failing to find himself in Guadeloupe (while at the same time 'not considering himself to be French') points to this idea: À vrai dire, Marie-Noëlle n'écoutait guère cette histoire, fastidieuse comme une rengaine. Combien étaient-ils à travers la planète Terre à partager la même mal-vie? Assez pour former une autre race, assez pour peupler un autre monde' [In fact, Marie-Noëlle was hardly listening to his story as tedious as a scratched record. How many were there across the planet Earth who shared the same tormented life? Enough to form another race, enough to form another world] (*Desirada*, 244; *DesiradaE*, 224).

31. For a discussion of the grandmother as an agent of obstruction in identitarian quests in Francophone Caribbean fiction see Lydie Moudileno, 'Le Rire de la grand-mère: Insolence et sérénité dans *Desirada* de Maryse Condé', *French Review: Journal of the American Association of Teachers of French*, 76 (2003), 1151–60.

32. In Pfaff, *Conversations*, Condé, commenting on the rationale behind the writing of the historical novel *Ségou*, observes: 'History [...] must henceforth be subordinated to the work of familial or collective memory' (p. 99).

33. Ludovic identifies family as a myth: 'Nos mythes ont la vie dure. Nous croyons que les liens de parenté sont les plus solides. [...].Tous ces enfants torturés, [...] nous sommes là à répéter [...] des choses que la réalité contredit' [Our myths are hard to dispel. We believe the ties of parenthood to be the strongest. [...]. All those tortured children, [...], and here we are repeating things that reality contradicts] (*Desirada*, 277; *DesiradaE*, 255).

34. For a fuller discussion of the role of elective relationships in the novel see Britton, *The Sense of Community*. pp. 136–39.

35. Britton, *The Sense of Community*, p. 137.

36. Mme Esmondas ne lui posait aucune question, comme si ce qui se passait au troisième étage ne lui importait pas. Elle ne lui demandait jamais de laver les assiettes sales, balayer, descendre la poubelle. Elle l'asseyait comme une princesse dans un fauteuil et lui racontait sans se vanter les cas les plus extraordinaires où elle avait montré sa force [Mme Esmondas never asked questions, as if what went on on the third floor was none of her business. She never asked M-N to wash the dishes, sweep or take the garbage down. She sat her down in an armchair like a princess and related to her in an unassuming way the most extraordinary cases in which she had demonstrated her powers] (*Desirada*, 46; *DesiradaE*, 35–36).

37. Marie-Noëlle's attitude of openness towards difference contrasts with the fear that her indecipherable difference inspires in the mourners at Ranélise's funeral in Guadeloupe. This suggests that the state of 'not belonging' in terms of the traditional markers of identity may have a positive value that translates into an openness to difference and, in contrast, that defining one's self in these traditional terms (national identity, ethnicity etc.) may limit one's capacity to be open to difference.

38. In addition to friendships, the novel features a number of mentoring-style relationships (both in the context of friendships and of professional relationships). Anthea, Marie-Noëlle's friend, also acts as her mentor, encouraging her to enrol for her doctorate and, eventually, finding her a permanent position at a New England university. Marie-Noëlle herself acts as a mentor to the students at the college at which she teaches (pp. 141–42).

39. In 'Le Rire', Moudileno observes: 'Marie-Noëlle trouve en effet sa place dans le monde à l'issue de sa quête parce qu'elle choisit de vivre aux États-Unis, en dehors du territoire de la mère, à "l'étranger" par rapport à l'origine. "Son" Amérique se définirait alors comme espace où s'est consommée la distance nécessaire à l'autonomie du sujet' [In fact, M-N finds her place in the world after the end of her identity quest because she choose to lives in the United States, outside of the mother's territory. 'Her' America can thus be defined as the space that allows the subject to attain autonomy through an estrangement from origins] (p. 1158).

40. Licops, 'Expériences diasporiques et migratoires', makes a similar argument, noting that Garvey produces 'un récit syncrétique qui rend l'espace urbain habitable' [a syncretic narrative that makes the urban space habitable] , p. 119.

41. See Condé, 'O Brave New World', p. 4.

42. It is also implied by means of the stranger who sits down at Garvey's and Ludovic's table and shares the story of his life with them that the experience of living 'pareille à des fourmis' [like ants] in the impersonal, frenetic metropolitan space means that the desire to tell the story of our lives to ourselves and others is all the more keenly felt: 'Finalement, un homme s'était assis à leur table et leur avait raconté l'histoire de sa vie. Histoire abracadabrante. Histoire sans doute à moitié imaginaire où il était question de la férocité des femmes' [Finally a man came and sat at their table and told them the story of his life. Some preposterous story that he must have made up, in part about the savagery of women] (*Desirada*, 242; *DesiradaE*, 222).

43. For a discussion of the role of gaps in identity, see Sourieau, 'Entretien avec Maryse Condé', pp. 1091–98.

44. See also Karin Schwerdtner, 'Wandering, Women and Writing', *Dalhousie French Studies*, 73 (2005), 129–37. Schwerdtner assigns prominence to the theme of wandering in the work arguing that 'the question of wandering [...] is linked to the problem of uncertainty — a mobility of affiliation [...]' (p. 136).

45. Sourieau, 'Entretien avec Maryse Condé'. Condé observes: 'Je pense c'est comme cela qu'il faut concevoir l'identité, comme un lien que l'on entretient avec un territoire réel ou imaginaire. Qu'il soit imaginaire n'a pas d'importance du moment qu'il fonctionne en tant que lieu auquel l'individu peut se rattacher' [I think that that is how you should conceive of identity, as a link that one maintains with a real or imaginary place. Whether the place is real or imaginary is of no importance, as long as it functions as a place to which the individual can form an attachment] (p. 1096).

CONCLUSION

Mapping the Future: Literature and Engagement

> Passé l'enthousiasme de mes vingt ans, je n'ai plus jamais envie de militer [...]. Je ne suis pas du tout quelqu'un qui a envie de militer mais on aime utiliser mon nom et je me laisse souvent prendre au jeu. (*EMC*, 133)

> [After the enthusiasm of my twenties, I no longer sought active political involvement [...]. I do not at all enjoy active (political) involvement, but people like to use my name, and I allow myself to get caught up in the game. (*CMC*, 90)]

> 'I see the mapping of a new world, a brave new world to quote Miranda in Shakespeare's *Tempest*.' ('O Brave New World', p. 6)

I started this book a with reflection on the complex sets of relationships that Condé's work establishes to notions of space, literature, identity and politics with a view to addressing the current critical debate in the field of Francophone Postcolonial Studies surrounding the relationship between various forms of political action or 'resistance' and literature. My various readings have presented Condé's practice of literature as shaped by a literal, rhetorical and generic mobility that disrupts the critical tendency in postcolonial studies to apply ready-made politicized readings to her work. In fact, as I have demonstrated, a central preoccupation that emerges in Condé's œuvre is a concern with the questioning of this field's key critical commonplaces: the representative role of the writer and literature, ideas of individual, collective identity and community as well as the notion of 'politics' and 'literature' itself. On the whole, however, this process of questioning of the critical assumptions of the field of postcolonial studies has been largely implicit and refracted through Condé's explicit and ongoing self-positioning in relation to the metropolitan French and Francophone Caribbean literary fields. Thus, while Condé's work undoubtedly offers a critique of the politicization of the role of literature and the author in the field of postcolonial studies, her critique raises broader questions concerning the traditions of literary and critical practice in which her work may be read.

Through its appeal to the freedom of literature, Condé's work offers an alternative vision of literary engagement that situates engagement in literature itself, configured as both a formal and creative practice. This practice is also distinctly critically conscious. Indeed, Condé's vision is infused with a type of postmodern scepticism towards the viability of all grand narratives including those concerning 'identity' and 'community' along with traditional identity and anti-colonial politics, This scepticism points to the central role that Condé envisages for literature: that of re-imagining these very notions along with critical practice itself. But as I have illustrated in Chapters 2 and 6, this process of re-imagining is marked by a perhaps necessarily unresolved emotional and intellectual implication in the very categories that are assumed to be outmoded. In a key sense then, Condé's practice of literature may be viewed as fundamentally utopian.

In 'The Impossible Space: Explorations of Utopia in French Writing' Angela Kershaw, Pamela Moore and Hélène Stafford characterize utopia as a 'concept and literary genre' that takes for granted a notion of space.[1] Drawing on Thomas More's reading of utopia as both a 'no-place' and a 'good place', Kershaw, Moore and Stafford point to the term's complex relationship to existing social and geographical contexts, noting that while 'utopian discourses are produced within specific geographical spaces', the very idea of utopia takes as its essential frame of reference a reformulation of notions of 'origins' and, with this, a disruption of the possibility for defining 'specific geographic spaces'.[2] In addition, Kershaw, Moore and Stafford's discussion of the notion's ambivalent relationship to questions of origins implies that a similar ambivalence is relevant to a consideration of the term's use as a critical concept. In this respect, they observe that utopia may serve as 'a conceptual tool to achieve social and political change in the real world by *adapting* or *transforming* what already is. It may also be used as a blueprint for the creation of a new community that rejects what already is.'[3] In this concluding chapter I shall draw on this reading of utopia to explore the implications of the process of re-imagining that is enacted in Condé's work.

The complex intertextual structuring of Condé's œuvre is suggestive of both ideas of 'no-place' and a good or ideal place, ideas that take as their starting point this work's implication in historically and culturally specific intellectual traditions. On the one hand, as I have observed, for example, in Chapters 2 and 4, Condé's texts undertake open-ended readings of various French, Francophone and Anglophone literary traditions in ways that also point to the creative incorporation and transformation of these traditions by her work. On the other hand, these readings foreground the role of key intellectual traditions for providing the conditions of possibility for the intertextual practice that defines Condé's literary writings and for the types of questions that are addressed within these. As I highlighted in my introduction, the major debates that emerged in the post-World War II French intellectual culture surrounding the relationship between Sartrean notions of 'littérature engagée' and freedom along with the reformulations of these ideas by French theorists such as the *nouveaux romanciers* and Maurice Blanchot have provided a particularly productive framework for Condé's creative and critical interventions.

At the centre of the reformulation of literary engagement that emerges in Condé's work is an attention to literature itself as a type of spatial practice, a practice that explores the process of globalization in its thematic and formal articulations. As I noted in Chapters 5 and 6, the possibilities presented by globalization for developing an extended conception of Francophone Caribbean identity is a key preoccupation of Condé's work. This focus is matched by an examination of globalization as a generic practice which is reflected in the complex cross-generic qualities of Condé's writings that blend fiction, autobiography, criticism, philosophy, theatre and 'spoken performances' in the interview. Such globalizing generic practices necessarily call into question the conventional definitions of literature as exclusively concerned with 'prose' or 'writing'.

Another important sense in which Condé's work can be viewed as serving as a space of engagement, then, is in terms of its mapping across these various sites (textual, visual, performative, etc.) of her own intellectual and experiential encounters with works from both metropolitan French and Francophone Caribbean literary traditions. This form of literary engagement is thus realized through explorations of the formal characteristics and generic boundaries of 'literature' along with a reflection on the routes of influence that link Francophone Caribbean and metropolitan French writing.

The ambiguous relationship to notions of autobiography and fiction that I identified as a defining characteristic of Condé's work in Chapters 4 and 6 is intrinsic to this process of mapping. As Condé's comments in the first quotation in the epigraph to this conclusion point out, the evolution of her thinking on engagement and literature has been inextricably linked to her own life experiences and, specifically, to her disillusionment with political action during her time in Africa. Condé's appeal to the freedom of literature thus emerges out of her personal experience of the failure of practical engagement, one that is put in to dialogue with her readings of key texts belonging to the metropolitan French and Francophone traditions that I highlighted above. But my discussion of the complex relationship between fiction and autobiography in Chapter 4 illustrates that this dialogue is itself filtered through a type of philosophical engagement that raises questions about the continuity between, on the one hand, the real author and, on the other, her autobiographical and fictional protagonists. It is this philosophical process which also frames the possibilities for re-imagining explored within Condé's work as a form of heuristic engagement based on confronting her own experiences with the utopian visions of metropolitan French and Francophone Caribbean works.

This would perhaps explain the importance that Condé ascribes to the reader's freedom. This freedom is not conceived in the political terms envisaged by Sartre but rather in the expression of individual choice and in the exercise of the individual imagination. In placing a notion of individual freedom of choice at the centre of her reformulation of engagement, Condé presents a challenge to the sectarian and collective logic of the traditional conception of politics that relies (as I highlighted, for example, in my discussion of the reception of *En attendant le bonheur* and of African–American identity politics in *Les Derniers Rois mages*) on an unambiguous choice of individual and group identity. Choice, as it is evinced in Condé's œuvre, points instead to the potential individual freedom to forge relationships across communitarian lines as well as cultural and intellectual traditions. Therefore, as I observed in Chapter 3, this focus creates the conditions for the emergence of a more fluid, organic conception of community. With this emphasis on forging relationships outside of established traditional social categories and systems and on fostering in the reader an openness to difference, Condé's work also points to an enlarged conception of engagement as an 'ethic of responsibility' that takes the author and the individual reader beyond their cultural, historical and identitarian determinations.

While the individual freedom evoked in Condé's work is necessarily actualized at the intersection of literature and the 'real world', for Condé, literature has a key role to play in serving as a site for dreaming on to which the reader projects his own individual experiences and imaginings. This process of engagement may be viewed as heuristic, realized through encounters between the reader's experiences and the text; it is also takes as its foundation a freeing of the reader to re-imagine existing categories and connections, as well as to dream or imagine connections that do not yet exist (and by extension to imagine him or herself in relation to these).

To read Condé's work at the intersection of these two interrelated views of engagement is therefore to track and also to participate in the work's interventions in key debates in the broader fields of French Studies and Postcolonial Studies, interventions that unsettle accepted critical and disciplinary boundaries. Through its emphasis on questioning, its formal restlessness as well as its permeability to a range of cultural influences, Condé's œuvre unleashes the creative and critical possibilities of the *questioning* of literature that Ann Jefferson suggests is intrinsic to the notion of 'littérature engagée' itself,[4] situating these within a broader, transatlantic creative-critical field constituted, amongst others, by theories of the French avant-garde, Francophone Caribbean literature and African-American literature. Such a process necessarily presents a challenge to re-read or perhaps to re-imagine polarized critical orthodoxies in the field of 'French Studies' and 'Postcolonial Studies' that cast 'committed writing' or 'politics' as incompatible with or opposed to 'the literary'. It also necessarily presents a challenge to the place of 'Francophone Caribbean literature' on the margins of the fields of 'French Literature' and of 'French Studies', one that speaks to the possibility of situating 'Francophone Caribbean literature' in what the signatories of the Manifeste 'pour une littérature-monde' characterize as 'un dialogue dans un vaste ensemble poly-phonique' [a dialogue in a vast polyphonic system].[5] Through what Condé's work presents as its essential involvement in this multi-cultural dialogue, the body of writing called 'Francophone Caribbean literature' potentially reverses its position as merely an object of study, claiming instead an 'engaged' position from which to comment creatively and critically on 'literature', 'criticism' and 'politics', in their broadest sense. To view this literature as a type of 'littérature-monde en français' is to re-activate the commitment to internationalist solidarity that connects the anti-colonial projects of Césaire, Sartre and Fanon with the French avant-garde and American modernisms, reconfiguring this solidarity as a type of worldly literary agency.[6] Such a project may well gesture towards the possibility of a mutual renewal of 'politics' and 'literature' by the energy of the imaginary. That this process of renewal may ultimately not be intelligible as 'political' or, for that matter, even 'literary' is, in a sense, the fullest realization of the ambiguous possibilities for mapping the future that the space of literature offers.

Notes to the Conclusion

1. Angela Kershaw, Pamela Moore and Hélène Stafford, 'Introduction', in *The Impossible Space: Explorations of Utopia in French Writing*, ed. by Angela Kershaw, Pamela Moore and Hélène Stafford (= *Strathclyde Modern Language Studies*, n.s., 6 (2000)), pp. 1–14 (p. 2).
2. Kershaw, Moore and Stafford, 'Introduction', p. 4.
3. Kershaw, Moore and Stafford, 'Introduction', p. 8.
4. Ann Jefferson, *Biography and the Question of Literature in France* (Oxford: Oxford University Press, 2007), p. 284.
5. 'Manifeste «pour une littérature-monde»', *Le Monde*, 19 March 2007, pp. 1–6 (p. 5) <http://www.étonnants-voyageurs.com/spip.php?article1574> [accessed 23 July 2010].
6. In using the term 'worldly', I am thinking of Said's reading of 'worldliness' as the essential engagement of the critic and the text in the world. See for example, Edward W. Said, *Reflections on Exile and Other Literary and Cultural Essays* (London: Granta Books, 2000). Said advocates a critical predisposition of worldliness, an attentiveness to how a work of literature is 'connected both to its specific historical and cultural situations and to a whole world of literature and formal articulations' (p. 382).

BIBLIOGRAPHY

Works of Maryse Condé

Novels

Moi, Tituba, sorcière... Noire de Salem (n.p.: Mercure de France, 1986)
I, Tituba, Black Witch of Salem, trans. by Richard Philcox (Charlottesville and London: University Press of Virginia, 1992)
Traversée de la Mangrove, Collection Folio (n.p.: Mercure de France, 1989)
Les Derniers Rois mages, Collection Folio (n.p.: Mercure de France, 1992)
The Last of the African Kings, trans. by Richard Philcox (Lincoln: University of Nebraska Press, 1997)
La Colonie du nouveau monde (Paris: Editions Robert Laffont, 1993)
En attendant le bonheur (Heremakhonon) (Paris: Robert Laffont, 1997)
Heremakhonon: A Novel, trans. by Richard Philcox (Boulder, CO: Lynne Rienner, 2000)
Desirada (Paris: Editions Robert Laffont, 1997)
Desirada: A Novel, trans. by Richard Philcox (New York: Soho, 2000)
Pays mêlé: Nouvelles (Paris: Editions Robert Laffont, 1997)
Le Cœur à rire et à pleurer: Contes vraies de mon enfance (Paris: Editions Robert Laffont, 1999)
Tales from the Heart: True Tales from my Childhood, trans. by Richard Philcox (New York: Soho, 2001)

Essays

'Parlez-moi d'amour...?', *Autrement*, 9 (1983), 206–12
'Notes sur un retour au pays natal', *Revue franco-haïtienne* (supplement), 176 (1987), 7–23
La Parole des femmes: Essais sur des romancières des Antilles de langue française (Paris: L'Harmattan: 1993)
'The Role of the Writer', *World Literature Today*, 67 (1993), 697–99
'Language and Power: Words as Miraculous Weapons', *CLA Journal*, 39 (1995), 18–25
'Chercher nos vérités', in *Penser la Créolité*, ed. by Maryse Condé and Madeleine Cottenet-Hage (Paris: Karthala, 1995), pp. 305–10
'O Brave New World', *Research in African Literatures*, 29 (1998), 1–7
'Order, Disorder, Freedom and the West Indian Writer', *Yale French Studies*, 83 (1993), 121–35
'The Tribulations of a Postcolonial Writer in New York', *PMLA*, 122 (2007), 336–37
'The Stealers of Fire: The French-Speaking Writers of the Caribbean and their Strategies of Liberation', *Journal of Black Studies*, 35 (2004), 154–64

Critical Texts

AIJAZ, AHMAD, *In Theory: Class, Nations, Literatures* (London: Verso, 1992)
ALESSANDRINI, ANTHONY C., ed., *Frantz Fanon: Critical Perspectives* (London and New York: Routledge, 1999)

AMIREH, AMAL, and LISA SUHAIR MAJAJ, eds, *Going Global: The Transnational Reception of Third World Women Writers* (New York and London: Garland Publishing Inc., 2000)

APTER, EMILY, *Continental Drift: From National Characters to Virtual Subjects* (Chicago, IL: Chicago University Press, 1999)

ARAUJO, NARA, ed., *L'Œuvre de Maryse Condé: Questions et Réponses à propos d'une écrivaine politiquement incorrecte* (Paris: L'Harmattan, 1996)

ARNOLD, A. J,, *Modernism and Negritude: The Poetics and Poetry of Aimé Césaire* (Cambridge, MA: Harvard University Press, 1998)

ARNOLD, JAMES, 'The Novelist as Critic', *World Literature Today*, 67 (1993) 711–16

ATTRIDGE, DEREK, *The Singularity of Literature* (London and New York: Routledge, 2004)

AWKWARD, MICHAEL, *Inspiriting Influences: Tradition, Revision and Afro-American Women's Novels* (New York and Oxford: Columbia University Press: 1989)

BAHRI, DEEPIKA, *Native Intelligence: Aesthetics, Politics and Postcolonial Literature* (Minneapolis and London: University of Minnesota Press, 2003)

BARBOUR, SARAH, and GERISE HERNDON, eds, *Emerging Perspectives on Maryse Condé: A Writer of her Own* (Trenton, NJ, and Asmara, Eritrea: Africa World Press, 2006)

BARTHES, ROLAND, *S/Z* (Paris: Seuil, 1970)

——*Le Bruissement de la langue: Essais Critiques IV* (Paris: Seuil, 1993)

——*Mythologies*, trans. by Annette Lavers (London: Vintage, 2000)

BARTOW, JOANNA R., *Subject to Change: The Lessons of Latin American Women's Testimonio for Truth, Fiction, and Theory* (Chapel Hill: University of North Carolina, 2005)

BÉCEL, PASCALE, '*Moi Tituba, sorcière... Noire de Salem*, A Tale of Petite Maronne', *Callaloo*, 18 (1995), 608–15

BÉRARD, STÉPHANIE, *Théâtres des Antilles, Traditions et Scènes Contemporaines* (préface d'Ina Césaire) (Paris: L'Harmattan, 2009)

BERGNER, GWEN, 'Who is that Masked Woman? Or, The Role of Gender in Fanon's *Black Skin, White Masks*', *Publications of the Modern Language Association*, 110 (1995), 75–88

BERNABÉ, JEAN, PATRICK CHAMOISEAU and RAPHAËL CONFIANT, *Éloge de la Créolité* (Paris: Gallimard, 1993)

——*In Praise of Creoleness*, trans. by Mohamed B. Taleb-Khyar (Baltimore, MD: Johns Hopkins University Press, 1990)

BEVERLEY, JOHN, 'The Margin at the Centre: On *Testimonio*', in *De/Colonizing the Subject: The Politics of Gender in Women's Autobiography*, ed. by Sidonie Smith and Julia Watson (Minneapolis: University of Minnesota Press, 1992), pp. 91–114

BHABHA, HOMI K., *The Location of Culture* (London and New York: Routledge, 1994)

BHAVNANI, KUM-KUM, ed., *Feminism and Race*, 1st edn, Oxford Readings in Feminism (Oxford: Oxford University Press, 2001)

BISHOP, MICHAEL, and CHRISTOPHER ELSON, eds, 'Transmigrations in Maryse Condé's True Tales', in *French Prose in 2000*, Faux Titre 231 (Amsterdam and New York: Rodopi, 2002), pp. 75–82

BLANCHOT, MAURICE, *L'Espace littéraire* (Paris: Gallimard, 1968)

BONGIE, CHRIS, *Friends and Enemies: The Scribal Politics of Post/Colonial Literature* (Liverpool: Liverpool University Press, 2008)

BOSE, PURNIMA, *Organizing Empire: Individualism, Collective Agency, and India* (Durham: Duke University Press, 2003)

BOURDIEU, PIERRE, *La Distinction: Critique sociale du jugement* (Paris: Minuit, 1979)

——*Les Règles de l'art: Génèse et structure du champ littéraire* (Paris: Seuil, 1992)

BOYCE DAVIES, CAROLE, and ELAINE SAVORY FIDO, eds, *Out of the Kumbla: Caribbean Women and Literature* (New Jersey: African World Press, 1990)

BOYCE DAVIES, CAROLE, *Black Women, Writing and Identity: Migrations of the Subject* (London and New York: Routledge, 1994)

BRAXTON, JOANNE M., *Black Women Writing Autobiography: A Tradition within a Tradition* (Philadelphia, PA: Temple University Press, 1989)

BRITTON, CELIA, *The Nouveau Roman: Fiction, Theory and Politics* (New York: St. Martin's Press Inc., 1992)

—— 'Structuralist and Post-Structuralist Psychoanalytic and Marxist Theories', in *The Cambridge History of Literary Criticism*, vol. VIII ('From Formalism to Post-Structuralism'), ed. by Raman Selden (Cambridge: Cambridge University Press, 1995), pp. 197–252

—— *Edouard Glissant and Postcolonial Theory: Strategies of Language and Resistance* (Charlottesville and London: University of Virginia Press, 1999)

—— 'The (De) Construction of Subjectivity in Daniel Maximin's *L'Ile et une nuit*', in *Francophone Texts and Postcolonial Theory*, ed. by Britton and Michael Syrotinski (= *Paragraph*, 24, 3 (2001)), 31–44

—— *Race and the Unconscious: Freudianism in French Caribbean Thought* (Oxford: Legenda and European Humanities Research Centre, University of Oxford, 2002)

—— 'New Approaches to Francophone Literature', *Francophone Postcolonial Studies*, 1 (2003), 29–32

—— 'Breaking the Rules: Irrelevance/ Irreverence in Maryse Condé's *Traversée de la Mangrove*', *French Cultural Studies*, 15 (2004), 35–47

—— *The Sense of Community in French Caribbean Fiction* (Liverpool: Liverpool University Press, 2008)

—— and MICHAEL SYROTINSKI, 'Introduction', in *Francophone Texts and Postcolonial Theory*, ed. by Britton and Syrotinski (= *Paragraph: A Journal of Modern Critical Theory*, 24, 3 (2001)), 1–11

BROWDY DE HERNANDEZ, JENNIFER, 'Of Tortillas and Texts: Postcolonial Dialogues in the Latin American Testimonial', in GHOSH, BOSE and MOHANTY, eds, *Feminist Dialogues on Third World Women's Literature and Film*, pp. 163–84

BUTLER, JUDITH, *Gender Trouble: Feminism and the Subversion of Identity* (New York and London, 1999)

CASE, FREDERICK IVOR, *Identity Crisis: Studies in the Guadeloupean and Martinican Novel* (Sherbrooke, Quebec: Naaman, 1985)

CÉSAIRE, AIMÉ, 'L'Homme de culture et ses responsabilités,' *Présence Africaine*, 24–25 (Feb– May 1956), 116–22

—— *Cahier d'un retour au pays natal* (Paris: Présence Africaine, 1983)

—— *Discours sur le Colonialisme* (Paris and Dakar: Présence Africaine, 1989)

—— *Notebook of a Return to My Native Land/ Cahier d'un retour au pays natal* (trans. by Mireille Rosello and Annie Pritchard and with intro by Mireille Rosello (Newcastle upon Tyne: Bloodaxe Books, 1995)

CHOW, REY, 'The Politics of Admittance: Female Sexual Agency, Miscegenation, and the Formation of Community in Frantz Fanon', in ALESSANDRINI, ed., *Frantz Fanon: Critical Perspectives*, pp. 34–56

CHRISTIAN, BARBARA, *Black Feminist Criticism: Perspectives on Black Women Writers* (New York: Pergamon Press, 1985)

COMBE, DOMINIQUE, *Aimé Césaire: Cahier d'un retour au pays natal*, Etudes Littéraires (Paris: Presses Universitaires de France, 1993)

CONDÉ, MARYSE, and MADELEINE COTTENET-HAGE, eds, *Penser la Créolité* (Paris: Karthala, 1995)

COTTENET-HAGE, MADELEINE, '*Traversée de la Mangrove*: Réflexion sur les interviews', in *L'Œuvre de Maryse Condé: Questions et réponses à propos d'une écrivaine politiquement incorrecte*, ed. by Nara Araujo (Paris: L'Harmattan, 1996), pp. 157–71

COTTENET-HAGE, MADELEINE, and LYDIE MOUDILENO, eds, *Maryse Condé: Une Nomade Inconvenante: Mélanges offerts à Maryse Condé* (Petit-Bourg, Guadeloupe: Ibis Rouge Editions, 2002)

CUDJOE, SELWYN, *Caribbean Women Writers: Essays from the First International Conference* (Wellesley, MA: Calaloux, 1990)

CULLER, JONATHAN, *On Deconstruction: Theory and Criticism after Structuralism* (London: Routledge, 1993)

DASH, MICHAEL J., *Edouard Glissant*, Cambridge Studies in African and Caribbean Literature (Cambridge: Cambridge University Press, 1995)

DAVIS, ANGELA Y., 'Foreword', in *I, Tituba, Black Witch of Salem*, by Maryse Condé, trans. by Richard Philcox (Charlottesville and London: University Press of Virginia, 1992), pp. xi–xiii

DAVIS, GREGSON, *Aimé Césaire* (Cambridge, New York and Melbourne: Cambridge University Press, 1997)

DELEUZE, GILLES, and FÉLIX GUATTARI, *L'Anti-Œdipe: Capitalisme et schizophrénie* (Paris: Minuit, 1972)

DEPESTRE, RENÉ, *Bonjour et adieu à la négritude suivi de Travaux d'identités; Essais* (Paris: Editions Robert Laffont, 1980)

DERRIDA, JACQUES, *Writing and Difference*, trans. by ALAN BASS (Chicago, IL: University of Chicago Press, 1978)

DJELAL, KADIR, 'Introduction: On Being at the Other End of the World', *World Literature Today* (Focus on Maryse Condé), 67, 4 (1993), 695–96

DONNELL, ALISON, and SARAH LAWSON WELSH, eds, *The Routledge Reader in Caribbean Literature*, 1st edn (London and New York: Routledge, 1996)

DOYLE, LAURA, and KENNETH SILVERMAN, eds, *Bodies of Resistance: New Phenomenologies of Politics, Agency, and Culture* (Evanston, IL: Northwestern University Press, 2001)

EAKIN, PAUL, JOHN, *Touching the World: Reference in Autobiography* (Princeton, NJ: Princeton University Press, 1992)

EDWARDS, BRENT HAYES, *The Practice of Diaspora: Literature, Translation and the Rise of Black Internationalism* (Cambridge, MA, and London: Harvard University Press, 2003)

ELLIOTT, ANTHONY, *Psychoanalytical Theory: An Introduction* (Basingstoke: Palgrave, 2000)

FABRE, MICHEL, *From Harlem to Paris: Black American Writers in France 1840–1980* (Urbana and Chicago: University of Illinois Press, 1991)

FANON, FRANTZ, *Peau noire, masques blancs* (Paris: Editions du Seuil, 1971)

—— *Black Skin, White Masks*, trans. by Charles Lam Markmann (London: Pluto Press, 2008)

—— *Les Damnés de la terre* (Paris: Gallimard, 1991)

—— *Pour la révolution africaine: Écrits politiques* (Paris: La Découverte, 2001)

FELSKI, RITA, *Beyond Feminist Aesthetics: Feminist Literature and Social Change* (London: Hutchinson Radius, 1989)

FORSDICK, CHARLES, *Victor Segalen and the Aesthetics of Diversity: Journeys between Cultures* (New York: Oxford University Press, 2000)

—— 'Travelling Concepts: Postcolonial Approaches to Exoticism', in *Francophone Texts and Postcolonial Theory*, ed. by Celia Britton and Michael Syrotinski (= *Paragraph*, 24, 3 (2001)), 12–29

—— 'État Present: Between "French" and "Francophone": French Studies and the Postcolonial Turn', *French Studies*, 59 (2005), 523–30

FORSDICK, CHARLES, and DAVID MURPHY, eds, *Francophone Postcolonial Studies: A Critical Introduction* (London and New York: Arnold, 2003)

FORSDICK, CHARLES, and DAVID MURPHY, eds, *Postcolonial Thought in the French-Speaking World* (Liverpool: Liverpool University Press, 2009)

FOUCAULT, MICHEL, *Histoire de la sexualité: La Volonté de savoir* (France: Editions Gallimard, 1976)

FULTON, DAWN, *Signs of Dissent: Maryse Condé and Postcolonial Criticism* (Charlottesville and London: University of Virginia Press, 2008)

GATES, HENRY LOUIS, JR, 'Critical Fanonism,' *Critical Inquiry*, 17 (1991), 457–70

——ed., *Race, Writing and Difference* (Chicago, IL, and London: University of Chicago Press, 1985)

GENETTE, GÉRARD, *Paratexts: Thresholds of Interpretation*, trans. by Jane E. Lewin, foreword by Richard Macksey (Cambridge and New York: Cambridge University Press, 1997)

GHOSH, BISHNUPRIYA, BRINDA BOSE and CHANDRA TALPADE MOHANTY, eds, *Feminist Dialogues on Third World Women's Literature and Film* (New York: Garland, 1997)

GIBSON, NIGEL C., ed., *Rethinking Fanon: The Continuing Dialogue* (New York: Humanity, 1999)

GILMORE, LEIGH, *Autobiographics: A Feminist Theory of Women's Self-Representation* (Ithaca, NY, and London: Cornell University Press, 1994)

GILROY, PAUL, *The Black Atlantic: Double Consciousness* (London and New York: Verso, 1993)

GLENDINNING, SIMON, and ROBERT EAGLESTON, eds, *Derrida's Legacy: Literature and Philosophy* (Abingdon: Routledge, 2008)

GLISSANT, EDOUARD, *Introduction à une poétique du divers* (Paris: Gallimard, 1996)

GOLDTHORPE, R., *Sartre: Literature and Theory* (Cambridge: Cambridge University Press, 1984)

GORDON, LEWIS R., *Fanon and the Crisis of the European Man: An Essay on Philosophy and the Human Sciences* (New York: Routledge, 1995)

GORDON, LEWIS, et al., eds, *Fanon: A Critical Reader* (Oxford: Blackwell, 1996), pp. 74–84

GREEN, KEITH, and JILL LEBIHAN, *Critical Theory and Practice: A Course Book* (London and New York: Routledge, 1996)

GREEN, MARY JEAN, et al., *Postcolonial Subjects: Francophone Women's Writers* (Minneapolis: Minnesota University Press, 1996)

GUÉRIN, DANIEL, *Les Antilles décolonisées* (Introduction par Aimé Césaire) (Paris: Présence Africaine, 1956)

HAIGH, SAMANTHA, *Mapping a Tradition: Francophone Women's Writing from Guadeloupe* (Leeds: Maney Publishing, 2001)

——ed., *An Introduction to Caribbean Francophone Writing: Guadeloupe and Martinique*, 1st edn (Oxford and New York: Berg, 1999)

HANDLEY, GEORGE B. 'It's an Unbelievable Story': Testimony and Truth in the Work of Rosario Ferré and Rigoberta Menchú', in LASHGARI, ed., *Violence, Silence, and Anger: Women's Writing as Transgression*, pp. 62–79

HALL, STUART, 'Race, Culture and Communications: Looking Backward and Forward at Cultural Studies', *Rethinking Marxism*, 5 (1992), 10–18

HALL, STUART, and PAUL DU GAY, eds, *Questions of Cultural Identity* (London, California and New Delhi: Sage, 1996)

HALL, STUART, DAVID HELD and TONY MCGREW, eds, *Modernity and its Futures*, Understanding Modern Societies, 4 (Cambridge: Polity Press, 1992)

HALLWARD, PETER, *Absolutely Postcolonial: Writing between the Singular and the Specific* (Manchester: Manchester University Press, 2001)

HANSEN, EMMANUEL, *Frantz Fanon: Social and Political Thought* (Ohio: Ohio State University Press, 1977)

HARGREAVES, ALEC, 'Exoticism in Literature and History', *Text and Context*, 1 (1986), 7–18

HARRISON, NICHOLAS, *Circles of Censorship: Censorship and its Metaphors in French Literature, History and Theory* (Oxford: Oxford University Press, 1995)

——*Postcolonial Criticism: History, Theory and the Work of Fiction* (Cambridge: Polity, 2003)

——ed., 'Who Needs an Idea of the Literary?', in *The Idea of the Literary*, ed. by Nicholas Harrison (= *Paragraph*, 28, 2 (2005)), 1–17

HAUSSER, MICHEL, *Essai sur la poétique de la négritude* (Paris: Editions Silex, 1986) (Atelier Nationale des Réproduction des Thèses, Université de Lille III)

HAWTHORN, JEREMY, *A Glossary of Contemporary Literary Theory*, 4th edn (Oxford and New York: Arnold Publishers, 2000)

HERNDON, GERISE, 'Gender Construction and Neocolonialism', *World Literature Today*, 67 (1993), 731–36

HEWITT, LEAH D., 'Condé's Critical Seesaw', *Callaloo*, 18 (1995), 641–51

——'Vérités des fictions autobiographiques', in COTTENET-HAGE and MOUDILENO, eds, *Maryse Condé: Une Nomade Inconvenante*, pp. 163–68

HILL, LESLIE, *Blanchot: Extreme Contemporary* (London and New York: Routledge, 1997)

HOPKINS, DAVID, *Surrealism: A Very Short Introduction* (Oxford: Oxford University Press, 2004)

HUGGAN, GRAHAM, *The Postcolonial Exotic: Marketing the Margins* (London and New York: Routledge, 2001)

HUTCHEON, LINDA, *Irony's Edge: The Theory and Politics of Irony* (London and New York: Routledge, 1995)

IPPOLITO, EMILIA, *Caribbean Women Writers: Identity and Gender*, 1st edn (Rochester, NY, and Woodbridge, Suffolk: Camden House, 2000)

JACK, BELINDA ELIZABETH, *Negritude and Literary Criticism: The History and Theory of "Negro-African" Literature in French* (Westport, CT, and London: Greenwood Press, 1996)

——*Francophone Literatures: An Introductory Survey* (New York: Oxford University Press, 1996)

JEFFERSON, ANN, *Biography and the Question of Literature in France* (Oxford: Oxford University Press, 2007)

JOHNSON, CHRISTOPHER, 'Introduction', in *Thinking in Dialogue: The Role of the Interview in Post-war French Thought*, ed. by Johnson (= *Nottingham French Studies*, 42 (2003)), 1–4

JOHNSON, ERICA L., 'Departures and Arrivals: Home in Maryse Condé's *Le Cœur à rire et à pleurer*', in *Gender and Displacement: Home in Contemporary Francophone Women's Autobiography*, ed. by Natalie Edwards and Christopher Hogarth (Newcastle: Cambridge Scholars Publishing, 2008), pp. 15–33

JUNEJA, RENU, ed., *Caribbean Transactions: West Indian Culture in Literature*, 1st edn, Warwick University Caribbean Studies (London and Basingstoke: Macmillan Education, Ltd, 1996)

KAPLAN, CAREN, 'Resisting Autobiography: Out-Law Genres and Transnational Feminist Subjects', in *De/Colonizing the Subject: The Politics of Gender in Women's Autobiography*, ed. by Sidonie Smith and Julia Watson (Minneapolis: University of Minnesota Press, 1992), pp. 115–38

——*Questions of Travel: Postmodern Discourses of Displacement* (Durham, NC, and London: Duke University Press, 1996)

KERSHAW, ANGELA, PAMELA MOORE and HÉLÈNE STAFFORD, 'Introduction', in *The Impossible Space: Explorations of Utopia in French Writing*, ed. by Kershaw, Moore and Stafford (= *Strathclyde Modern Language Studies*, n.s., 6 (2000)), 1–14

KINNAHAN, LINDA A., *A Poetics of the Feminine: Authority and Literary Tradition in William Carlos Williams, Mina Loy, Denise Levertov and Kathleen Fraser* (Cambridge and New York: Cambridge University Press: 1994)

KRISTEVA, JULIA, *Etrangers à nous-mêmes* (Paris: Gallimard, 1998)

KYOORE, PASCHAL B., *The African and Caribbean Historical Novel in French: A Quest for Identity* (New York, Washington, DC, and Baltimore: Peter Lang: 1996)

LACAN, JACQUES, 'Le Stade du miroir comme formateur de la fonction du Je telle qu'elle nous est révélée dans l'expérience psychanalytique', in *Ecrits I* (Paris: Seuil, 1966), pp. 89–97

LARSON, KATHERINE, 'Resistance from the Margins in George Elliott Clarke's *Beatrice Chancy*', *Canadian Literature*, 189 (2006), 103–18

LASHGARI, DEIRDRE, ed., *Violence, Silence, and Anger: Women's Writing as Transgression* (Charlottesville: University Press of Virginia, 1995)

LEINER, JACQUELINE, *Aimé Césaire: Le terreau primordial*, Etudes littéraires françaises, 56 (Tübingen: GNV, 1993)

LEJEUNE, PHILIPPE, *Je est un autre: L'Autobiographie, de la littérature aux médias* (Paris: Seuil, 1980)

LEQUIN, LUCIE, and MAVRIKAKIS CATHERINE, eds , *La Francophonie sans frontière: Une nouvelle cartographie de l'imaginaire au féminin* (Paris, Budapest and Torino: L'Harmattan, 2001)

LEWIS, BARBARA, 'No Silence: An Interview with Maryse Condé', *Callaloo* (Maryse Condé: A Special Edition), 18 (1995), 543–50

LEWIS, GORDON R., ET AL., eds, *Fanon: A Critical Reader* (Oxford and Cambridge, MA: Blackwell Publishers, 1996)

LICOPS, DOMINIQUE, 'Expériences diasporiques et migratoires des villes dans *La Vie scélérate* and *Desirada* de Maryse Condé', *Nottingham French Studies*, 39 (2000), 110–20

LIONNET, FRANÇOISE, *Postcolonial Representations: Women, Literature, Identity*, 1st edn, Reading Women Writing (Ithaca, NY, and London: Cornell University Press, 1995)

——*Autobiographical Voices: Race, Gender and Self-Portraiture* (Ithaca, NY, and London: Cornell University Press, 1989)

LOOMBA, ANIA, *Colonialism/Postcolonialism* (London and New York: Routledge: 1998)

LYON, JANET, *Manifestoes: Provocations of the Modern* (Ithaca, NY: Cornell University Press, 1999)

MACEY, DAVID, *Frantz Fanon: A Life* (London: Granta Books, 2000)

MAKWARD, CHRISTIANE P., *Mayotte Capécia ou l'Aliénation selon Fanon* (Paris: Editions Karthala, 1999)

MALENA, ANNE, *The Negotiated Self: The Dynamics of Identity in the Francophone Caribbean Narrative*, Francophone Cultures and Literatures, 24 (New York: Peter Lang, 1999)

MANZOR-COATS, LILLIAN, 'Of Witches and Other Things: Maryse Condé's Challenges to Feminist Discourse', *World Literature Today*, 67 (1993), 737–44

MAXIMIN, COLETTE, *Littératures caribéennes comparées* (Pointe-à-Pitre and Paris: Editions Jasor-Karthala, 1996)

McCLINTOCK, ANNE, *Imperial Leather: Race, Gender and Sexuality in the Colonial Contest* (New York and London: Routledge, 1995)

McCUSKER, MAEVE, '"This Creole culture, miraculously forged": The Contradictions of Créolité', in *Francophone Postcolonial Studies: A Critical Introduction*, ed. by Charles Forsdick and David Murphy (London and New York: Arnold, 2003), pp. 112–21

——'Troubler l'ordre de l'oubli: Memory and Forgetting in French Caribbean Literature', *Forum for Modern Languages Studies*, 40 (2004), 438–50

MILLER, CHRISTOPHER, L., *Blank Darkness: Africanist Discourse in French* (Chicago, IL, and London, 1985)

——'After Negation: Africa in Two Novels by Maryse Condé', in GREEN, GOULD and RICE-MAXIMIN, eds, *Postcolonial Subjects: Francophone Women Writers*, pp. 173–85

MILNE, LORNA, 'Gare au gauffrier: Literature and Postcolonial Studies', *Francophone Postcolonial Studies*, 1 (2003), 60–63

MOI, TORIL, *Sexual/Textual Politics: Feminist Literary Theory* (London and New York: Routledge, 1985)

——ed., *The Kristeva Reader* (Oxford: Basil Blackwell, 1986)

MOORE-GILBERT, BART, et al., eds, *Postcolonial Criticism* (London and New York: Longman, 1997)

MORRISON, TONI, *Playing in the Dark: Whiteness and the Literary Imagination* (Cambridge, MA: Harvard University Press, 1982)

MORTIMER, MILDRED, 'A Sense of Space and Place in Maryse Condé's *Les Derniers Rois mages*', *World Literature Today* (Focus on Maryse Condé), 67, 4 (1993), 757–62

MOUDILENO, LYDIE, 'Le Rire de la grand-mère: Insolence et sérénité dans *Désirada* de

Maryse Condé', *French Review: Journal of the American Association of Teachers of French*, 76 (2003), 1151–60

MOUDILENO, LYDIE, and FRANCIS HIGGINSON, 'Portrait of the Artist as Dreamer: Maryse Condé's *Traversée de la mangrove* and *Les Derniers Rois mages*', *Callaloo*, 18 (1995), 626–40

MUDIMBÉ-BOYI, ELISABETH, 'Giving a Voice to Tituba: The Death of the Author', *World Literature Today*, 67 (1993), 751–56

MURDOCH, H. ADLAI, 'Divided Desire: Biculturality and the Representation of Identity in *En attendant le bonheur*', *Callaloo*, 18 (1995), 579–92

—— *Creole Identity and the French Caribbean Novel* (Gainsville: University Press of Florida, 2001)

MURPHY, DAVID, 'Choosing a Framework: The Limits of French Studies/Francophone Studies/ Postcolonial Studies', *Francophone Postcolonial Studies*, 1 (2003), 72–80

NARAYAN, UMA, *Dislocating Cultures: Identities, Traditions and Third World Feminism* (London and New York: Routledge, 1997)

NESBITT, NICK F., 'Le Sujet de l'histoire: Mémoires troublées dans *Traversée de la mangrove* et *Le Cœur à rire et à pleurer*', in COTTENET-HAGE and LYDIE MOUDILENO, eds, *Maryse Condé: Une nomade inconvenante*, pp. 113–19

NORRIS, CHRISTOPHER, *Deconstruction: Theory and Practice* (London: Methuen, 1982)

O'CALLAGHAN, EVELYN, *Woman Version: Theoretical Approaches to West Indian Fiction by Women*, Warwick University Caribbean Studies (London and Basingstoke: Macmillan Caribbean, 1993)

PARAVISINI-GEBERT, LIZABETH, 'Feminism, Race and Difference in the Works of Mayotte Capécia, Michèle Lacrosil and Jacqueline Manicom,' *Callaloo*, 15(1992), 66–74

PERRET, DELPHINE, 'Dialogue with the Ancestors', trans. by Steve Arkin, *Callaloo* 18 (1995), 626–40

PFAFF, FRANÇOISE, *Entretiens avec Maryse Condé* (Paris: Karthala, 1993)

—— *Conversations with Maryse Condé*, trans. by Pfaff (London and Lincoln: University of Nebraska Press, 1996)

POOLE, SARA, *Elise ou la vraie vie*, Critical Guides to French Texts (London: Grant & Cutler, 1994)

PROULX, PATRICE J., 'Inscriptions of Female Community and Liberation in Maryse Condé's *Moi, Tituba sorcière...*', *Ecrivaines Françaises et Francophones: Europe Plurilingue*, 1997 (March), 148–61

READ, ALAN, ed., *The Fact of Blackness: Frantz Fanon and Visual Representation* (Seattle, WA, Bay Press; London: Institute of Contemporary Arts, 1996)

RÉGIS, ANTOINE, *La Littérature franco-antillaise: Haïti, Guadeloupe et Martinique* (Paris: Karthala, 1992)

ROACH, PAUL, 'Introduction', *Elise ou la vraie vie* (London: Routledge, 1987), pp. 1–50

ROBBE-GRILLET, ALAIN, *Pour un nouveau roman* (Paris: Gallimard, 1947; repr. Les Editions de Minuit, 1964)

RODY, CAROLINE, *Daughter's Return: African-American and Caribbean Women's Fictions of History* (New York and London: Oxford University Press, 2001)

ROSELLO, MIREILLE, 'Caribbean Insularization of Identities in Maryse Condé's Work From *En attendant le bonheur* to *Les Derniers Rois mages*', *Callaloo*(Maryse Condé: A Special Edition), 18 (1993), 565–78

—— *Littérature et identité créole aux Antilles* (Paris: Karthala, 1992)

SALHI, KAMAL, ed., *Francophone Postcolonial Cultures* (Oxford and Lanham, MD: Lexington, 2003)

SAID, EDWARD W., *Orientalism* [1978] (Harmondsworth: Penguin, 1991)

—— *Culture and Imperialism* (London: Vintage, 1994)

—— *Reflections on Exile and Other Literary and Cultural Essays* (London: Granta Books, 2000)

SANSAVIOR, EVA, 'Entretien avec Maryse Condé', *Francophone Postcolonial Studie*s, 2 (2004), 7–33

SARTRE, JEAN-PAUL, 'Orphée Noir', in *Anthologie de la nouvelle poésie nègre et malgache de langue française*, ed. by Léopold S. Senghor (Paris: Presses Universitaires de France, 1948), pp. 9–44

—— *Qu'est-ce que la littérature?* (Paris: Editions Gallimard, 2008)

—— *What is Literature?*, trans. by Bernard Frechtman (with an introduction by David Caute) (London and New York: Routledge, 2006)

SCHWERDTNER, KARIN, 'Wandering, Women and Writing', *Dalhousie French Studies*, 73 (2005), 129–37

SELDEN, RAMAN, ed., *The Cambridge History of Literary Criticism, vol. VIII: From Formalism to Post-Structuralism* (Cambridge: Cambridge University Press, 1995)

SERRANO, RICHARD, *'Francophone' Writers at the Ends of the French Empire* (Lanham, MD: Lexington Books, 2005)

SHOWALTER, ELAINE, ed., *The New Feminist Criticism: Essays on Women, Literature and Theory* (Virago: London, 1986)

SHARPLEY-WHITING, DENEAN, 'Fanon and Capécia', in ALESSANDRINI, ed., *Frantz Fanon: Critical Perspectives*, pp. 57–74

SIMEK, NICOLE, *Eating Well, Reading Well: Maryse Condé and the Ethics of Interpretation* (Amsterdam and New York: Rodopi, 2008)

SMITH, ARLETTE M., 'Maryse Condé's *Hérémakhonon*: A Triangular Structure of Alienation', *CLA*, 32 (Sept 1988), 45–54

—— 'The Semiotics of Exile in Maryse Condé's Fictional Works', *Callaloo*, 14 (1991), 381–88

SMITH, MICHELLE, 'Reading in Circles: Sexuality and/as History in *I, Tituba, Black Witch of Salem*', *Callaloo*, 18 (1995), 602–07

SMITH, SIDONIE, and JULIA WATSON, eds, *De/Colonizing the Subject: The Politics of Women's Autobiography* (Minneapolis: University of Minnesota Press, 1992)

SMITH, SIDONIE, and JULIA WATSON, eds, *Women, Autobiography, Theory: A Reader* (Madison and London: University of Wisconsin Press, 1998)

SMOCK, ANN, 'Marsye Condé's *Les Derniers Rois mages*', *Callaloo* , 18 (1995), 668–80

SOMMER, DORIS, ' "Not Just a Personal Story": Women's *Testimonios* and the Plural Self', in *Life/Lines: Theorizing Women's Autobiography*, ed. by Bella Brodzki and Celeste Schenck (Ithaca, NY, and London: Cornell University Press, 1988), pp. 107–30

SOURIEAU, MARIE-AGNÈS, 'Entretien avec Maryse Condé: De l'identité culturelle', *The French Review*, 72 (1999), 1091–98

SPIVAK, GAYATRI CHAKRAVORTY, 'Can the Subaltern Speak?', in *Colonial Discourse and Post-colonial Theory*, ed. by Patrick Williams and Laura Chrisman (Hemel Hempstead: Harvester Wheatsheaf, 1993), pp. 66–111

—— *A Critique of Postcolonial Reason: Toward a History of the Vanishing Present* (Cambridge, MA, and London: Harvard University Press, 1999)

SQUIRES, JUDITH, ed., *Principled Positions: Postmodernism and the Rediscovery of Value* (London: Lawrence and Wishart, 1993)

STEEDMAN, CAROLYN, *Past Tenses: Essays on Writing Autobiography and History* (London: Rivers Oram Press, 1992)

STOVER, JOHNNIE M., *Rhetoric and Resistance in Black Women's Autobiography* (Gainesville: University Press of Florida, 2003)

SUK, JEANNIE, *Postcolonial Paradoxes in French Caribbean Writing: Césaire, Glissant, Condé* (Oxford: Clarendon Press, 2001)

VERGÈS, FRANÇOISE, 'Labyrinthes', in COTTENET-HAGE and LYDIE MOUDILENO, eds, *Maryse Condé: Une nomade inconvenante*, pp. 185–90

WA NYATETU-WAIGWA, WANGARI, 'From Liminality to a Home of Her Own? The Quest Motif in Maryse Condé's Fiction from *En attendant le bonheur* to *Les Derniers Rois mages*', *Callaloo* (Maryse Condé: A Special Edition), 18 (1995), 551–64

WEBB, BARBARA, *Myth and History in Caribbean Fiction: Alejo Carpentier, Wilson Harris and Edouard Glissant* (Amherst: University of Massachusetts Press, 1992)

WHITLOCK, GILLIAN, *The Intimate Empire: Reading Women's Autobiography* (London and New York: Cassell, 2000)

WILLIAMS, PATRICK, and LAURA CHRISMAN, eds, *Colonial Discourse and Post-Colonial Theory: A Reader*, with introduction by authors (Essex: Pearson Education: 1994)

WILLIAMS, RAYMOND, *Marxism and Literature* (Oxford: Oxford University Press, 1977)

WILSON, ELIZABETH, ' "Le Voyage et l'Espace clos" — Island and Journey Metaphor: Aspects of Women's Experience in the Works of Francophone Caribbean Women Novelists', in *Out of the Kumbla: Caribbean Women and Literature*, ed. by Carole Boyce Davies and Elaine Savory Fido (Trenton, NJ: Africa World Press, 1990), pp. 45–58

YOUNG, LOLA, 'Missing Persons: Fantasising Black Women in *Black Skin, White Masks*', in READ, ed., *The Fact of Blackness: Frantz Fanon and Visual Representation*, pp. 86–101

YOUNG, ROBERT, 'Ideologies of the Postcolonial', Editorial in *Interventions*, 1 (1998/99), 4–8

ZIMRA, CLARISSE, 'Daughters of Mayotte, Sons of Frantz: The Unrequited Self in Caribbean Literature', in HAIGH, ed., *An Introduction to Caribbean Francophone Writing: Guadeloupe and Martinique*, pp. 177–94

INDEX